INSECTS OF HAWAII

INSECTS OF HAWAII

A Manual of the Insects of the Hawaiian Islands, including an Enumeration of the Species and Notes on their Origin, Distribution, Hosts, Parasites, etc.

by **ELWOOD C. ZIMMERMAN**

Associate Entomologist, Experiment Station,
Hawaiian Sugar Planters' Association; Curator
of Entomology, Bernice P. Bishop Museum

VOLUME 4

HOMOPTERA: AUCHENORHYNCHA

Sponsored by

BERNICE P. BISHOP MUSEUM • EXPERIMENT
STATION, HAWAIIAN SUGAR PLANTERS'
ASSOCIATION • UNIVERSITY OF HAWAII

University of Hawaii Press, Honolulu
1948

Issued October 19, 1948

PRINTED IN THE UNITED STATES OF AMERICA
BY THE HONOLULU STAR-BULLETIN

PREFACE TO VOLUME 4

This is the fourth volume of *Insects of Hawaii*. In it are recorded 313 species of auchenorhynchus Homoptera, most of which are referred to commonly as leafhoppers. Only 16 of these species are not native insects, and the group forms one of the major sections of the endemic Hawaiian fauna. Comparatively little is known about any except a few of the native species; a vast amount of information concerning the group is yet to be recorded and a large number of new species remains to be described. The 16 immigrant species include such well-known pests as the sugarcane leafhopper, corn leafhopper, bean leafhopper and taro leafhopper which have caused damage to Hawaiian crops amounting to millions of dollars.

Reference should be made to the "Preface to the First Five Volumes," in Volume 1 of this work, for a detailed outline of these volumes and for general acknowledgments and comment. The other volumes of this series are: 1, *Introduction;* 2, *Apterygota–Thysanoptera;* 3, *Heteroptera;* and 5, *Homoptera: Sternorhyncha.*

The drawings for this volume were made mostly by Frieda Abernathy, University of California; Arthur Smith, British Museum (Natural History); and the author. The photographs were made by W. Twigg-Smith and J. T. Yamamoto, Experiment Station, H.S.P.A., most of them by Mr. Yamamoto.

In addition to the acknowledgments made in Volume 1, I wish to thank W. E. China, British Museum (Natural History), for answering a number of questions and for supervising the drawing of the types of several species. Paul Oman, U. S. National Museum, and R. H. Beamer, University of Kansas, read the manuscript and helped with several problems. My colleague, R. H. Van Zwaluwenburg, Experiment Station, H.S.P.A., read all the manuscript and proof.

E.C.Z.

Honolulu
August, 1948

CONTENTS

INSECTS OF HAWAII

CHECKLIST OF THE INSECTS IN THIS VOLUME

Order HEMIPTERA

Suborder HOMOPTERA
Series AUCHENORHYNCHA
Superfamily CICADOIDEA

Family CERCOPIDAE
Subfamily APHROPHORINAE

Genus **PHILAENUS** Stål
    spumarius (Linnaeus)

Family CICADELLIDAE
Subfamily TETTIGELLINAE

Genus **ACOPSIS** Amyot and Serville
    minerva (Ball)
    mollipes (Say)

Subfamily MACROPSINAE

Genus **MACROPSIS** Lewis
    occidentalis (Van Duzee)

Subfamily TYPHLOCYBINAE

Genus **EMPOASCA** Walsh
    solana DeLong

Subfamily JASSINAE

Genus **STRAGANIA** Stål
    Subgenus **Penestragania** Beamer and Lawson
        robusta (Uhler)

[1]

Subfamily Euscelinae

Genus **NESOPHRYNE** Kirkaldy
   kaiamamao (Kirkaldy)
   kukanaroa (Kirkaldy)

Genus **KIRKALDIELLA** Osborn
   euphorbiae Osborn
   ewana Osborn

Genus **NESOPHROSYNE** Kirkaldy
   Subgenus **Nesophrosyne** Kirkaldy
      affinis Osborn
      albicosta Osborn
      angulifera Osborn
      bicolorata Osborn
      bobeae Kirkaldy
      caelicola Kirkaldy
      cinerea Osborn
      craterigena Kirkaldy
      cuprescens Osborn
      ehu Kirkaldy
      furculata Osborn
      giffardi giffardi Kirkaldy
      giffardi interrupta Osborn
      gouldiae Kirkaldy
      haleakala Kirkaldy
      halemanu Kirkaldy
      ignigena Kirkaldy
      imbricola Kirkaldy
      lineata Osborn
      mabae Osborn
      maritima Kirkaldy
      milu Kirkaldy
      monticola Kirkaldy
      montium Kirkaldy
      montivaga Kirkaldy
      myrsines Kirkaldy
      nimbicola Kirkaldy
      nimbigena Kirkaldy
      notatula Osborn
      nubigena Kirkaldy
      nuenue Kirkaldy
      obliqua Osborn
      oneanea Kirkaldy

       opalescens Kirkaldy
       oreadis Kirkaldy
       palolo Osborn
       paludicola Kirkaldy
       palustris Kirkaldy
       pele Kirkaldy
       peleae Osborn
       perkinsi (Kirkaldy)
       pipturi Kirkaldy
       pluvialis Kirkaldy
       ponapona Kirkaldy
       procellaris Kirkaldy
       signatula Osborn
       silvicola Kirkaldy
       silvigena Kirkaldy
       sinuata Osborn
       touchardii Osborn
       ulaula ulaula Kirkaldy
       ulaula nigrolineata Kirkaldy
       umbratilis Kirkaldy
       umbricola Kirkaldy
       umbrigena Kirkaldy

    Subgenus **Nesoreias** Kirkaldy
       comma Osborn
       eburneola Osborn
       insularis Kirkaldy
       koleae (Kirkaldy)
       marginalis Osborn
       oceanides Kirkaldy
       sanguinea Osborn

Genus **DELTOCEPHALUS** Burmeister
    hospes Kirkaldy

Genus **OPSIUS** Fieber
    stactogalus (Amyot)

Genus **BALCLUTHA** Kirkaldy
    hospes (Kirkaldy)
    kilaueae (Kirkaldy)
    peregrina (Kirkaldy)
    plutonis (Kirkaldy)
    timberlakei (Osborn)
    volcanicola (Kirkaldy)

Genus **NESOLINA** Osborn
  lineata Osborn

Family MEMBRACIDAE

Subfamily SMILIINAE

Tribe CERESINI

Genus **STICTOCEPHALA** Stål
  festina (Say)

Subfamily CENTROTINAE

Genus **TRICENTRUS** Stål
  albomaculatus Distant

Superfamily FULGOROIDEA

Family CIXIIDAE

Subfamily CIXIINAE

Tribe CIXIINI

Genus **OLIARUS** Stål
  acaciae Kirkaldy
  albatus Giffard
  consimilis Giffard
  discrepans Giffard
  euphorbiae Giffard
  filicicola Kirkaldy
  haleakalae Kirkaldy
  halehaku Giffard
  halemanu Giffard
  hevaheva Kirkaldy
  immaculatus Giffard
  inaequalis inaequalis Giffard
  inaequalis koebelei Metcalf
  inaequalis kohala Metcalf
  inaequalis konana Metcalf
  inconstans Giffard
  instabilis instabilis Giffard

instabilis bryani Metcalf
instabilis crawi Metcalf
instabilis ehrhorni Metcalf
instabilis osborni Metcalf
instabilis terryi Metcalf
instabilis williamsi Metcalf
intermedius Giffard
kahavalu Kirkaldy
kaiulani Giffard
kanakanus kanakanus Kirkaldy
kanakanus punaensis Metcalf
kaohinani kaohinani Kirkaldy
kaohinani perkinsi Metcalf
kaonohi Kirkaldy
kauaiensis Kirkaldy
kaumuahona Giffard
kirkaldyi Giffard
koae Giffard
koanoa Kirkaldy
koele Giffard
kulanus Giffard
lihue Giffard
likelike Giffard
makaala Giffard
mauiensis Giffard
montanus Giffard
monticola Kirkaldy
morai (Kirkaldy)
muiri Giffard
myoporicola Giffard
neomorai neomorai Giffard
neomorai oahuana Metcalf
nemoricola Kirkaldy
neotarai Giffard
niger Giffard
nubigenus Kirkaldy
olympus olympus Giffard
olympus paliensis Metcalf
opuna Kirkaldy
orono orono Kirkaldy
orono molokaiensis Kirkaldy
orono oahuensis Kirkaldy
paludicola Kirkaldy
pele pele Kirkaldy

pele alpha Metcalf
pele beta Metcalf
pluvialis Kirkaldy
procellaris Kirkaldy
silvestris Kirkaldy
similis similis Giffard
similis lanaiana Metcalf
similis mauiana Metcalf
similis molokaiana Metcalf
swezeyi Giffard
tamehameha Kirkaldy
tantalus Giffard
tarai tarai Kirkaldy
tarai hawaiiensis Metcalf
tarai kohalana Metcalf
waialeale Giffard
wailupensis Giffard

Genus **IOLANIA** Kirkaldy
koolauensis Giffard
lanaiensis Giffard
mauiensis Giffard
oahuensis Giffard
perkinsi perkinsi Kirkaldy
perkinsi notata Kirkaldy

Family DELPHACIDAE

Subfamily DELPHACINAE

Tribe ALOHINI

Genus **LEIALOHA** (Kirkaldy)
hawaiiensis (Muir)
kauaiensis (Muir)
lanaiensis (Muir)
lehuae (Kirkaldy)
mauiensis (Muir)
naniicola (Kirkaldy)
oahuensis (Muir)
oceanides (Kirkaldy)
ohiae (Kirkaldy)
pacifica (Kirkaldy)
scaevolae Muir
suttoniae Muir

Genus **NESOTHOË** Kirkaldy
    antidesmae (Muir)
    bobeae Kirkaldy
    dodonaeae (Muir)
    dryope (Kirkaldy)
    elaeocarpi (Kirkaldy)
    eugeniae (Kirkaldy)
    fletus Kirkaldy
    frigidula Kirkaldy
    giffardi (Kirkaldy)
    gulicki (Muir)
    haa (Muir)
    hula Kirkaldy
    laka Kirkaldy
    maculata (Muir)
    munroi (Muir)
    perkinsi Kirkaldy
    piilani Kirkaldy
    pluvialis Kirkaldy
    semialba (Muir)
    seminigrofrons (Muir)
    silvestris Kirkaldy
    terryi Kirkaldy

Genus **NESODRYAS** Kirkaldy
    freycinetiae Kirkaldy
    swezeyi Zimmerman

Genus **ALOHA** Kirkaldy
    artemisiae (Kirkaldy)
    campylothecae Muir
    dubautiae (Kirkaldy)
    flavocollaris Muir
    ipomoeae Kirkaldy
    kirkaldyi Muir
    myoporicola Kirkaldy
    plectranthi Muir
    swezeyi Muir

Genus **NESORESTIAS** Kirkaldy
    filicicola Kirkaldy
    nimbata (Kirkaldy)

Genus **NOTHORESTIAS** Muir
    badia Muir
    swezeyi Muir

Genus **DICTYOPHORODELPHAX** Swezey
    mirabilis Swezey
    praedicta Bridwell
    swezeyi Bridwell
    usingeri Swezey

Genus **NESOSYDNE** Kirkaldy
    acuta (Muir)
    ahinahina (Muir)
    aku (Muir)
    amaumau (Muir)
    anceps Muir
    argyroxiphii Kirkaldy
    asteliae Muir
    boehmeria (Muir)
    bridwelli (Muir)
    campylothecae (Muir)
    chambersi Kirkaldy
    coprosmicola (Muir)
    cyathodis Kirkaldy
    cyrtandrae Muir
    cyrtandricola Muir
    dubautiae (Muir)
    eeke (Muir)
    fullawayi (Muir)
    geranii (Muir)
    giffardi Muir
    gigantea (Muir)
    gouldiae Kirkaldy
    gunnerae Muir
    haleakala Kirkaldy
    halia Kirkaldy
    hamadryas Kirkaldy
    hamata Muir
    imbricola Kirkaldy
    incommoda Muir
    ipomoeicola Kirkaldy
    koae Kirkaldy
    koae-phyllodii Muir
    koebelei Muir
    kokolau (Muir)
    kuschei (Muir)
    lanaiensis (Muir)
    leahi (Kirkaldy)

lobeliae Muir
longipes (Muir)
mamake (Muir)
mauiensis (Muir)
monticola Kirkaldy
montis-tantalus Muir
naenae (Muir)
neocyrtandrae (Muir)
neoraillardiae (Muir)
neowailupensis (Muir)
nephelias Kirkaldy
nephrolepidis Kirkaldy
nesogunnerae Muir
nesopele (Muir)
nigriceps Muir
nigrinervis (Muir)
nubigena Kirkaldy
oahuensis Muir
olympica (Muir)
osborni Muir
painiu (Muir)
palustris Kirkaldy
perkinsi Muir
phyllostegiae Muir
pilo (Muir)
pipturi Kirkaldy
procellaris Kirkaldy
pseudorubescens Muir
raillardiae Kirkaldy
raillardiicola (Muir)
rocki Muir
rubescens (Kirkaldy)
rubescens pele (Kirkaldy)
sharpi Muir
sola Muir
stenogynicola (Muir)
sulcata (Muir)
swezeyi Muir
tetramolopii (Muir)
timberlakei Muir
ulehihi (Muir)
umbratica Kirkaldy
viridis (Muir)
waikamoiensis (Muir)
wailupensis (Muir)

Tribe DELPHACINI

Genus **PERKINSIELLA** Kirkaldy
 saccharicida Kirkaldy

Genus **PEREGRINUS** Kirkaldy
 maidis (Ashmead)

Genus **LIBURNIA** Stål
 paludum (Kirkaldy)

Genus **KELISIA** Fieber
 emoloa Muir
 eragrosticola Muir
 sporobolicola sporobolicola Kirkaldy
 sporobolicola immaculata Muir
 swezeyi Kirkaldy

Genus **TAROPHAGUS** Zimmerman
 proserpina (Kirkaldy)

Genus **MEGAMELUS** Fieber
 angulatus Osborn

Family FLATIDAE

Subfamily FLATINAE

Genus **SIPHANTA** Stål
 acuta (Walker)

Order **HEMIPTERA,** continued

Suborder **HOMOPTERA** (Leach, 1815) Latreille, 1817

Omoptera Leach, 1815.

Leafhoppers, Treehoppers, Spittlebugs, Psyllids, White Flies, Aphids,
Mealybugs, Scales

This suborder is distinguished from the Heteroptera chiefly as follows: wings usually held roof-like over the abdomen, fore pair without two fields, of nearly uniform texture throughout, although frequently more rigid than the hind pair, usually membranous; rostrum appearing to arise between the fore coxae; gular region indistinct; wingless forms common.

Minute to large insects of many forms; body soft to heavily sclerotized; active or sedentary, many saltatorial. Head hypognathous, ventral part abutting fore coxae in many groups; cephalic sutures variably modified, often obscure; compound eyes present or absent; ocelli two or three or none; antennae variable, moniliform, filiform or styliform, reduced to three or four or fewer segments in some groups and obsolete in others, with a maximum of 25 segments in some male coccids, usually with variformed sensoria; mouth parts, as in the Heteroptera, highly modified for piercing plant tissue and sucking fluids, produced into a variable beak which usually projects caudad between the legs; clypeus, labrum and epipharynx variable, often fused and/or variously modified; stylets usually very long, retractile and coiled within the body in some forms. Thorax variable, distinctly divided in winged forms, not greatly differentiated from abdomen in some apterous forms. Legs ambulatory or saltatory, reduced or absent in many female scales; tarsi one- to three-segmented, absent in some forms, with one or two claws, or none. Wings present or absent and variously modified, the hind pair reduced to halteres in male coccids, apterous forms common, brachypterous and long-winged forms frequently occurring in same species; venation usually greatly reduced. Abdomen usually much modified, basically 11-segmented, but frequently much reduced, cerci absent; ovipositor well developed to absent. Metamorphosis gradual; eggs laid free, inserted in plant tissue, deposited in waxy ovisacs formed by the female, or developed ovoviviparously; parthenogenetic forms common, predominant in some groups. Some families containing species with highly developed wax-forming glands, many forms great honeydew producers; a highly variable group of herbivores, many active, many saltatorial, many immobile in adult female state.

[11]

It is impossible to write an adequate description of the Homoptera without going into great detail because the group consists of so many variable and complex groups. The notes above are only a bare outline. Because of this diversity, the suborder as a whole has a less well-coordinated literature than does the Heteroptera. In fact, many of the families have attracted specialists who have limited themselves, by necessity, to single groups as other workers have attached themselves to entire orders.

Homoptera have been traced back in the fossil record to the Triassic. Today the suborder is well represented over all of the world.

Although Hawaii has a magnificently developed endemic homopterous fauna, insofar as species go, none of the native forms was described until 1902 when Kirkaldy wrote his first paper for *Fauna Hawaiiensis*. Certain immigrant species, especially coccids, were listed by name from the islands some years previously, however. After Kirkaldy's first report, our knowledge of the native Homoptera grew rapidly. The establishment of the sugarcane leafhopper gave impetus to the study of local forms and resulted in the transfer of the specialists Kirkaldy and Muir from England to Hawaii. The bulk of our native Homoptera was described by these two workers, but Crawford entered the field to expand our knowledge of the Psyllidae, Giffard revised the Cixiidae, and Osborn revised the Cicadellidae. Since Kirkaldy and Muir left the scene, the native Homoptera have received little attention by writers. The interest and activities pertaining to the economic forms have continued and have been increasing in the last few years. However, before these volumes no attempt had been made to gather data pertinent to the entire suborder in one place.

Although we have a specifically well-developed endemic homopterous fauna, it is an "unbalanced" one, as compared to continental faunas. I refer to it as "unbalanced" because, of the series known elsewhere, only a few groups are represented. The only families represented by endemic species are the Cicadellidae, Cixiidae, Delphacidae, Psyllidae and the Pseudococcidae. The characteristic groups of the continents—Cicadidae, Cercopidae, Membracidae, Flatidae, Issidae, Ricaniidae, Fulgoridae, Aphididae, the many families of Coccoidea—are wanting from the native fauna. The few families which are surely represented by native species are further limited. The native Cicadellidae are represented by only five or six genera. Two genera represent the Cixiidae. Seven genera represent the Delphacidae, and six of these are closely interrelated endemics. The endemic Pseudococcidae are contained in six genera.

One unusual feature of the endemic homopterous fauna is the almost entire lack of grass- and sedge-feeding species which are so dominant in continental areas. With the exception of the few species of *Kelisia* (Delphacidae) and *Balclutha* (*Nesosteles*) (Cicadellidae), all of our many positively native Homoptera feed upon trees (mostly), shrubs, herbs, vines or ferns. The locally abnormal habit of the grass-feeding *Kelisia* and *Balclutha* has been a factor in leading some workers to consider them as non-endemic, but the data now assembled are adequate to establish their endemicity beyond a doubt. *Nesolina* will have to be added to this group if it proves to be endemic.

The suborder Homoptera contains many of the most serious of agricultural pests. Our two best-known species are the sugarcane leafhopper and the pineapple mealybug, each of which has caused damage that can only be estimated in millions of dollars. The many scales and aphids now established in the islands confront all agriculturists with a constant and ever-growing series of control problems. There are no homopterous insects in these islands which can be called obviously beneficial to man, although the native forms are mostly "neutral." Many species carry various kinds of plant diseases, and some forms become so abundant on their hostplants as literally to suck the life out of them. They are mostly prolific, fast-growing creatures—some incredibly so. Some have yielded to biological control, but others have withstood all attempts to control them satisfactorily by natural means.

TABULAR ANALYSIS OF THE HAWAIIAN HOMOPTERA

FAMILY	GENERA	ENDEMIC GENERA	NON-ENDEMIC GENERA	SPECIES	ENDEMIC SPECIES	ADVENTIVE SPECIES
Cercopidae	1	0	1	1	0	1
Cicadellidae	12	4	8	80	73	7
Membracidae	2	0	2	2	0	2
Cixiidae	2	1	1	84	84	0
Delphacidae	14	8	6	145	140	5
Flatidae	1	0	1	1	0	1
Psyllidae	8	5	3	31	31	0
Aleyrodidae	5	0	5	7	0	7
Aphididae	24	0	24	47	0	47
Margarodidae	1	0	1	1	0	1
Ortheziidae	1	0	1	1	0	1
Pseudococcidae	12	3	9	35	14	21
Asterolecaniidae	1	0	1	4	0	4
Kermidae	1	0	1	2	0	2
Coccidae	5	0	5	15	0	15
Diaspididae	25	0	25	49	0	49
Totals	115	21	94	505	342	163

Percentage of endemism in native group: genera, 88 percent; species, 100 percent.
Percentage of present-day fauna native: 68 percent.
Percentage of present-day fauna adventive: 32 percent.
Average number of species per genus in native group: 12.
Average number of species per genus in adventive group: 2.

KEY TO THE SERIES OF HOMOPTERA

(Adults)

1. Tarsi three-segmented; antennae short, with a terminal arista
 .... **Auchenorhyncha.**
2. Tarsi one- or two-segmented; antennae without a terminal arista; often immobile forms (scales, etc.)...............
 ....**Sternorhyncha.**

Series AUCHENORHYNCHA Duméril, 1806

This division includes the larger, less-specialized Homoptera. The wing venation is not reduced as it is in the Sternorhyncha.

KEY TO THE SUPERFAMILIES

1. Mesocoxae not elongate, their points of articulation' subcontiguous and distant from wings; tegulae absent......**Cicadoidea.**
2. Mesocoxae conspicuously elongate, often twice as long as broad, their points of articulation much farther apart than greatest chord of a coxa, toward sides of body and often near wings; tegulae present................................**Fulgoroidea.**

Superfamily CICADOIDEA Ashmead, 1904

KEY TO THE FAMILIES FOUND IN HAWAII

1. Pronotum unusually large, produced backward as a sharp process over abdomen and nearly or entirely hiding scutellum......
....**Membracidae.**
Pronotum not so formed, scutellum visible.................. 2
2. At least hind tibiae conspicuously multispinose or serially spinose; hind coxae strongly expanded laterad, reaching to sides of sterna or to edges of wings..............**Cicadellidae.**
Tibiae with at most two stout spur-like spines on outer edge (in addition to terminal spines) and never multispinose in our species; hind coxae subconical and not expanded to sides of sterna................................**Cercopidae.**

The nymphs may be separated as follows:

1. Dorsum granulate............................**Membracidae.**
Dorsum not granulate..................................... 2
2. Tibiae multispinose; nymphs free and active.........**Cicadellidae.**
Tibiae not multispinose along their lengths; nymphs normally hidden by surrounding masses of froth............**Cercopidae.**

NOTES ON KIRKALDY'S TYPES OF HAWAIIAN LEAFHOPPERS

(Cicadellidae and Delphacidae)

The natural difficulties encountered in attempting a study of the extensively speciated Hawaiian leafhoppers are intensified by confusion caused largely by carelessness on the part of certain of the authors of the known species. Fortunately, some private notes written by Dr. Perkins have served to clarify some muddled situations. Dr. Swezey has kindly made available to me a letter written by Perkins to Muir on January 31, 1922, which contains this invaluable information. It is of such importance that I believe that most of it should be printed here and thus preserved for future workers. The letter is in the files of the Hawaiian Sugar Planters' Association Experiment Station. It is divided into two principal parts, the first a narrative, the second a list of species with notes on their types and other remarks. Nearly all of the narrative is printed below, but the notes are segregated and are placed under the species headings farther along in the text, and I have added some comments where additional information has been available.

I am sending herewith...a box containing a number of Hawaiian leafhoppers, containing a considerable number of actual types of Kirkaldy's, and others which were certainly cotypes and some which I compared with his actual types, but which he did not see....

The specimens look more untidy than mine usually do. I did not care in this case to remount any, nor to remove the very untidy MS. labels of K's, as I think they ought to be left on, until some one better informed than myself on the species has examined them. The flaring red labels I am quite sure must indicate the specimen or specimens that would have been labelled as the actual types. In some cases there are specimens without this peculiar label, which were actual types, I believe.

When the final proofs of the Suppl. to Hemiptera [in *Fauna Hawaiiensis*] came to Honolulu after K's death, I went through all the specimens I could find. It is very likely I missed some, since so far as I remember, they were scattered here and there in a score or more of boxes mixed up more or less with things not Hawaiian. Kershaw helped me a good deal with Kirkaldy's boxes.

I kept one of the duplicate copies of the proofs of F. H. [*Fauna Hawaiiensis*] and wrote on these a lot of remarks about both the Homops. and Heterop. In a number of cases the MS. name on an evident type did not occur in the proofs at all, the name having evidently been changed for what he considered a better one by K.—or for some other reason. In such cases it was easy to fix which printed name belonged to the (different) MS. name, by considering the date and locality and the description. These together furnished positive evidence of the valid name of the doubly-named specimens.

I think I failed to find any representative of some described species at all, probably because these had been eaten up, as a vast number of specimens were, during K's illnesses. You will easily see signs of "frass" of *Psocus* etc. on some of the cards now, though I cleaned off the worst of this. I have no specimens, that I have had sole charge of, that show any signs of this, though some of Blackburn's are bad and he let many of his Neuroptera be almost entirely destroyed.

The notes which I made on K's species at the time indicate chiefly the destination of the type, but in some cases there are other remarks. I may have sent these notes out before, but in any case I have copied them again. Type S.I.C. = belonging to Sandwich Is. Committee and no doubt these are all in the Brit. Mus. now. K. agreed to make types of S.I.C. specimens before all others, as he had undertaken those first....

I think I told you I collected leafhoppers most particularly on Molokai and Lanai, much more than elsewhere, as also the land shells of those Islands. Unfortunately these were nearly all destroyed and there were hundreds of cards of these and also of smaller Heterops. (chiefly Capsidae) entirely cleared of their contents or with only remnants left. K. must have described only a fraction of what I got. I particularly remember the great numbers of Delphacids on Molokai, when I was beating for Coleops. etc., but Jassids were more numerous in individuals on Hawaii. One year they were dead of some fungus disease in countless thousands in the Kona district and in a few minutes I remember filling several pill boxes, as they stuck, dead, but lifelike, on the trees. No doubt these were mostly one species. I never saw another epidemic like this, and if the fungus attacked the species indiscriminately, it would go hard with the rarer ones on such an occasion!...

There are signs of verdigris on some of the beasts I pinned with silver wires, as happens when they put in too much alloy. I think it was only specimens that were pinned from Molokai that escaped being eaten up, all the carded ones were cleared off, so pinning has some advantages in this case and I wish I had pinned more.

It is quite possible that I may have overlooked some species, not specially labelled, in the (named) collection I possess, as I have not examined the specimens critically on this occasion, but I took a very great deal of trouble over them at the time I corrected K's last proofs. Casually examined, they appear to me correct....

Family **CERCOPIDAE** (Leach, 1815)

Spittlebugs, Froghoppers

This group is not represented in the native Hawaiian fauna, and it was only recently (1944) that a foreign species was reported to have become established here.

The name "spittlebug" is derived from the frothy material produced by the nymphs and in which they live on their hostplants. These peculiar masses of "cuckoo-spit" are characteristic of the family and are usually conspicuous in the areas in which the insects occur. The frothy substance is considered to protect the pale, delicate nymphs from drying and, at least to a considerable degree, from their enemies. Cecil (1930:125) describes the formation of the froth in *Philaenus leucophthalmus* Linnaeus as follows:

> The nymph increases in size as it feeds, and after feeding from 1 to 2 minutes it excretes a clear fluid from the anus. In from 5 to 12 minutes the nymph is completely covered with the fluid. The position of the tip of the abdomen when the fluid is excreted, causes the fluid to flood the dorsal surface of the abdomen and run off the sides of the body. When the nymph is covered with clear fluid the tip of the abdomen is extended outside the fluid. While outside the fluid, the posterior lateral folds are opened to allow entry of air, then closed as the abdomen is retracted into the fluid. The body of the nymph is then contracted and a bubble of air is released into the fluid. This process is performed repeatedly until the clear fluid becomes a white frothy mass or spittle. In the method of forming the spittle I agree with Morse [A Bubble-blowing Insect, *Popular Science Monthly*, 57:23–29, figs. 1–6, 1900] but do not agree with him that the anal appendages serve as gills when the nymph is covered with spittle.

The family characters of the single species established in Hawaii may be summarized briefly as follows: head with two ocelli; antennae appearing to have an enlarged, two-segmented basal part upon which is articulated a long, fine seta which arises from a bulbous base which simulates a third segment to the basal segments; hind coxae subconical and at all parts distant from the lateral edges of the pleura; tibiae subcylindrical, posterior pair with two stout spines on the outer side and a cluster of spines at the apex.

The cercopids are thought to be most closely allied to the Cicadidae, a group which is not represented in Hawaii. In our fauna, they most closely resemble the Cicadellidae, from which family they are most easily distinguished by their comparatively simple hind tibiae which lack rows of numerous, conspicuous spines.

The family is fairly well represented elsewhere in Oceania, especially by the genus *Lallemandana*.

[17]

Subfamily APHROPHORINAE (Amyot and Serville, 1843)

Genus PHILAENUS Stål, 1864

Philaenus spumarius (Linnaeus) (fig. 1).
Cicada spumaria Linnaeus, 1758:437.

Figure 1—*Philaenus spumarius* (Linnaeus). The meadow froghopper, a spittlebug.

The meadow froghopper.

Hawaii.

Immigrant. A widespread species in Europe and North America. First found in the Territory at Kilauea, Hawaii, by W. C. Goolsby in 1944 and reported by Richard Faxon, *Proc. Hawaiian Ent. Soc.* 12(2):219, 1945, as *P. leucophthalmus* (Linnaeus).

Hostplants: *Anagallis arvensis, Artemisia vulgaris, Bidens pilosa minor, Brassica oleracea botrytis,* celery, *Centaurium umbellatum, Chrysanthemum maximum, Coix lacryma-jobi, Commelina diffusa, Coprosma ernodioides typica, Coprosma rhynchocarpa, Cordyline terminalis, Cynodon dactylon, Cyperus brevifolius, Dactylis glomerata, Dahlia, Daucus carota sativa, Dianthus chinensis, Digitaria pruriens, Erigeron albidus, Fuchsia magellanica, Geranium carolinianum australe, Gnaphalium purpureum, Hebe salicifolia, Hibiscus tiliaceus, Holcus lanatus, Hypericum moserianum, Hypochaeris radicata, Ilex anomala, Ipomoea batatas, Lactuca sativa, Lythrum maritimum, Medicago hispida, Mentha, Mesembryanthemum, Metrosideros collina polymorpha, Modiola caroliniana, Myosotis azorica, Oenothera striata, Panicum purpurascens,* parsley, *Pastinaca sativa, Physalis peruviana, Plantago lanceolata, Pluchea odorata, Raillardia scabra, Raphanus sativus longipinnatus* (daikon radish), *Rheum rhaponticum, Rubus penetrans, Rumex acetosella, Sacciolepis contracta,* satsuma orange, *Senecio mikanioides, Solidago altissima, Sonchus oleraceus, Stachytarpheta,* strawberry, *Tibouchina semidecandra, Trifolium procumbens, Tritonia crocosmaeflora, Verbena litoralis, Veronica plebia, Vinca, Wikstroemia phillyreaefolia.*

This comparatively stout species is a brownish insect about 6 mm. long. The dorsum is densely and conspicuously clothed with short golden pubescence, and the hind margin of the pronotum is conspicuously concave at the middle. It is reported to damage various meadow plants in the United States (see Osborn and Knull 1939:101). The nymphs are soft, pale-greenish creatures.

Family **CICADELLIDAE** (Latreille, 1802) Latreille, 1850

Tettigonidae (Spinola, 1850) Uhler, 1876.
Jassidae (Stål, 1858) Fieber, 1866.

Cicadellids, Jassids, Leafhoppers, Sharpshooters

This family is one of the largest of the order. It is well represented in Hawaii by a large number of endemic species as well as by several immigrant forms.

The common names leafhopper and sharpshooter are derived from the active and agile way the bugs jump when disturbed.

The group is an economically important one, because certain of its species cause much damage to crop plants, not only by sucking their juices but by serving as vectors of certain plant diseases. The individuals of some species become excessively abundant and swarm on their hostplants. Fortunately, we have few species of economic importance in Hawaii, but we are in constant danger of having serious pest species break through our quarantine barriers.

Two ocelli normally are present; the antennae consist of two enlarged basal segments and a long, setaceous flagellum which is microscopically and usually indistinctly multisegmented; sides of the face explanate and extending at least over part of the fore coxae; hind coxae greatly expanded, their sides reaching to the sides of the pleura or to the edges of the wings; at least the hind tibiae with rows of numerous, conspicuous spurs and spines.

The literature containing descriptions of the native Hawaiian cicadellids is largely confined to three papers, two by Kirkaldy (1902:114–116; 1910:555–576) and one by Osborn (1935:1–62). Osborn's paper is illustrated, contains some keys and summarizes all of the group occurring in the islands. The family is a taxonomically difficult one and has been largely neglected by local entomologists. It is in considerable need of additional study, and the supra-generic nomenclature has not been stabilized. Evans' revised classification (1946–1947) was received after the manuscript for this section was written, but I have made some major changes while "in press" to follow him more closely.

KEY TO THE SUBFAMILIES OF CICADELLIDAE FOUND IN HAWAII

1. Ocelli on crown (head long and triangular in our species)
.... **Tettigellinae.**
   Ocelli not on crown.................................... 2

2(1). Fore margin of pronotum in our species produced forward
   at middle to beyond a line drawn between apices of eyes
   as seen from above; lora narrow and tumescent; genae
   reduced to narrow strips................... **Macropsinae.**

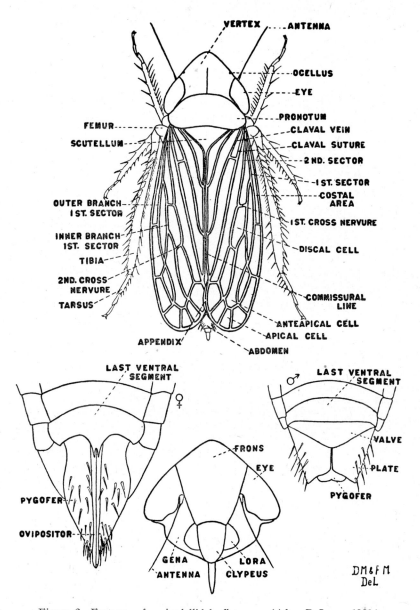

Figure 2—Features of a cicadellid leafhopper. (After DeLong, 1923.)

Fore margin of pronotum not so produced, middle of fore
margin behind a line drawn between fore margins of eyes;
lora broad and flat; genae large and expanded........... 3

3(2). Antennae comparatively deeply inserted in a concavity
which is margined on its dorsal edge by an "antennal
ledge" which runs from eye onto frons; frontal sutures
(from ocelli downward) obsolete; pronotum distinctly
broader than head across eyes and tegminal membrane set
with conspicuous spines in our species............**Jassinae.**
Antennal ledges vestigial or obsolete; frontal sutures distinct from ocelli downward; otherwise not as above....... 4

4(3). Tegminal venation reduced, appendix absent, veins forking
near base and without cross-veins before apex of clavus
(our species a small, slender, delicate, pale-green form)
.... **Typhlocybinae.**
Tegminal venation either complete or partially reduced
(*Balclutha* and *Nesolina*), but with an appendix on inner
side of membrane, veins forking on disc and usually (but
not always) with cross-veins before apex of clavus, thus
forming discal cells........................**Euscelinae.**

Subfamily TETTIGELLINAE

This group, which is not represented here by any native species, may be distinguished from the other Cicadellidae found in Hawaii by the positions of the
ocelli. These organs are situated on the disc of the vertex (see the illustrations).
The heads of our immigrant representatives, as viewed from above, are conspicuously triangular.

Genus **ACOPSIS** Amyot and Serville, 1843

Draeculacephala Ball, 1901.

These insects are referred to as "sharpshooters" because of their leaping ability.
The nymphs do not have the abdominal tergites armed with long setae. These
are our largest cicadellids; they attain a maximum length of 9 mm. or more. They
are among the few of our species which retain their green color after preservation,
and are among the commonest and most easily recognized of the group in Hawaii.
The conspicuously triangular head is distinct (see the illustrations). The top of
the head, the anterior and lateral borders of the pronotum, and the scutellum are
greenish-yellow, and the remainder of the dorsum is grass-green. They frequently
come to light in large numbers and are most abundant in areas where there is lush
vegetation.

I follow Evans in the use of *Acopsis*.

KEY TO THE SPECIES OF ACOPSIS FOUND IN HAWAII

1. Median length of vertex of head of female, as measured from above, distinctly longer than median line of pronotum; male mostly pale beneath (dried specimens)........**mollipes** (Say).
2. Median length of vertex of female subequal to length of pronotum; male mostly dark beneath (dried specimens).........
....**minerva** (Ball).

Acopsis minerva (Ball) (fig. 3).

Draeculacephala minerva Ball, 1927:36.

Draeculacephala mollipes, in Hawaiian literature as the result of misidentification.

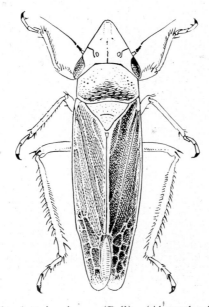

Figure 3—*Acopsis minerva* (Ball). (Abernathy drawing.)

Kauai, Oahu, Molokai, Maui, Hawaii.

Immigrant. A North American species. First found in Hawaii in Honolulu in 1912 by J. Nunes.

Hostplants: Bermuda grass, grasses, rice, sedges, sugarcane.

Parasites: *Gonatocerus mexicanus* Perkins (Hymenoptera: Mymaridae); *Oligosita caerulocephala* (Fullaway) and *Brachystella lutea* (Fullaway) (Hymenoptera: Trichogrammatidae); *Ootetrastichus beatus* Perkins (Hymenoptera: Eulophidae). These are all egg parasites.

Van Duzee identified the first examples of this species taken in Hawaii as *A. mollipes* (Say), but in 1942 Oman identified the species as *A. minerva*. See Swezey, O. H., *Proc. Hawaiian Ent. Soc.,* 11(3):263–264, 1943.

The eggs are long and curved. When laid in sugarcane, the tissues around the oviposition sites turn red and make conspicuous colored spots on the cane leaves.

Acopsis mollipes (Say) (fig. 4).

Tettigonia mollipes Say, 1831:312.

Draeculacephala mollipes (Say), of authors.

Kauai, Oahu, Hawaii.

Immigrant. A native of the United States. This form is a more recent arrival in the Territory than *minerva*. The earliest captures I have seen are as follows: Oahu, Honouliuli Beach, sand dunes, June 9, 1934 (E. Y. Hosaka); Hawaii, Hilo Sugar Planters' Substation, December, 1936 (F. X. Williams); Kauai, Lihue, January 28, 1939 (C. E. Pemberton).

Hostplants: watercress, and other plants not yet recorded as hosts in Hawaii.

In 1945 this species was reported to be causing serious damage to watercress near Honolulu where it swarmed on the plant. Growers reported the loss of several crops, but control was obtained by the use of rotenone.

Osborn and Knull (1939:111–114, fig. 42) give a detailed account of this species in North America. There it is called the "tenderfoot leafhopper" or the "sharp headed leafhopper."

Figure 4—*Acopsis mollipes* (Say), lateral and dorsal views of female.

Subfamily MACROPSINAE Evans, 1938

Genus **MACROPSIS** Lewis, 1835

This genus may be distinguished most easily in Hawaii because the middle point of the anterior margin of the pronotum projects forward beyond a line drawn between the anterior edges of the eyes as indicated in the figure. It is a nearly cosmopolitan group. It is doubtfully represented in our fauna by a possibly immigrant species.

Macropsis occidentalis (Van Duzee) (fig. 5).

Pediopsis occidentalis Van Duzee, 1889:238.

Macropsis hawaiiensis Osborn, 1935:11, fig. 1. New synonym.

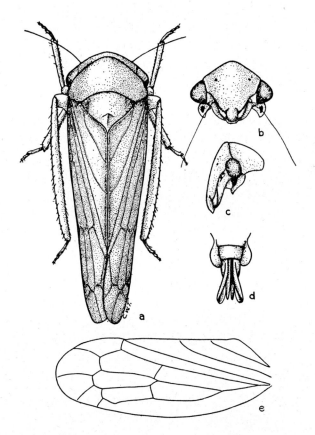

Figure 5—*Macropsis occidentalis* (Van Duzee) (from the holotype male of *hawaiiensis* Osborn). (After Osborn, 1935.)

Hawaii (?).

Immigrant (?). A species from southwestern United States. This species was redescribed as a Hawaiian species by Osborn from a single male specimen supposedly taken by Giffard at 29 miles, Kilauea, 4,000 feet, on *Coprosma pubens* (?), and to my knowledge it has not been recovered in Hawaii since Giffard supposedly collected the type in 1917. Osborn noted the close relationship of his type with certain species, especially North American, and he said (1935:12), "Were it not for the very definite record given with this specimen, I should think best to omit description [of it] as it would seem possibly a straggler or accidental immigrant." The "definite record" does not remove it from the realm of an accidental immigrant. Dr. Paul Oman has kindly sent me material of *M. occidentalis* which I have compared with Osborn's type at the Bishop Museum, and the above synonymy is the result. It is doubtful that Osborn's type was collected in Hawaii. Giffard collected extensively in California and it is probable that the specimen in question is mislabeled; perhaps it got mixed with some Kilauea material by accident.

Subfamily TYPHLOCYBINAE

Eupteryginae.

We have only a single immigrant species to represent this group in our Territory. The absence of tegminal cross-veins in the basal half or more of the wing and the subbasal forking instead of discal forking of the veins serve to distinguish it from the other subfamilies found in Hawaii.

Genus EMPOASCA Walsh, 1862

This large, widespread genus contains a number of species of economic importance. A good review of the genus in North America will be found in Poos and Wheeler, 1943. In our fauna, the single representative species can only be confused with *Balclutha*. However, the venation of the tegmina is conspicuously different. The veins run from the base to the cross-veins without forking and are weakly defined basad of the middle.

Empoasca solana DeLong (figs. 7, f; 27).
    Empoasca solana DeLong, 1931:50, fig. 10 (male terminalia). Osborn, 1935: 61, fig. 27, *a–c*.

The bean leafhopper (amaranth jassid, in local literature).
Kauai, Oahu, Molokai, Maui, Lanai, Hawaii.
Immigrant. A widespread North American pest. First found in the Territory by Ehrhorn at Honolulu in 1918 at a light.

Hostplants: amaranth, beet, blackeye bean, castor bean, celery, celtuce, cowpea, *Datura,* eggplant, garden bean, lettuce, lima bean, melon, papaya, peanut, potato, summer squash, Swiss chard, tomato, watermelon, yellow cosmos.

This green, transparent-winged leafhopper is one of our most important bean pests, and it has been reported damaging eggplant, peanuts, lettuce and other truck crops. It feeds principally on the undersurfaces of the leaves and causes "burning," yellowing, stippling and shriveling. It frequently becomes excessively abundant and artificial control must be resorted to to save the crops attacked. Beans are most severely attacked in hot, dry, lowland areas. It has not been proved to carry any plant diseases in Hawaii as yet.

Control: Spraying with Bordeaux mixture has been used with some success, but sulphur dust or a pyrethrum–sulphur dust is more highly recommended and has given good control. Satisfactory control is also reported from the use of pyrethrum–talc dust.

Subfamily JASSINAE

Bythoscopidae Dohrn, 1859.

Bythoscopinae, of authors.

This subfamily is not represented by endemic species in Hawaii, although some of our native leafhoppers formerly were placed here. The one immigrant species is easily distinguished from all our other leafhoppers because of the numerous small spines on the tegmina. The more fundamental character, however, is the comparatively deeply set bases of the antennae which are narrowly covered above by an "antennal ledge." The head is very broad with a short vertex, and the pronotum is strongly striolated transversely. Some of our *Nesophryne* may be confused with this subfamily, but the characters outlined in the key and under *Nesophryne* will serve to separate the groups.

Genus **STRAGANIA** Stål, 1862

This is a widespread genus represented in our Territory by a single immigrant species. The combination of the pronotum being broader than the head across the eyes and the conspicuous elytral setulae will serve as a ready means of separating it from the other genera of the subfamily in Hawaii.

Bythoscopus has been used for this group in Hawaii. The two species *Bythoscopus viduus* Stål and *Bythoscopus peregrinans* Stål were reported from Hawaii in error in the "Eugenie's Resa." (See Stål, 1859.)

Subgenus **Penestragania** Beamer and Lawson, 1945

Stragania robusta (Uhler) (fig. 6).

Pachyopsis robustus Uhler, Bull. U. S. Geol. Geog. Survey 3:467, 1877 (I have not seen this reference).

Bythoscopus robustus (Uhler) Osborn, 1935:12.

Stragania (Penestragania) robusta (Uhler) Beamer and Lawson, 1945:53, pl. 1, figs. 1, 1a.

Figure 6—*Stragania robusta* (Uhler).

Oahu, Molokai.

Immigrant. A North American species common from Florida to California. First found by Swezey at Kawela Bay, Oahu, in 1933.

Hostplants: *Ambrosia artemisiaefolia* (ragweed), Bermuda grass, *Prosopis* (algaroba), *Scaevola frutescens*.

In our fauna, this is a distinct species. Perhaps the most outstanding character is the conspicuous dark spines which cover the pale-greenish or yellowish fore-wing membrane. It is between 4 and 5 mm. in length. I have not examined any nymphs. The adults are attracted to lights.

Subfamily EUSCELINAE

This is the largest subfamily of jassids, and it is the only one represented by native species in Hawaii.

With the exception of *Deltocephalus, Balclutha* and *Nesolina,* which feed upon grasses, all of the other representatives of the group found in Hawaii feed upon shrubs or trees.

The following combination of characters serves to distinguish our species from the other subfamilies now found in Hawaii: ocelli at the apices of the frontal sutures and between crown and front, not on crown; lora and genae broad and flat; antennal ledges obsolete and antennal depressions shallow; with the exception of *Balclutha* and *Nesolina,* which may have partially reduced tegminal venation, the venation of the tegmina is complete; there is a membranous "appendix" along the inner margin of the tegminal membrane. With the exception of *Balclutha,* which are pale green or yellowish species without tegminal marking, the other species have prominent color patterns and many are beautiful and striking in color and pattern.

Our species of *Nesophryne* might be confused with the Jassinae because of their broad heads, short crowns and strongly striolated pronota, but the character of the insertions of the antennae will separate the groups. The slender, pale *Balclutha* might be confused with *Empoasca* in the Typhlocybinae, but the more complete

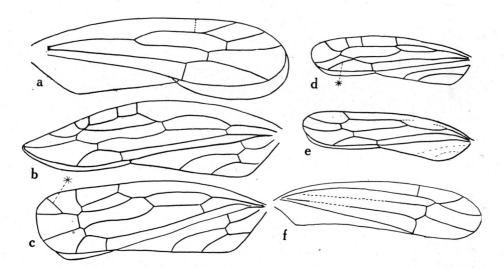

Figure 7—Diagrams of wings of some Cicadellidae: **a,** right tegmen of holotype female of *Balclutha kilaueae* (Kirkaldy) (claval veins omitted); **b,** left tegmen of *Kirkaldiella ewana* Osborn, from the type series; **c,** left tegmen of *Kirkaldiella euphorbiae* Osborn, from the type series (vein marked with asterisk may or may not be present, thus altering the number of apical cells); **d,** left tegmen of *Nesolina lineata* Osborn, from the type series (vein marked with asterisk may be absent); **e,** left tegmen of *Balclutha timberlakei* (Osborn), paratype; **f,** right tegmen of *Empoasca solana* DeLong (claval veins omitted).

tegminal venation plus the presence of an appendix on the tegminal membrane will serve to distinguish *Balclutha.* Also, on *Balclutha,* the tegmina overlap strongly behind and on the hind margin there is a distinct angle formed by the junction of the clavus and membrane as the illustrations show.

KEY TO THE GENERA OF EUSCELINAE FOUND IN HAWAII

1. Pronotum coarsely and conspicuously transversely striolate; head broad, crown usually short and broad; comparatively stout, heavy species to very stout species...
.... **Nesophryne** Kirkaldy.
Not such species..................................... 2

2(1). Fore wings with three anteapical cells (check carefully;
the outer anteapical cell may be small and obscured by
coloring) 3
Fore wings with two anteapical cells...................... 6

3(2). Outer anteapical cell (often much reduced in size) well isolated from outer apical cell and normally connected to
it by a longitudinal vein which is usually longer than
breadth of outer apical cell (see fig. 9, center)........
.... **Nesophrosyne** Kirkaldy.
Outer anteapical cell not so formed, but broadly joining
outer apical cell (see fig. 9, top)...................... 4

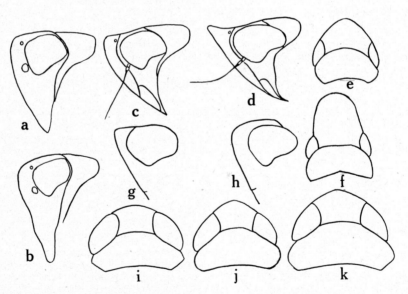

Figure 8—Outlines of heads of some Cicadellidae: **a,** *Nesophrosyne pipturi* Kirkaldy; **b,** *Nesophrosyne gouldiae* Kirkaldy; **c,** *Kirkaldiella ewana* Osborn, paratype; **d,** *Kirkaldiella euphorbiae* Osborn, paratype; **e,** *Nesolina lineata* Osborn, adult; **f,** *Nesolina lineata* Osborn, nymph; **g,** *Nesophrosyne signatula* Osborn, holotype; **h,** *Nesophrosyne notatula* Osborn, holotype; **i,** *Nesophrosyne perkinsi* (Kirkaldy), cotype; **j,** *Nesophrosyne ponapona* Kirkaldy, cotype; **k,** *Nesophrosyne pipturi* Kirkaldy, cotype (?).

4(3).   Vertex broadly rounded (in anterior outline as viewed
          from above), short, very little longer at middle than
          near eyes, only about one-half as long as pronotum;
          green species ....**Opsius** Fieber.

        Vertex rounded, pointed or roundly pointed in front, but
          distinctly longer at middle than at sides and at least
          three-fourths as long as pronotum................... 5

5(4).   Vertex broadly rounded or roundly pointed (then exten-
          sively and broadly depressed behind the thin apical
          margin), but not sharply pointed; tegmina densely
          opaque and with numerous pale spots..............
          ....**Kirkaldiella** Osborn.

        Vertex prolonged and sharply pointed, not strongly de-
          pressed behind fore margin; tegmina subhyaline, not
          pale-spotted..................**Deltocephalus** Burmeister.

6(2).   Fore wings with two discal cells...................
          ....**Nesophrosyne** subgenus **Nesoreias** Kirkaldy.
        Fore wings with only one discal cell................... 7

7(6).   Head, as measured from directly above, equal or subequal
          in length along median line to median line of pronotum,
          conspicuously pointed..................**Nesolina** Osborn.

        Head rounded or roundly pointed and obviously shorter
          along median line than pronotum......**Balclutha** Kirkaldy.

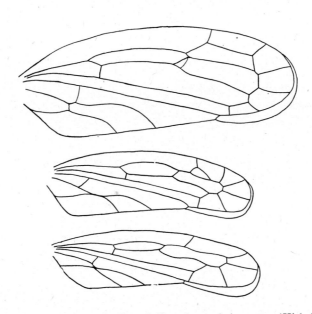

Figure 9—Outlines of tegminal venation of *Nesophryne kaiamamao* (Kirkaldy), top; *Neso-phrosyne* (*Nesophrosyne*) *perkinsi* (Kirkaldy), center; and *Nesophrosyne* (*Nesoreias*) *insularis* Kirkaldy, bottom.

Genus **NESOPHRYNE** Kirkaldy, 1907a:160

This is an endemic genus which Kirkaldy (1907:160) said was "Allied to *Eutettix,* but the habitus is quite different, and the vertex much shorter, more declivous, with the eyes scarcely so wide as the transversely striolate pronotum." In 1910 (p. 556) Kirkaldy gave an expanded description. Osborn (1935:8–9) gave no other notes on the relationships of the genus. *Eutettix* and other allied genera occur in the islands southwest of Hawaii. W. E. China has recently examined the genus for me and writes that it seems to have been "derived from *Goniagnathus* Fieb., a genus widespread in Europe and Asia . . ." I have found the male genitalia to be of the same type as *Nesophrosyne* and *Kirkaldiella.* In fact, I do not see how these three genera can be separated on the basis of their genitalia. The venation of the tegmina is similar to that of *Kirkaldiella.* Perhaps all three genera have sprung from the same basic stock.

It is remarkable that most of the species of this group (considering the undescribed species, too) so closely resemble *Bythoscopus* yet belong to a distinct subfamily. They are our only native species to have coarse transverse striolations on the pronotum.

The described species are from Kauai, but I have seen new species from Oahu, Lanai and Maui, and these include the most divergent forms.

Two species were described by Kirkaldy (1902:114–115) in *Bythoscopus,* but when he described *Nesophryne* (1907:160) and later (1910:557) when he added a new species, he did not have access to the types of the two species described under *Bythoscopus* and suggested that he might have redescribed those species. Osborn (1935:8) thought that he had identified three of Kirkaldy's four "species" among the fairly large number of specimens examined by him, but he was misled by the literature.

In Perkins' letter (January 31, 1922), referred to above, he stated:

Nesophryne. I cannot furnish any information as to types of this genus. The types of *kukanaroa* and *kaiamamao* ought to be in the B[ritish] M[useum] as apparently K[irkaldy] did not have them in Honolulu. *Filicicola* and *microlepiae* should be amongst Giffard's specimens, but I doubt whether K[irkaldy] labelled these distinctively, as he had no need to send them back to England like the others. Types from my collection he evidently partly labelled as such [by attaching pieces of red paper] but at the time he knew it was my intention to send these back with those belonging to the "Sandwich Is. Committee." One or two specimens of *Nesophryne* (as I suppose) in my collection were not named at all by him.

With these valuable notes to guide me, I have been successful in finding Kirkaldy's holotype specimens in Giffard's material at the Bishop Museum. As Perkins surmised, they bear no type labels. I have labeled these specimens as the holotypes and have placed them in the type collection at the Bishop Museum. Three nymphs of *filicicola,* including the one mislabeled "Kilauea, Hawaii," instead of "Kilauea, Kauai," as noted by Kirkaldy in his original description, have been placed with the holotype.

A comparison of these types, *filicicola* and *microlepiae,* has led me to consider
them to be synonyms as is indicated later in the text. Kirkaldy described *microlepiae*
a few years after *filicicola,* and he said (1910:557), "This may be only a dark var.
of the preceding [*filicicola*], but I do not think so." The type of *microlepiae* is
closely similar to that of *filicicola,* but it has the dark maculations intensified so that
it is considerably darker than *filicicola,* but the color pattern is essentially duplicated.
The type of *filicicola* may be a teneral individual. I have examined the external
male terminalia and find that they are alike, as the illustrations indicate. In the
series of specimens of the various species which I have examined there is considerable variation in color and intensity of the color, and it appears that the difference
in color of the two types comes within the range of variation for a single species.
The two names are therefore considered to apply to one species, and these in turn
fall as synonyms of *kaiamamao.*

Osborn's description of the male terminalia of *filicicola* is erroneous. I have the
specimen before me from which he evidently drew his description. It is not *filicicola*
but appears to be *kukanaroa,* a species not recognized by Osborn amongst the material he examined. Osborn described the male terminalia of *filicicola* as follows:
"valve small, triangular; plates triangular, tips acute." From a glance at the figure
of the terminalia of the type of *filicicola* presented here, it will be obvious that

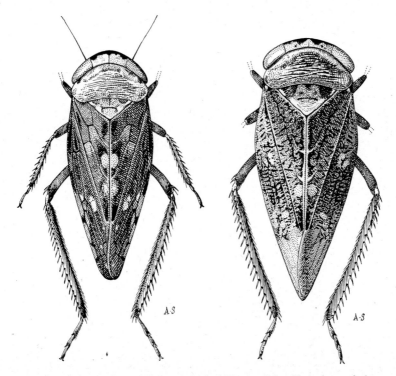

Figure 10—*Nesophryne kaiamamao* (Kirkaldy), holotype, left; *Nesophryne kukanaroa* (Kirkaldy), holotype, right. (Drawn at the British Museum of Natural History by Smith.)

Osborn described the terminalia of a different species. The terminalia of the specimen confused with *filicicola* are illustrated here under the name of *kukanaroa*.

The specimens of the several species of the genus examined by me have been taken on *Elaeocarpus, Myrsine (Suttonia), Cheirodendron, Osmanthus* and evidently other unidentified trees.

The nymphs are stout creatures and do not have numerous long bristles on the abdominal tergites.

KEY TO THE SPECIES OF NESOPHRYNE

1. Male with head as viewed from directly above with front margin bluntly pointed and projecting distinctly beyond anterior margin of eyes, as illustrated; hind margin between inner corners of eyes only slightly longer than greatest chord of an eye (1.5:1.3); when viewed from side, front and vertex form an angle.....................**kaiamamao** (Kirkaldy).

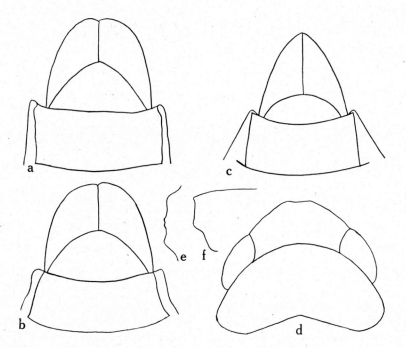

Figure 11—Details of Cicadellidae: **a,** ventral view of male terminalia of *Nesophryne kaiamamao* (Kirkaldy) (from the type of *microlepiae* Kirkaldy, and here considered the same as *filicicola*—compare with **b**); **b,** the same of the type of *Nesophryne filicicola* Kirkaldy (now a synonym of *kaiamamao*); **c,** the same of *Nesophryne kukanaroa* (Kirkaldy); **d,** head and pronotum of *Balclutha kilaueae* (Kirkaldy), holotype female (the head appears unnaturally blunted, but it is variable in shape); **e,** outline of last ventral segment of *Balclutha kilaueae* (Kirkaldy), holotype, from directly beneath; **f,** the same in side view. (Contours in **e** and **f** are somewhat variable, especially the median point.)

2. Male with front margin of head broadly and flatly arcuate and hardly projecting forward of eyes, as figured; hind margin between inner corners of eyes much longer than greatest chord of an eye (2 : 1.5) ; when viewed from side, front and vertex not angulate but together forming a broad, smooth curve.............................**kukanaroa** (Kirkaldy).

Nesophryne kaiamamao (Kirkaldy) (figs. 9; 10; 11, a, b; 14, d).

Bythoscopus kaiamamao Kirkaldy, 1902: 115.

Nesophryne kaiamamao (Kirkaldy) Kirkaldy, 1910:557. Osborn, 1935:10.

Nesophryne filicicola Kirkaldy, 1907a:160. Osborn, 1935:9. Genotype. New synonym.

Nesophryne microlepiae Kirkaldy, 1910: 557. Osborn, 1935:9. New synonym.

Endemic. Kauai (type locality: "high plateau").

Hostplants: *Microlepia strigosa* (not *Gleichenia dichotoma* as reported in the original description; correction of error by Kirkaldy, 1910: 557), *Elaeocarpus bifidus*. It is probable that *Microlepia* is not a hostplant.

The holotype is in the British Museum, and a drawing of it is presented herewith.

Nesophryne kukanaroa (Kirkaldy) (figs. 10; 11, c).

Bythoscopus kukanaroa Kirkaldy, 1902: 114.

Nesophryne kukanaroa (Kirkaldy) Kirkaldy, 1910: 557. Osborn, 1935: 10.

Endemic. Kauai (type locality: Halemanu, 4,000 feet).

Hostplant: *Cheirodendron*.

The holotype is in the British Museum, and it is figured here.

Genus **KIRKALDIELLA** Osborn, 1935:13

This genus was described to receive two Hawaiian species and is endemic. Osborn thought it resembled or was allied to the non-Hawaiian genera *Eutettix, Mesamia* and *Megabyzus*. However, he stated (1935:17) that *Nesophrosyne halemanu* Kirkaldy and *Nesophrosyne haleakala* Kirkaldy ". . . seem to be somewhat intermediate between the species of *Kirkaldiella* and *Nesophrosyne* as the head is more flattened and the vertex margin sharper than in those species, but the outer anteapical approaches the form common in *Nesophrosyne*." It appears to me that *Kirkaldiella* is a local offshoot of *Nesophrosyne*. The male genitalia are similar to *Nesophrosyne* and *Nesophryne*.

The two included species differ from each other in several conspicuous characters. I do not feel that the generic characters outlined by Osborn entirely fit the second (*ewana*), and the formation of the vertex of the head, as used by Osborn in his key to the genera of Jassinae (p. 13) does not apply to *ewana*, although it is applicable to *euphorbiae*.

The nymphs have two rows of long bristles on each side of the dorsum of the abdomen, a feature in common with *Nesophrosyne*.

KEY TO THE SPECIES OF KIRKALDIELLA

1. Median line of vertex of head slightly longer than median line of pronotum; head, in side view as in figure 8, d; tegmina broadly rounded at apex.................**euphorbiae** Osborn.
2. Median line of vertex distinctly shorter than median line of pronotum; head in side view as in figure 8, c; tegmina sharply pointed at apex............................**ewana** Osborn.

Kirkaldiella euphorbiae Osborn (figs. 7, c; 8, d; 12).

Kirkaldiella euphorbiae Osborn, 1935:14, fig. 2. Genotype.

Figure 12—*Kirkaldiella euphorbiae* Osborn, paratype, left; *Kirkaldiella ewana* Osborn, paratype, right (tips of wings damaged).

Endemic. Molokai (type locality: Moomomi).

Hostplant: *Euphorbia*.

The types are in the Bishop Museum.

Kirkaldiella ewana Osborn (figs. 7, b; 8, c; 12).

Kirkaldiella ewana Osborn, 1935:15, fig. 3.

Endemic. Oahu (type locality: Ewa).

Hostplant: *Euphorbia multiformis*.

The types are in the Bishop Museum.

Genus **NESOPHROSYNE** Kirkaldy, 1907a:160

Kirkaldy, 1910:558, expanded description.

This native genus is our largest complex of the family. W. E. China is of the opinion that it is a possible derivative of the *Thamnotettix* complex. The tegminal venation is slightly simplified from that of *Nesophryne* and *Kirkaldiella* by the reduction of the outer anteapical cell, and it is further reduced in the subgenus *Nesoreias* in which this cell is lost (see the illustrations). The male genitalia are of the same type as those of *Kirkaldiella* and *Nesophryne*. It would appear that in spite of the different facies of some of the broad species of *Nesophryne* (unde-scribed) these genera may be much more closely allied than has heretofore been believed and that perhaps they may have come from the same stem.

Prof. Dwight DeLong has given me the following note on a comparison of the male genitalia: "The genus *Scaphoideus* has male plates which are elongated and rounded at the tip. The genus *Osbornellus* has plates which are long, tapered to filamentous tips which are covered with spines. The plates of *Nesophrosyne* are like those of *Osbornellus*. The internal genital structures are distinct. The aedeagus is usually Y-shaped in ventral view in *Nesophrosyne* and in all the species which I have examined the apex of each arm of the aedeagus is bent shortly with a slender terminal process. This seems to be characteristic of the genus. . . . I consider these two genera distinct."

In spite of the fact that 62 forms have been described, the genus is comparatively poorly known, and I believe that it includes well over 100 species. No key has been written to separate the species. It is a difficult group. Kirkaldy (1910:558) said, "This genus—*Nesophrosyne*—is the most difficult of the Hemipterous genera of these islands to deal with specifically. It is impossible in some instances, from the material before me, to say whether certain forms are species or only local varieties. A much more adequate material, a knowledge of the range of variation, of the foodplants, and of the nymphs, is necessary before the synonymy can be settled. The variation in some forms known to me is quite bewildering." The difficulties now facing the student who wishes to identify his collections are great in spite of the fact that only Kirkaldy and Osborn have described the known species. The genus is in need of critical and much more careful study than it has received heretofore.

The nymphs have two rows of conspicuous bristles on each side of the dorsum of the abdomen, and they are often very different one from another and should furnish good characters for separation of the species.

Our native *Nesomimesa* wasps sometimes provision their nests with these leafhoppers. Unidentified *Gonatopus* (Dryinidae) wasps attack some of the species.

I have not recorded full lists of hostplants from series which I have considered might be mixed species. The hostplant relationships of the group are not well known.

KEY TO THE SUBGENERA OF NESOPHROSYNE

1. Tegmina with three anteapical cells (fig. 9, center)..**Nesophrosyne.**
2. Tegmina with only two anteapical cells (fig. 9, bottom)..**Nesoreias.**

Subgenus **Nesophrosyne** Kirkaldy

The construction of a key to the many described forms of *Nesophrosyne* is a most difficult task. Not only is the genus a confusing natural complex of complexes, but the workers who have described the known species have added not a little to the confusion. Under *Nesoreias* I have noted some of the confusing variation that is encountered in tegminal venation. To one as inexperienced with the leafhoppers as I, the task has been almost overwhelming. I believe that the entire group must be gone over with great care by a skilled, broad-minded, biologist-systematist beginning with a careful revision of the type specimens of all of the known species before

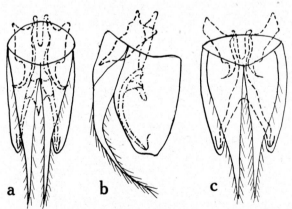

Figure 13—Sketches of male genitalia of *Nesophrosyne*: **a, b,** ventral and lateral views of *N. perkinsi* (Kirkaldy), genotype of *Nesophrosyne*; **c,** ventral view of parts of *N. nuenue* Kirkaldy. (Kindly drawn for me by Dwight DeLong from specimens determined by Osborn and now in the Ohio State University collection.)

we can hope to obtain even a fair understanding of the genus. The internal genitalia of not a single species has been illustrated heretofore, yet today these organs are considered of primary importance to identification by workers on continental faunas. Much confusion is caused by teneral specimens which usually are paler and have color patterns distinct from fully matured individuals. The types of certain species possibly are teneral specimens, and this fact may make the recognition of the species difficult.

In Osborn's text, obviously allied species frequently are separated widely, and there are remarkably few notes on the relationships of the species. Brief summaries explaining how the species were interrelated and how they differed from one another would have saved us many hours of toil. Many of his descriptive comments are almost meaningless, as applied to individual species, or they are generic. The failure to standardize the descriptions so that the same characters were given equal treatment for each species is most confusing, and it makes it difficult or impossible to assemble diagnostic differences from the series of descriptions. Some of his series of specimens (*bicolorata,* and others, for example) obviously contain more than one species. He failed frequently to take into account and describe the variability of color and color pattern and usually arbitrarily described the color and color pattern of a single individual.

None of Kirkaldy's 40 species included in his *Fauna Hawaiiensis* report of 1910 was illustrated, and Kirkaldy's carelessness with the specimens and his failure to designate types properly adds to the difficulties. Osborn's comments on Kirkaldy's report indicate that he also found the report difficult to work with, for he said (1935:5), "It is unfortunate considering this difficulty that Kirkaldy did not make his descriptions more complete and specific so that comparisons would be more satisfactory. Many descriptions he has confined to a few words, referring to some other species for comparison, and, without positive identification for his other species, the description is of course almost valueless. Kirkaldy of course made

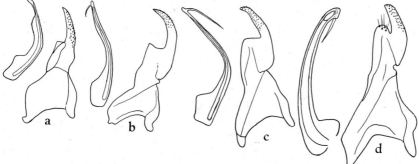

Figure 14—Male genital structures of *Nesophrosyne* and *Nesophryne*: **a,** *Nesophrosyne angulifera* Osborn; **b,** *Nesophrosyne furculata* Osborn, paratype; **c,** *Nesophrosyne peleae* Osborn, paratype; **d,** *Nesophryne kaiamamao* (Kirkaldy). The left figure in each pair of drawings is one arm of the aedeagus, the right figure is a paramere. The drawings were made from glycerine mounts pressed down tightly with a cover slip. The contours of the arms of the aedeagus are somewhat different when seen from the side in their natural positions, and this difference should be allowed for when comparisons are made.

his descriptions from a small number of individuals, many from single specimens representing one sex, or with no evidence concerning the sexes belonging to the same species."

The following key cannot be taken as a final piece of work. It is a first attempt, nothing more. It is, I realize, difficult to use, and it may not work for all species or all specimens of single species. I had been inclined not to include it here, but I have found that it has at least some use and some species can be readily identified by it, and as it may serve as a building block for some future monographer, I have considered its inclusion worth while. In the light of this difficulty, I have written a second series of keys based primarily upon geographical distribution and which follows the main key hereafter and which will be found easier to use for localized lots of material. It is to be regretted, however, that time was not available to enable me to make detailed studies of the genitalia and to incorporate the characters in the keys.

I have, unfortunately, been unable to see authentic specimens of the following six Kirkaldy species and have had to omit them from the key: *nubigena, opalescens, paludicola, silvigena, umbricola,* and *umbrigena* (but see our figures made from the types). All except *umbrigena* and *silvigena* were also unknown to Osborn. I would not rely upon Kirkaldy's descriptions for the identification of these species from our assemblage of unidentified material. Osborn was unable to find the types of any of these species in the British Museum in 1932, but they have been located and drawn for this text at the British Museum. Osborn gave some notes and comments on these species in his 1935 report and redescribed what he considered representatives of *silvigena* and *umbrigena.* The series of specimens returned by Osborn to the Bishop Museum under the name *silvigena* contains several species and cannot be relied upon. The material I have had before me possibly contains a few species which have been misnamed, and these, if any, will cause confusion in the key.

Tentative General Key to the Species of Nesophrosyne

(excluding the species listed above)

See also the individual island keys below.

Where membrane is referred to, I mean the spaces between the veins, not just the apical part of the corium.

1.   Head with vertex distinctly produced and pointed (see fig. 17 of *lineata*), when measured from side, distance between anterior edge of an eye and apex is about one-half length of an eye, and when measured from directly above, the distance between middle of base to a line drawn between apices of eyes is about equal to or shorter than length of vertex beyond this line; vertex with a narrow, white, median vitta bounded on each side by a broad, dark vitta in all species excepting *angulifera*...... 2

Head not so formed, vertex shorter and more rounded, although pointed in some forms, when measured from side the distance beyond fore edge of an eye is distinctly less than one-half of length of an eye, usually about one-third or less, and when measured from directly above, the distance between middle of base and a line drawn between anterior edges of eyes is greater than length from this line to apex of vertex; vertex rarely with such a color pattern as above................ 5

2(1).   Face with grill of dark transverse lines conspicuous; vertex without a pale median vitta bounded on either side by a dark vitta...................**angulifera** Osborn.
Face without a grill of dark lines; vertex with a narrow, pale, median vitta bounded on either side by a broad, dark vitta 3

3(2).   Costal margin almost entirely pale, adjacent membrane mostly hyaline or subhyaline excepting at apex and on cross-veins..........................**albicosta** Osborn.
Costal margin and adjacent membrane almost entirely dark colored 4

4(3).   Abdominal ventrites mostly black..........**lineata** Osborn.
Abdominal ventrites with broad bands of yellow or largely yellow ....**affinis** Osborn.

5(1).   Head comparatively peculiarly formed when viewed from side or in front, appearing longer and more nearly vertical than is usual for the genus (fig. 8, b); face measured from top of apex of vertex to apex of clypeus (as seen from front) longer than greatest distance across head (including eyes) as measured from front (host-plant *Cyrtandra*)....................**gouldiae** Kirkaldy.
Head not so formed................................. 6

6(5).   Wings and pronotum pale and densely flecked with minute, dark specks but without prominent maculae and without prominent, dark-colored veins except toward apex 7
Wings without such dense, minute flecks, usually with dark maculae and/or dark veins, or, if pale, never flecked as above................................. 8

7(6).   Vertex flattened and forming a distinct angle with front, as in figure 8, g, as seen from side.......**signatula** Osborn.
Vertex rounded off into front as seen from side, as in figure 8, h..........................**notatula** Osborn.

8(6).   Undersurface, including pleura and venter, almost entirely or entirely pale (excluding ovipositor), not colored, not even with narrow dark bands on abdominal ventrites 9
Undersurface partly or largely colored, dark colored or conspicuously maculate, or with broad or narrow abdominal bands, never pale and immaculate...........19

9(8).   Head, measured from side, with distance from suture between ocellus and an eye to apex of vertex divided into length of an eye equals less than 4...............10
This measurement equals 4.5 or more..................16

10(9).   Tegminal membrane without conspicuous dark maculae
          other than an apical infuscation; dorsum usually pale-
          yellow or amber colored..........................11
          Tegmina with distinct dark maculae and in some species
          with veins conspicuously dark......................13

11(10).   Pronotum obviously broader than head across eyes; teg-
          mina with rather obscure white patches.....**ehu** Kirkaldy.
          Pronotum subequal in breadth to head.................12

12(11).   Vertex, as viewed from side, distinctly concave; last ven-
          tral segment of female very slightly, hardly concave
          on sides..........................**cuprescens** Osborn.
          Vertex not concave, rounded off to front; last ventral
          segment of female deeply concave on each side.......
          .... **ignigena** Kirkaldy.

13(10).   Tegminal veins mostly conspicuously dark from base to
          apex, even those on clavus largely dark, and making a
          characteristic and outstanding dark, net-like pattern..
          .... **furculata** Osborn.
          Tegminal veins not so colored, sometimes partly dark,
          but never so conspicuously so as above...............14

14(13).   Tegminal membrane not milky and without distinct milky
          spots, more yellowish or transparent amber in color
          and typically with only the following dark maculae:
          tip of clavus dark, costal margin with a brown blotch
          about midway between base and nodus where there is a
          similar blotch, bounding veins of outer apical cell em-
          browned and dark color extending over most of next
          to outer apical cell; pronotum dark on either side or
          over most of disc....................**touchardii** Osborn.
          Tegmina not as described above, membrane largely milky
          or with distinct milky spots and typically with more
          brown maculae 15

15(14).   Hind wings moderately transparent and with dark veins;
          tegminal membrane and veins tinged with brown.....
          .... **ponapona** Kirkaldy.
          Hind wings usually milky white, opaque, veins largely
          pale; tegmina distinctly paler (Note: This is very
          closely allied to the preceding, but it is a paler insect.)
          .... **pipturi** Kirkaldy.

16(9).   Clavus with a conspicuous yellow saddle mark bordered
          before and behind with black, most of tegminal veins
          dark colored..........................**mabae** Osborn.
          Not such species....................................17

17(16).   Tegmina with three or four nodal veins..**maritima** Kirkaldy.
          Tegmina with only a single nodal vein.................18

18(17).   Very pallid species, usually milky-white above or with a
          pale-yellowish or brownish tinge, but tegmina always
          at least with milky areas or spots, although the spots
          may be obscure (on *Sida*)...........**perkinsi** (Kirkaldy).
          Yellowish-brown species with amber-colored tegmina...
          .... **procellaris** Kirkaldy.

19(8). Median length of vertex divided into extreme breadth of head to outer edges of eyes equals 2.9 or more (measure very carefully with an eyepiece micrometer with vertex level) 20

This measurement equals less than 2.9, usually less than 2.8..40

20(19). Pronotum (by actual and careful measurement) slightly but distinctly and measurably broader than greatest breadth of head across greatest convexity of eyes (not at their hind edges).............................21

Pronotum narrower, about as broad as head across eyes, or just perceptibly broader, but not obviously broader (an optical illusion may confuse one into thinking that it is distinctly broader owing to the narrowing of the hind edges of the eyes, so measure carefully)..........24

21(20). Most or all of veins of tegmina individually mostly distinct and dark colored and forming a conspicuous reticulate pattern overall (a small slender species).......
.... **montivaga** Kirkaldy.

Few or none of veins separately dark colored and not forming such a pattern, and not especially distinct individually 22

22(21). Legs extensively dark or infuscated, especially femora; tegmina normally with a very conspicuous yellow saddle mark margined by black and with beautiful purplish-coppery reflections when rotated against light
.................................**myrsines** Kirkaldy.

Legs, excepting posterior tibiae, entirely pale; tegmina without a distinct saddle mark......................23

23(22). Head with a pale median vitta bounded on each side by a dark stripe; tegmina extensively dark or black with costal area subhyaline or milky-white..............
.............................**umbratilis** Kirkaldy.

Head not so colored, irregularly maculate; tegmina with dark maculae, but not extensively dark; costal area not subhyaline or white much before middle and with a large dark macula before middle.........**sinuata** Osborn.

24(20). Vertex conspicuously depressed behind apex (a Kauai species with a simple reticulate pattern on tegmina formed by dark veins).............**halemanu** Kirkaldy.

Vertex not so formed, usually obviously convex, but flattened in some species.............................25

25(24). Tegmina with a distinct and conspicuous color pattern which consists principally of numerous dashes of dark brown on yellow membrane with veins pale colored except caudad.........................**pele** Kirkaldy.

Tegmina not so colored.............................26

26(25). Tegmina with nearly all of color pattern made up by usually very conspicuous dark-colored veins on a greenish-yellow background or infuscations on veins but with some small dark areas in some cells or on clavus, but without a conspicuous saddle mark..................27

Tegmina either with extensive dark maculations or without such dark-colored veins or with a distinct saddle
mark 29

27(26). Tegmina with three or four nodal veins.............
....**nimbigena** Kirkaldy.
Tegmina with only a single nodal vein................28

28(27). Median length from fore edge of vertex to apex of scutellum (excluding the apical spine) divided into length
of tegmina equals about 2.6............**bobeae** Kirkaldy.
Median length from apex of scutellum to apex of vertex
divided into length of tegmina equals about 3.0.......
................................**silvicola** Kirkaldy.

29(26). Tegmina with costal area hyaline, or hyaline and partly
whitish from almost at base nearly to apex; clavus
typically greenish-yellow, area between this and pale
costal area dark; clavus without a diagonal dark mark
across greenish-yellow membrane.......**giffardi** Kirkaldy.
Tegmina with a different color pattern, if costal area is
paler than surrounding membrane, it is less extensively
so than above 30

30(29). Tegmina with color pattern somewhat similar to *giffardi,*
as described above, but with clavus with a conspicuous
dark band along base which obliquely crosses greenish-
yellow background dividing it into two pale maculae;
occasionally dark color is restricted to oblique mark
and is not present along base of clavus.............
........................**giffardi interrupta** Osborn.
Color pattern of tegmina distinct from that described
above 31

31(30). Almost entirely black species; tegmina usually with a
yellow saddle mark and a few pale or subhyaline spots
behind middle.........................**milu** Kirkaldy.
Not black species....................................32

32(31). Tegmina amber-colored or tinged with reddish, without
a saddle mark and not otherwise distinctly maculate....33
Tegmina maculate and usually with a conspicuous saddle
mark 35

33(32). Pronotum and clavus extensively and conspicuously red
.... **palustris** Kirkaldy.
Not so, largely amber-colored above...................34

34(33). Front of head without a transverse dark band below
ocelli ....**ulaula** Kirkaldy.
Front with a continuous dark transverse band just below
ocelli....................**ulaula nigrolineata** Kirkaldy.

35(32). Vertex black, pronotum, excepting anterior margin, yellow; each element of the yellow saddle mark elongate-
triangular and extending to less than one-half its
length from claval apex; area in front of bright saddle
mark with coppery reflections; an unusually bright-
colored species...................**nimbicola** Kirkaldy.
Not so colored, vertex usually not much darker than pronotum, or saddle mark is broader and does not extend
so near to claval apex............................36

36(35). Veins of tegmina conspicuously dark colored and tegmina
 with few to several white maculae in cells behind middle. 37
 Tegminal veins not mostly distinctly darker than membrane, or only partly so or largely masked by equally
 dark or darker membrane..........................38

37(36). Saddle mark hardly if any longer than length of pronotum ....**monticola** Kirkaldy.
 Saddle mark about twice as long as length of pronotum
 ....**mabae** Osborn.

38(36). Saddle mark of tegmina open, more or less C-shaped or
 broken and inconspicuous, not bordered by black.....
 .... **imbricola** Kirkaldy.
 Saddle mark of tegmina solid, bordered at least partially
 before and behind by black.........................39

39(38). Vertex and pronotum extensively black, tegmina with
 extensive black areas...............**myrsines** Kirkaldy.
 Vertex and pronotum largely pale, tegmina with only
 limited dark area; a rather brownish-orange species..
 .... **oreadis** Kirkaldy.

40(19). Pronotum (by careful measurement) slightly but distinctly broader than greatest breadth of head across eyes..41
 Pronotum narrower, about as broad, or hardly perceptibly
 broader than greatest breadth of head, but never obviously broader 43

41(40). Dorsum with an extensive amount of continuous dark or
 black coloring; tegmina with a strongly contrasted,
 yellow saddle mark (variable in extent).............
 .... **pluvialis** Kirkaldy.
 Dorsal color pattern not as above; tegmina without a distinct saddle mark, only veins and scattered maculae
 dark colored 42

42(41). Clypeus and lora almost or entirely dark; tegmina with
 extensive dark coloring in discal and adjacent cells...
 ....**montium** Kirkaldy.
 Clypeus and lora at most each with a dark apical spot;
 tegmina without such extensive dark coloring.......
 .... **ponapona** Kirkaldy.

43(40). Vertex distinctly, broadly depressed before apex, distinctly concave in longitudinal outline when viewed
 from side 44
 Vertex not so formed, usually distinctly convex, but flattened in some forms or obscurely depressed, but never
 distinctly so 45

44(43). Tegminal veins all or nearly all conspicuously dark colored
 ....**haleakala** Kirkaldy.
 Tegminal veins almost entirely pale..........**palolo** Osborn.

45(43). Membrane of tegmina extensively dark with large areas
 continuously dark or black and with or without a yellow saddle mark 46
 Tegmina not extensively dark, excepting veins and local
 infuscations and without a saddle mark..............49

46(45). Clavus extensively yellow, dark only at apex.. **peleae** Osborn.
Clavus dark at base as well as apex or more extensively
dark colored 47

47(46). Dorsum extensively dark or black; tegmina without a
pale saddle mark....................**bicolorata** Osborn.
Clavus with a distinct yellow area or saddle mark.......48

48(47). Yellow area of clavus distinctly elongate, extending from
base nearly to apex, clavus usually dark only outwardly
at base and at apex, at least without a saddle mark as
described below for *koleae* (the species confused with
myrsines by Osborn; see discussion under *myrsines*)...
....species ?
Clavus with a subrounded, well-defined yellow saddle
mark which is ringed with dark color and is normally
well isolated from base of clavus...................
..........................**Nesoreias koleae** (Kirkaldy).

49(45). Tegminal veins all or nearly all, including those on clavus,
conspicuously dark colored and forming a conspicu-
ous, somewhat net-like pattern......................50
Tegminal veins mostly pale, those on clavus never conspicuously dark colored............................52

50(49). Legs and face mostly pale...............**furculata** Osborn.
Legs and/or face with extensive dark coloring...........51

51(50). Lanai species with tegmina predominantly yellowish-
brown between veins.................**oneanea** Kirkaldy.
Maui species with tegmina clear or grayish between
veins, wings showing through to add to the grayish or
whitish cast........................**cinerea** Osborn.

52(49). At least hind tibiae with dark spots or dark coloring,
femora usually partly dark..........................53
Legs quite pale, without conspicuous dark areas..........54

53(52). Tegmina each with a large distinct milk-white blotch
(sometimes yellowish-white) at about middle of corium
(really a blend of three spots in adjacent cells), and
some milk-white spots above these on clavus........
....................................**obliqua** Osborn.
Tegmina without any such spots......**oneanea** Kirkaldy (?)

54(52). Vertex broadly arcuate in front as illustrated (fig. 19 of
nuenue) 55
Vertex more roundly pointed than arcuate (fig. 21 of
touchardii) 56

55(54). Outer anteapical cell reduced, only about one-half as
broad as narrowest part of adjacent anteapical cell, a
single nodal arising from near its base. (Note: There
is only one example under this name at the Bishop
Museum, identified by Osborn, and it may not be correctly named.)....................**craterigena** Kirkaldy.
Outer anteapical cell well developed, about as broad as
narrower part of adjacent anteapical cell, usually (always?) with two nodals..............**nuenue** Kirkaldy.

56(54). Tegmina with a small but prominent dark spot on nodal
from outer anteapical cell, but without dark areas
cephalad of this..................**oneanea** Kirkaldy (?)

Tegmina with one or more dark spots or blotches anterior
    to nodal dark patch...............................57
57(56). Pronotum with a large, variable dark blotch on each
    side; tip of clavus dark..............**touchardii** Osborn.
    Pronotum without such a dark colored patch.........
    .... **caelicola** Kirkaldy.

The following set of keys has been broken up according to island. Our knowledge of the distribution of the species is incomplete, and some confusion may result if representatives of certain species are found in new localities. However, these keys should be of aid in placing most of the described species, but it should not be assumed that because a specimen runs to a particular name in the key that it is automatically correctly identified. Further careful checking often may be needed, and there is no substitute for accurately named specimens to use for final comparison. The keys will serve, however, to eliminate many species from the list of possible name assignments.

ISLAND KEYS FOR THE SEPARATION OF THE SPECIES OF NESOPHROSYNE

KEY TO THE KAUAI NESOPHROSYNE

Although only three species have been recorded from Kauai, I have collected or examined probably a dozen or more species from that island, most of which appear to be new.

1. Face entirely pale; vertex black with a yellow median line; pronotum black; tegmina largely black with pale longitudinal maculae on clavus, some pale spots distad on clavus, and costal margin broadly pale from near base to near apex; a slender species.................**umbratilis** Kirkaldy.

2. Face with much dark coloring, clypeus dark, front with grill dark and distinct; vertex depressed behind apex, mostly pale, with a fine, dark median line which expands slightly just before apex, and a pair of subapical dark spots and a similar but less well-defined pair of dark subbasal spots; pronotum mostly pale; tegmina basically pale with contrasting dark (brown) veins, apices dark, and with some variable dark marks elsewhere, but veins outstanding; a stout species.........................**halemanu** Kirkaldy.

3. Pale ferruginous, face black, color encroaching on vertex, grill only visible at sides, ferruginous; sterna (entirely ?), femora (except apically) blackish, hind tibiae striped longitudinally with black, bristles pale ferruginous; membrane clouded with black inwardly (from original description; I have not seen this species, but see fig. 22, a)............
    ....**silvigena** Kirkaldy.

KEY TO THE OAHU NESOPHROSYNE

(20 forms)

(*N. opalescens* omitted, but see fig. 18.)

1.   Vertex strongly pointed, produced, distance along median line from line drawn between fore edges of eyes to apex about as long as distance from this line to base, median line pale, expanded slightly distad, flanked on either side from base to apex by a nearly black vitta, which occupies entire area between median line and eye at base, pale outside this vitta; pronotum and scutellum nearly all dark; tegmina mostly dark but with pale costal band from near base to apical cells...........
.....................................**albicosta** Osborn.
Not such species..................................... 2

2(1).   Pale species with vertex, thoracic nota and tegmina almost entirely covered with minute spatter-like flecks of dark color suggesting a dusting of sand, most distinct on tegmina and forming an unusual color pattern for *Nesophrosyne* 3
Not such species..................................... 4

3(2).   Vertex short and broadly rounded, its median length less than three-fourths as long as narrowest interocular breadth ....**notatula** Osborn.
Vertex pointed, nearly as long as shortest distance between eyes...........................**signatula** Osborn.

4(2).   Vertex pointed, produced, with a well-marked transverse depression between anterior edges of eyes; face with grill well-defined; vertex, pronotum and scutellum pale
....**palolo** Osborn.
Vertex not so depressed in combination with a produced, pointed vertex 5

5(4).   Head appearing longer and more nearly vertical than usual for genus (see fig. 8, b); face measured from top of apex of vertex to apex of clypeus (as seen from front) as long or longer than greatest distance across head (including eyes) as measured from front (on *Cytandra*) ....**gouldiae** Kirkaldy.
Head shorter and broader, usually distinctly broader across eyes than length in front (including frons and clypeus) 6

6(5).   Undersurface, including pleura and venter almost entirely or entirely pale (excluding ovipositor).......... 7
Undersurface partly or largely colored, dark colored or conspicuously maculate or with broad or narrow abdominal bands, never very pale and immaculate........12

7(6).   Vertex either depressed behind apex or with a subapical, impressed, transverse line........................... 8
Vertex convex, not so impressed subapically........... 9

8(7).   Vertex pointedly produced; tegmina with only one nodal vein ....**cuprescens** Osborn.

Vertex short and broadly rounded; tegmina with two or
more nodal veins.....................**maritima** Kirkaldy.

9(7).   Vertex very short, arcuate, only slightly produced beyond
eyes...............................**perkinsi** Kirkaldy.
Vertex pointed or roundly pointed, distinctly produced
beyond eyes 10

10(9).   Tegminal membrane not milky and without distinct milky
spots, more yellowish or transparent amber in color
and typically with only the following dark maculae:
tip of clavus dark, costal margin with a brown blotch
about midway between base and nodus where there is
a similar blotch, bounding veins of outer apical cell
embrowned and dark color extending over most of
next to outer apical cell; pronotum dark on either side
or over most of disc..................**touchardii** Osborn.
Tegmina not as described above, membrane largely milky
or with distinct milky spots and typically with more,
brown maculae 11

11(10). Hind wings moderately transparent and with dark veins;
tegminal membrane and veins tinged with brown.....
......................................**ponapona** Kirkaldy.
Hind wings usually milky-white, opaque, veins largely
pale; tegmina distinctly pale (Note: This is very
closely allied to the preceding, but it is a paler insect.)
....................................**pipturi** Kirkaldy.

12(6).   Pronotum mostly or entirely black or dark brown.......13
Pronotum largely pale, never mostly dark..............15

13(12). Vertex mostly yellow, with a narrow, sinuous, subapical
transverse dark band; scutellum mostly pale, yellow;
tegmina with clavi broadly and conspicuously yellow
from base to about apical fourth, thence black, remainder of tegmina black excepting some large pale maculae behind middle; a striking black and yellow species
....**peleae** Osborn.
Without such a color pattern........................14

14(13). Face dark; clavi with a common, transversely ovate, pale
saddle mark at middle which is about as long along
median line as pronotum and is very conspicuous to
unaided eyes in fully matured examples.............
................................**monticola** Kirkaldy.
Face pale; clavi without a saddle mark and almost or entirely dark or black, or rather mottled or irregularly
colored in teneral specimens especially..**bicolorata** Osborn.

15(12). Predominantly reddish or brownish-orange species without extensive dark coloring on tegmina and without
conspicuous dark veins.............................16
Basically yellowish species, normally with extensive dark
coloring on tegmina or with prominent dark-colored
veins or both.....................................18

16(15). Clavi with a common, median, white or creamy, subovate
saddle mark.........................**oreadis** Kirkaldy.
Tegmina without saddle mark........................17

17(16). Front of head without a transverse dark band beneath
ocelli.................................**ulaula** Kirkaldy.
Front with a continuous, narrow, transverse, dark band
just below ocelli...........**ulaula nigrolineata** Kirkaldy.

18(15). Tegmina of fully mature specimens with subcostal area
hyaline or partly whitish, in any case pale, area between this pale area and clavus black or dark; clavus
typically entirely or almost entirely greenish-yellow..
..................................**giffardi** Kirkaldy.
Without such a color pattern, veins usually outstanding,
at least in part, and making up much of color pattern..
..................................**bobeae** Kirkaldy.

KEY TO THE MOLOKAI NESOPHROSYNE

(5 species)

1. Female. Blackish; a yellowish ferrugineous grill on a pur-
plish-brown frons; a whitish spot on pronotum near
lateral margins; scutellum sordid whitish, more or less
suffused (especially apically) with brownish; tegmina
whitish hyaline, claval veins suffused brown, apical
angle brown; inner half of corium brownish except a
narrow claval margin and one or two apical spots,
whitish, exterior half whitish, apical cells mostly
brownish; abdomen mostly blackish-brown; hind
tibiae blackish-brown, spines white; pygophore pale
with pale hairs; ovipositor sheath blackish; length 4.5
mm. (from original description; I do not know the
species, but see fig. 18)...............**paludicola** Kirkaldy.
Not such species....................................... 2

2(1). Vertex produced, sharply pointed, depressed behind apex... 3
Vertex short, arcuate, not depressed behind apex......... 4

3(2). Almost entirely dark above; vertex with a pale, narrow
median line, thence with a dark vitta on either side from
base to apex, its base as wide as distance from median
line to eye, but narrowing to apex, and with sides of
vertex in front of eyes pale; pronotum for most part
dark; tegmina largely dark..............**lineata** Osborn.
Vertex mostly pale with some dark spots; pronotum
largely pale; tegmina basically yellowish with prominent dark and pale maculae and dark veins, with some
variable coalesced white maculae in usual saddle mark
position on clavus and with a cluster of four outstanding rounded white spots in cells arranged as an extension
from those on clavus and together with them forming
an oblique series across tegmina, with a white spot at
apices of inner and middle preapical cells, outer apical
cells largely white..................**angulifera** Osborn.

4(2). A stout reddish species; undersurfaces with black coloring..............................**palustris** Kirkaldy.
A slender yellowish species; undersurfaces pale........
..................................**procellaris** Kirkaldy.

(12 species)

(excepting *nubigena* and *umbricola,* but see figs. 18 and 22, b)

1.   Vertex strongly pointed, produced, distance along median
        line from line drawn between fore edges of eyes to
        apex about as long as distance from this line to base,
        median line pale and flanked on either side with a dark
        vitta from base to apex, base of each dark vitta as wide
        as distance from median line to eye; pronotum and
        scutellum mostly dark; tegmina dark excepting for
        some pale spots which are mostly behind middle; a
        sharp-headed, dark-colored species.........**lineata** Osborn.
      Not such species................................... 2

2(1). Almost entirely black, with a variable yellow saddle mark
        on clavi, and with a submedian costal hyaline macula
        and some variable hyaline patches between and behind
        apex of clavi and costal margin; an unusually dark,
        striking species with a short, arcuate vertex; some ex-
        amples with a bluish cast on tegmina.......**milu** Kirkaldy.
      Not such dark-colored species......................... 3

3(2). A beautiful and strikingly colored species; vertex black;
        pronotum almost entirely yellow, darker only along fore
        margin, and sharply contrasting in color with vertex;
        scutellum orange; tegmina largely brownish tinged with
        orange and in part infuscated, clavi with a large, prom-
        inent, elongate, yellow saddle mark; face, legs and
        venter almost entirely dark...........**nimbicola** Kirkaldy.
      Not such highly colored species...................... 4

4(3). Tegmina with two or more nodal veins; clavi each with a
        vague, interrupted, variable, zigzag, dark, longitudinal
        line in fully mature examples from near base to near
        apex near inner claval margin enclosing a more opaque
        area, but often obscure and not or hardly traceable in
        teneral specimens....................**nuenue** Kirkaldy.
      Tegmina with only one nodal vein and that usually hidden
        in an infuscation and obscure........................ 5

5(4). Tegmina with a milk-white or yellowish blotch composed
        of three or four spots in adjacent cells at about middle
        of corium and with a pair or more of similar patches
        above those on clavus, entire group arranged in an
        oblique manner across tegmen, and those on clavus
        margined anteriorly by black, those on corium abutted
        caudad by black and with pale patches in cells caudad
        ....**obliqua** Osborn.
      Not such species..................................... 6

6(5). Median length of vertex, carefully measured, divided into
        breadth of head across eyes at widest point equals
        nearer 2.5 or 2.6 than 3.0........................... 7
      This measurement equals about 3.0 or more than 3.0....... 8

7(5).   Veins almost all prominent and dark colored, those on
        clavi also conspicuous and dark excepting in a vague,
        variable saddle mark, tegmina thus conspicuously lined
        ....**furculata** Osborn.
        Veins at most only partly or irregularly dark, those on
        clavi never conspicuously dark.........**caelicola** Kirkaldy.

8(6).   Basal half or more of femora black; each clavus with a
        variable, open, more or less C-shaped saddle mark; veins
        not especially prominent..............**imbricola** Kirkaldy.
        Femora pale; veins of coria dark and mostly prominent
        to apex of tegmina.................................. 9

9(8).   Tegmina with a dark subcostal macula just before middle
        and rather similar to nodal infuscation...**silvicola** Kirkaldy.
        Tegmina without a dark patch anterior to nodal infusca-
        tion.................................. **oneanea** Kirkaldy.

KEY TO THE MAUI NESOPHROSYNE

(6 species)

1.   Vertex produced, pointed, concave subapically, median
        line as long or longer than its narrowest interocular
        breadth... 2
        Vertex shorter and more rounded, its median line always
        shorter than its narrowest part between eyes........... 3

2(1).   A short, stumpy, abbreviated-winged species; tegmina not
        or hardly surpassing terminalia, distance from end of
        clavus to apex distinctly shorter than median length of
        head and pronotum combined.........**haleakala** Kirkaldy.
        Wings fully developed, length of tegmina beyond apex
        of clavus distinctly longer than median length of head
        and pronotum combined; with an oblique series of white
        maculae from middle of clavus to costal margin......
        .... **angulifera** Osborn.

3(1).   A predominantly reddish or brownish-orange colored spe-
        cies; dorsum nearly immaculate and veins not dark ex-
        cept apically.........................**ulaula** Kirkaldy.
        Not reddish species, dorsum conspicuously maculate and
        veins mostly dark.................................. 4

4(3).   Vertex short and broad, broadly arcuate (length of median
        line divided into shortest distance between eyes equals
        about 1.6); pronotum pale caudad, black cepahalad; teg-
        mina with three or four nodal veins not hidden by infus-
        cation; a large stout species...........**nimbigena** Kirkaldy.
        Vertex roundly pointed (length of median line divided
        into shortest distance between eyes equals about 1.0–
        1.2); pronotum without a black anterior marginal band;
        tegmina with nodal veins largely hidden by infuscation;
        relatively slender forms............................. 5

5(4).   Tegmina with an oblique series of white or yellowish
        maculae from middle of clavus to costal margin, those
        on clavus bordered anteriorly with dark coloring, those

on corium followed by dark coloring which may be in form of a dark fascia when extensive, this color pattern distinct to unaided eyes..............**obliqua** Osborn.

Tegmina without such a color pattern, a rather grayish appearing species whose tegminal color pattern is largely made up of prominent dark veins on a predominantly pale background..............**cinerea** Osborn.

KEY TO THE HAWAII NESOPHROSYNE

(20 forms)

(excluding *umbrigena,* but see fig. 22, c)

1.   Vertex produced and sharply pointed, dorsally shallowly concave, with a narrow, yellow median line which expands at apex and is flanked on either side by a broad black vitta which occupies entire space between median line and eyes at base but narrows forward; pronotum and scutellum almost or entirely dark or black; tegmina, excepting some pale marginal or submarginal maculae from middle caudad, dark or black........**affinis** Osborn.
    Not such species................................... 2

2(1).   Tegmina with a striking color pattern consisting of irregular dark longitudinal dashes on pale-yellowish (green when living?) background on clavi and coria; veins pale or pale yellow except at apex; vertex broadly arcuate, its median length only about three-fourths as long as shortest interocular breadth; vertex, pronotum and scutellum yellowish with variable, restricted dark marks; face dark and grill well developed............
.... **pele** Kirkaldy.
    Not such species................................... 3

3(2).   Legs partly or largely dark, femora always with dark coloring 4
    Femora entirely pale, legs all pale excepting at most some dark spots or areas on hind tibiae................... 7

4(3).   A predominantly reddish or brownish-orange species, tegmina without distinct color pattern....**ulaula** Kirkaldy.
    Not such concolorous species, but distinctly maculate above, even if reddish or orange in color; tegmina normally with saddle mark......................... 5

5(4).   Vertex, pronotum, scutellum and tegmina all with extensive black coloring; saddle mark of tegmina solid and extending entirely across clavi; a predominantly dark but brightly marked species..............**myrsines** Kirkaldy.
    Predominantly brownish-yellow or orange-colored species, black marks restricted or absent................ 6

6(5).   Saddle mark of clavi when best developed only a C-shaped line on each clavus, open inwardly, not solid, often obscure.....................**imbricola** Kirkaldy.

Saddle mark extending conspicuously and solidly across entire clavus, variably bordered with black in front.. ....**oreadis** Kirkaldy.

7(3). Tegmina with two or more distinct nodal veins, clavi in fully mature examples with a characteristic, narrow, elongate, saddle mark extending nearly from base to apex, its outer edge irregular, more or less scalloped, sometimes edged with black, this black edging then assuming a zigzag course; veins and apices of tegmina in part dark, but otherwise a yellowish species without extensive dark maculae above.........**nuenue** Kirkaldy.

Not such species, tegmina normally with a single nodal concealed in an infuscation......................... 8

8(7). Face, sternum and venter of abdomen pale, yellowish or whitish, excluding ovipositor which may be dark and a possible dark median patch on last ventrite and a restricted dark area just above and behind fore coxae, without extensive dark areas...................... 9

Face, sternum and venter of abdomen at least in part with extensive dark or black areas, at least with dark facial markings even if no other dark marks are present......12

9(8). Clavi with a large, conspicuous, solid, somewhat diamond-shaped, yellowish saddle mark, in part edged with black ....**mabae** Osborn.

Without such a saddle mark...........................10

10(9). Vertex, as measured from side, almost half as long from fore edge of an eye to apex as length of eye, rather sharply, roundly pointed.................**ehu** Kirkaldy.

Vertex shorter, either more arcuate, or as above, but closer to one-third or one-fourth as long as an eye as measured from side.................................11

11(10). Veins of tegmina yellow and none infuscate or dark except at apex and tegmina without dark maculae except at apex, clavus opaque greenish-yellow, corium mostly hyaline............................**ignigena** Kirkaldy.

Tegmina with veins at least partly dark or infuscate and with small dark maculae on clavus and corium........ ....**craterigena** Kirkaldy.

12(8). Note: The following species are extremely difficult to separate in a key based upon external characters, especially color, because of their variability and the fact that teneral specimens may have quite distinct color patterns from normal, fully matured individuals.

Small, slender species not or barely more than 4 mm. long, all with rather pointed heads, tegmina maculate but without extensive solid black areas..............13

Stouter forms usually at least 4.5 or 5 mm. long, vertex either arcuate or pointed, but if smaller than 4.5 mm. then with solid black areas on tegmina, or dorsa largely black 15

13(12). Tegmina with veins mostly pale, dark only caudad, with dark maculae restricted to a vague humeral mark, tip of clavus dark, apex of corium dark and with a dark

costal patch at about middle, another on nodal vein
and a narrower one on vein of outer apical cell, tegmina
otherwise almost immaculate and hyaline; face without grill, with only a pair of dark bands between eyes
(these may be fused into one band); (these characters
are from typical form which may not occur on Hawaii)
....**touchardii** Osborn.

Tegmina with more extensive dark veins and more dark
maculations; face with extensive dark coloring.........14

14(13). Genae broadly pale outwardly; costal area of tegmina
almost entirely pale, hyaline from base to apical cell,
nodal vein inconspicuously marked.....**montium** Kirkaldy.

Genae entirely dark; costal area of tegmina with well-
developed dark maculae, nodal vein enclosed in a
broad dark patch.................**montivaga** Kirkaldy.

15(12). Corium adjacent to clavus continuously and conspicuously black or nearly black.........................16

Corium adjacent to clavus mostly pale.................19

16(15). Front of head extensively or almost entirely black; variable in dorsal color pattern but typically with vertex,
pronotum and scutellum largely black, although usually
with some yellow markings; clavi extensively black but
with a variable yellow saddle mark; vertex more
pointed than species of next couplet, distance from fore
edge of eye to apex, as measured from side, about one-
third as long as an eye...........:.....**pluvialis** Kirkaldy.

Front of head yellowish, at most with only small dark
areas (excepting in male of *sinuata* which is dark and
which has almost entirely yellow clavi and otherwise
is distinct); vertex arcuate, only about one-fourth or
less as long on sides before eyes as length of an eye.....17

17(16). Face almost entirely black, grill evident; corial veins
dark...........................male **sinuata** Osborn.

Face pale, grill wanting; corial veins not dark..........18

18(17). Clavi almost entirely yellow, not dark except at most at
base and apex; scutellum without three dark marks
.... **giffardi** Kirkaldy.

Clavi each with a conspicuous, oblique, black band running from inner anterior corner to outer middle thus
dividing each clavus into two yellow zones; scutellum
with three dark maculae.......**giffardi interrupta** Osborn.

19(15). Apex of clavus with a long, slender, more or less linelike infuscation along inner margin only, dark color
extending entirely across apex; apex of last abdominal
ventrite of female pointed, usually not notched in
middle; tegmina largely hyaline, veins all dark and
prominent (Note: The male of this species may run
to the next section which applies, however, to female
sinuata)..........................**silvicola** Kirkaldy.

Apex of clavus with a larger dark mark which extends entirely or almost entirely across apex, not thin and linelike; apex of last ventrite of female notched in middle; tegmina at least in part subopaque, specimens with color pattern similar to holotype have a large dark blotch at about basal third extending from costal margin nearly to clavus, but many examples lack this large macula or may have it greatly reduced, in which case corial veins are darker than surrounding membrane but not particularly prominent.....female **sinuata** Osborn.

Nesophrosyne affinis Osborn (fig. 15).
Nesophrosyne affinis Osborn, 1935:21, fig. 7.

Endemic. Hawaii (type locality: "Olaa, Crater Road, 27 miles, altitude 3,600 feet").
Holotype and allotype in the Bishop Museum.
This is a Hawaii representative of the *albicosta-lineata* group.

Nesophrosyne albicosta Osborn (fig. 15).
Nesophrosyne albicosta Osborn, 1935:19, fig. 5.

Endemic. Oahu (type locality: Manoa Cliff Trail).
Hostplant: *Kadua acuminata.*
Holotype in the Bishop Museum.

At least one of Osborn's paratypes is *N. gouldiae* instead of *albicosta.* This species is much like *lineata,* but its head is differently shaped and the color pattern of the tegmina is distinct.

Nesophrosyne angulifera Osborn (figs. 14, a; 15).
Nesophrosyne angulifera Osborn, 1935:22, fig. 8.

Endemic. Molokai, Maui (type locality: Olinda, 4,200 feet).
Hostplant: *Coprosma.*
Holotype and allotype in the Bishop Museum.

This species has a color pattern like that of *obliqua,* but the vertex is produced and more pointed and is subapically impressed.

Nesophrosyne bicolorata Osborn (fig. 15).
Nesophrosyne bicolorata Osborn, 1935:25, fig. 11.

Endemic. Oahu (type locality: Punaluu).
Hostplant: *Kadua.*

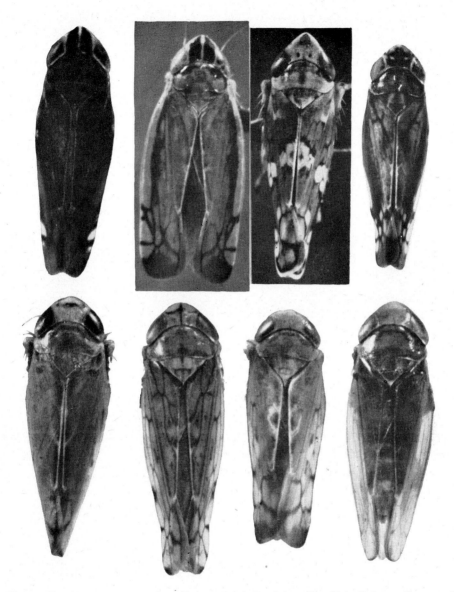

Figure 15—*Nesophrosyne* species. Top row, left to right: *N. affinis* Osborn, allotype; *N. albicosta* Osborn, paratype; *N. angulifera* Osborn, paratype; *N. bicolorata* Osborn, paratype. Bottom row, left to right: *N. bobeae* Kirkaldy; *N. cinerea* Osborn, holotype; *N. craterigena* Kirkaldy; *N. cuprescens* Osborn, holotype.

The holotype and allotype mounts, each containing two specimens on the same pin, are in the Bishop Museum. Some of the paratypes are different species from Osborn's holotype.

Nesophrosyne bobeae Kirkaldy (fig. 15).

Nesophrosyne bobeae Kirkaldy, 1910:564. Osborn, 1935:38.

Endemic. Oahu (type locality: Mount Tantalus, 1,800 feet).
Hostplant: *Bobea elatior*.
The type mount in Perkins' collection, now in the Bishop Museum, consists of four examples mounted together on an elongate card. Perkins notes in his letter: "We found no other specimens of this species" [in the Kirkaldy collection, that is]. Osborn notes that no type material was found in the British Museum. It is closely allied to the Lanai *oneanea*. Perhaps the two forms may prove not to be distinct full species.

Nesophrosyne caelicola Kirkaldy.

Nesophrosyne caelicola Kirkaldy, 1910:566. Osborn, 1935:39.

Endemic. Lanai (type locality: 3,000 feet).
Type in the British Museum, where it was examined by Osborn.
Osborn identified specimens from Oahu and Hawaii as this species, but as I am not sure that all of these specimens are the same as the Lanai type, I prefer to limit the species to the type locality pending further study.

Nesophrosyne cinerea Osborn (fig. 15).

Nesophrosyne cinerea Osborn, 1935:35, fig. 16.

Endemic. Maui (type locality: Olinda, 4,200 feet).
Hostplant: *Coprosma montana*.
Although not mentioned in the original description, this species is obviously related to *furculata*. However, it is closely similar to our cotype (?) of *oneanea* and may be only a teneral specimen of that species or a pale color form of it. More material must be seen to ascertain its status. The holotype is in the Bishop Museum.

Nesophrosyne craterigena Kirkaldy (fig. 15).

Nesophrosyne craterigena Kirkaldy, 1910:571. Osborn, 1935:37.

Endemic. Hawaii (type locality: Kona).
Osborn examined the male holotype in the British Museum. Perkins said in his letter that "The description of this and of *pele* was left incomplete (with blank

spaces in the proof). I attempted to fill in the gaps in *craterigena,* but could not do so in *pele.*" I am not sure that the material determined by Osborn as this species and used by me for the keys has been correctly determined.

Nesophrosyne cuprescens Osborn (fig. 15).
Nesophrosyne cuprescens Osborn, 1935:26, fig. 13.

Endemic. Oahu (type locality: "Palolo Hill").
Hostplant: *Metrosideros.*
The holotype is in the Bishop Museum.

Nesophrosyne ehu Kirkaldy.
Nesophrosyne ehu Kirkaldy, 1910:569. Osborn, 1935:31.

Endemic. Hawaii (type locality: Kilauea).
Although Perkins said in his letter that the type should be in the British Museum, Osborn stated that it could not be found in that collection. The specimen referred to by Osborn in his revision and there redescribed is in the Bishop Museum. It is the Hilo cotype collected by Swezey as mentioned by Kirkaldy. However, it bears the following label "? same sp. cotype. R.C.L.P.," indicating that Perkins was not sure that it represented the same species as Kirkaldy's type from Kilauea.

Nesophrosyne furculata Osborn (figs. 14, b; 16).
Nesophrosyne furculata Osborn, 1935:29, fig. 14.

Endemic. Lanai (type locality: 2,500–3,500 feet).
This species is an associate of *cinerea.* The holotype and allotype are in the Bishop Museum.

Nesophrosyne giffardi Kirkaldy (fig. 16).
Nesophrosyne giffardi Kirkaldy, 1910:563. Osborn, 1935:31.

Endemic. Oahu (?), Hawaii (type locality: Kailua).
Osborn examined the type in the British Museum. The large series he returned to Bishop Museum under this name contains several forms from several islands and requires careful revision.

Nesophrosyne giffardi interrupta Osborn (fig. 16).
Nesophrosyne giffardi variety *interrupta* Osborn, 1935:32.

Endemic. Hawaii (type locality: Kona, 4,000 feet).
Hostplant: *Myoporum.*

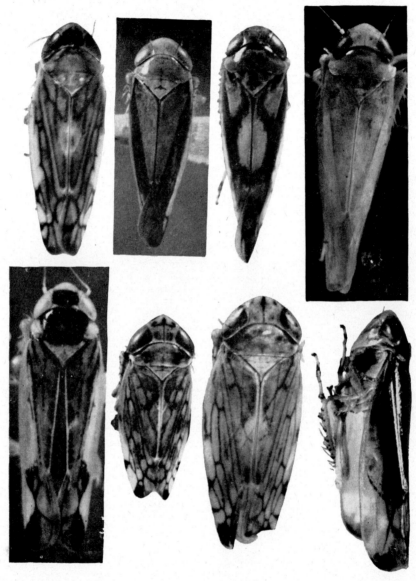

Figure 16—Species of *Nesophrosyne*. Top row, left to right: *N. furculata* Osborn, paratype; *N. giffardi* Kirkaldy; *N. giffardi interrupta* Osborn; *N. gouldiae* Kirkaldy, pale form. Bottom row, left to right: *N. gouldiae* Kirkaldy, dark form; *N. haleakala* Kirkaldy; *N. halemanu* Kirkaldy; *N. ignigena* Kirkaldy.

The holotype and allotype are in the Bishop Museum. I have seen examples of the typical form taken with this color variety from the same hostplant. Some examples of the typical form show a tendency toward assuming the tegminal color pattern of the variety.

Nesophrosyne gouldiae Kirkaldy (figs. 8, b; 16).
Nesophrosyne gouldiae Kirkaldy, 1910:560. Osborn, 1935:28.

Endemic. Oahu (type series from Mount Tantalus, 1,400 feet, and Palolo, 1,400 feet).

Hostplant: *Cyrtandra cordifolia.* (The hostplant was erroneously given in *Fauna Hawaiiensis* as *Gouldia.* The error was corrected by Swezey in a footnote in Osborn, 1935:28).

The type mount is in the Bishop Museum and consists of two specimens, one of the pale immaculate forms (female) and one which has extensive dark coloring on the dorsum (male).

This species belongs to the *ponapona–pipturi* complex and has the pronotum wider than the head, but it may be distinguished because of the unusual shape of the head as seen from the side. The latter character is best appreciated by observation, and it is difficult to describe adequately.

Nesophrosyne haleakala Kirkaldy (fig. 16).
Nesophrosyne haleakala Kirkaldy, 1910:567. Osborn, 1935:17.

Endemic. Maui (type locality: Haleakala, 9,000 feet).

Hostplant: *Coprosma* or *Vaccinium.*

The type was seen in the British Museum by Osborn. Perkins notes that it was labeled with the manuscript name *"nivata,"* not *haleakala,* by Kirkaldy.

Osborn identified specimens from Kauai (on *Campylotheca*) as this species, but I believe that they represent another species. I have seen another new species from Maui which belongs to this group of short species, and which has a more rounded vertex.

I have collected this species from the high slopes of Haleakala (8,500 feet) from a mixed growth of *Coprosma* and *Vaccinium.* The tendency toward brachyptery is particularly noteworthy.

Nesophrosyne halemanu Kirkaldy (fig. 16).
Nesophrosyne halemanu Kirkaldy, 1910:559. Osborn, 1935:16.

Endemic. Kauai (type locality: Halemanu, 4,000 feet).

Osborn examined the type at the British Museum.

Nesophrosyne ignigena Kirkaldy (fig. 16).
Nesophrosyne ignigena Kirkaldy, 1910:570. Osborn, 1935:37.

Endemic. Hawaii (type locality: Kilauea).
Hostplant: *Pittosporum longifolia.*
Perkins said in his letter that the type should be in the British Museum, and that "Giffard's specimen (only one) is not quite like the type." Osborn said, "I have not found any specimens to refer to this species and it seems probable that it should rank as a variety only, perhaps one of the many forms of *N. silvicola,* though smaller." However, there is a single example of this species in Perkins' collection at the Bishop Museum, and I have determined a good series of specimens, including nymphs, from the above mentioned hostplant, collected by Timberlake in Kau, Hawaii. The clavi are more opaque than the remainder of the tegmina and are more yellow in appearance.

Nesophrosyne imbricola Kirkaldy (fig. 17).
Nesophrosyne imbricola Kirkaldy, 1910:566. Osborn, 1935:46.

Endemic. Lanai (type locality: over 2,000 feet), Hawaii (?).
The type was examined by Osborn in the British Museum.

Nesophrosyne lineata Osborn (fig. 17).
Nesophrosyne lineata Osborn, 1935:20, fig. 6.

Endemic. Molokai, Lanai (type locality: 1,900 feet).
The holotype and allotype are in the Bishop Museum.
Osborn's description of the female genitalia does not agree with his figure. The "last" ventral segment of the female is longer than the preceding and is distinctly concave at the sides.
I have seen what appears to be an offshoot of this species from Oahu, but it has the wing venation of *Nesoreias.* The species, or a new ally of it, occurs also on Maui, but more material is required to ascertain the true status of the Maui form. It is closely allied to, but distinct from *albicosta* from Oahu.

Nesophrosyne mabae Osborn (fig. 17).
Nesophrosyne mabae Osborn, 1935:49, fig. 19.

Endemic. Hawaii (type locality: South Kona Road, 1,900 feet).
Hostplant: *Maba sandwicensis.*
The holotype and allotype are in the Bishop Museum.

Nesophrosyne maritima Kirkaldy (fig. 17).
Nesophrosyne maritima Kirkaldy, 1910:560. Osborn, 1935:31.

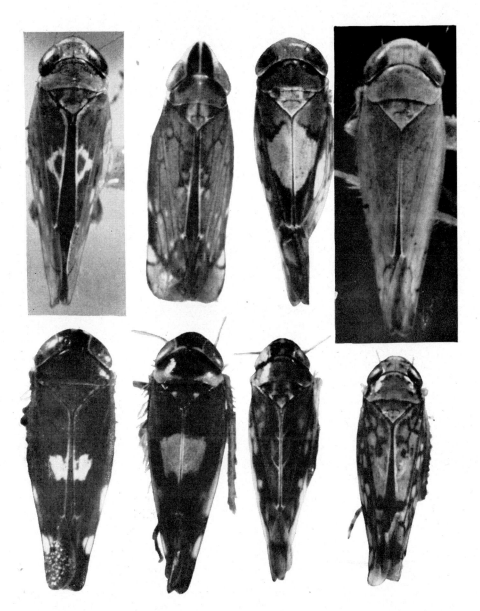

Figure 17—*Nesophrosyne* species. Top row, left to right: *N. imbricola* Kirkaldy; *N. lineata* Osborn; *N. mabae* Osborn, paratype; *N. maritima* Kirkaldy. Bottom row, left to right: *N. milu* Kirkaldy; *N. myrsines* Kirkaldy; *N. montium* Kirkaldy (compared with type); *N. montivaga* Kirkaldy, cotype.

Endemic. Oahu (type locality: Waianae Coast).
Hostplant: *Dodonaea viscosa.*
The type was examined at the British Museum by Osborn.

Nesophrosyne milu Kirkaldy (fig. 17).
Nesophrosyne milu Kirkaldy, 1910:565. Osborn, 1935:45.

Endemic. Lanai (type locality: 3,000 feet).
Osborn examined the type at the British Museum.

Nesophrosyne monticola Kirkaldy.
Nesophrosyne monticola Kirkaldy, 1910:562. Osborn, 1935:46.

Endemic. Oahu (type locality: Mount Kaala, over 2,000 feet).
Hostplant: *Perrottetia, Wikstroemia* (?).
The type should be in the British Museum, according to Perkins.

Nesophrosyne montium Kirkaldy (fig. 17).
Nesophrosyne montium Kirkaldy, 1910:569. Osborn, 1935:42.

Endemic. Hawaii (type locality: Mountain View).

There are in the Bishop Museum two specimens, a male and a female, mounted on the same pin, collected by Swezey at Mountain View, Hawaii, March 31, 1906, which are labeled "Type of *Nesophrosyne montium* Kirk" with a large red type label. These specimens are those mentioned as the type material by Kirkaldy in his original description. However, Perkins, in his letter, says that the type from Puna, Hawaii, is in the British Museum, and that "Swezey's specimens appeared to me to be doubtfully the same, according to my note." Osborn stated that "A specimen in the Natural History Museum, London, presumably the type, is smaller than those in hand." He redescribed the species from one of Swezey's Mountain View specimens which he considered to be a cotype. Kirkaldy does not mention any Puna specimens in his original description, and I would consider that only those specimens specifically mentioned by him in his original description could rightfully belong to his cotype series. I thus feel that the Bishop Museum specimens labeled "type" from Mountain View should be considered the true type rather than the specimen in the British Museum from Puna. See also the discussion under *ponapona.*

Nesophrosyne montivaga Kirkaldy (fig. 17).
Nesophrosyne montivaga Kirkaldy, 1910:569. Osborn, 1935:41.

Endemic. Hawaii (type locality: Kilauea).

Perkins says in his letter that the type should be in the British Museum, but Osborn states, "Type location not known but specimens probably from type material in HSPA collection." The Hamakua cotypes (three examples on one pin) and a specimen from Kilauea are in the Bishop Museum. The Kilauea example bears the data listed by Kirkaldy for the holotype, and although it bears no type label, it may be the holotype. Further checking at the British Museum is needed to settle the question.

Nesophrosyne myrsines Kirkaldy (fig. 17).

Nesophrosyne myrsines Kirkaldy, 1910:568.

Nesophrosyne arcadiicola Kirkaldy, 1910:571 (Hawaii, type locality: Hilo). Osborn, 1935:44. New synonym.

Endemic. Hawaii (type locality: Kilauea).

Hostplants: *Coprosma pubens, Myrsine, Sadleria* fern.

The holotypes of both *myrsines* and *arcadiicola* are in the Bishop Museum and are now before me. They represent the same species, and the above synonymy is necessary.

Kirkaldy (1910:568) described the beautiful yellow, black and crimson nymph. The specimen of the nymph described is mounted on the same card as his holotype.

Osborn (1935:40) described another species under this name, because he did not know *myrsines,* and he erroneously identified a series of specimens of another species as *myrsines.* He said, "No type specimen was found in Natural History Museum, London. Type probably lost as there is no specimen in the collection so labeled as to distinguish it." The holotype is preserved in good condition in the type collection of Bishop Museum and is from Perkins' collection. I have been unable to identify the species confused with *myrsines* by Osborn, and it appears to be new.

Although superficially different because of its dark color, this species has affinities with such species as *Nesoreias eburneola.* In fact, I have seen a specimen in which one wing is typical of *Nesophrosyne,* the other of *Nesoreias.*

Nesophrosyne nimbicola Kirkaldy (fig. 19).

Nesophrosyne nimbicola Kirkaldy, 1910:565. Osborn, 1935:44.

Endemic. Lanai (type locality: "over 2000–3000 ft.").

Hostplant: *Myrsine (Suttonia) lessertiana.*

The type is in the British Museum where it was examined by Osborn.

Nesophrosyne nimbigena Kirkaldy (fig. 19).

Nesophrosyne nimbigena Kirkaldy, 1910:567.

Endemic. Maui (type locality: Mount Haleakala, over 5,000 feet).

Perkins notes in his letter that the type should be in the British Museum, but it was not located there when Osborn studied the group. One of Perkins' specimens from Haleakala is in the Bishop Museum and bears the following label written by Perkins: "clearly—nimbigena." The specimens returned by Osborn identified and described as this species (1935:38) represent different species.

Nesophrosyne notatula Osborn (figs. 8, h; 19).

Nesophrosyne notatula Osborn, 1935:47, fig. 17.

Endemic. Oahu (type locality: Mount Kaala, 1,500–1,600 feet).
Hostplant: *Metrosideros*.
Holotype and allotype in the Bishop Museum.

Nesophrosyne nubigena Kirkaldy (fig. 18).

Nesophrosyne nubigena Kirkaldy, 1910:567.

Endemic. Lanai (type locality: 2,000 feet).
This species was overlooked by Osborn and not included in his 1935 revision. The unique holotype is in rather poor condition, as is indicated by our illustration made at the British Museum. I have not recognized any specimens of this species in the material I have seen.

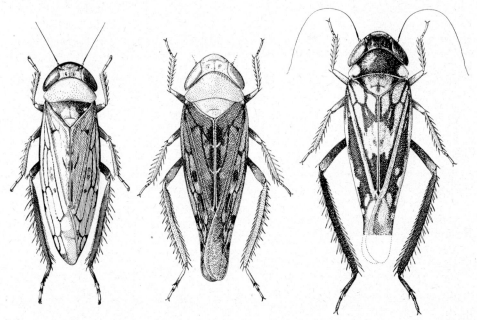

Figure 18—Holotypes of *Nesophrosyne*: *N. nubigena* Kirkaldy, left (type in poor condition); *N. opalescens* Kirkaldy, middle; *N. paludicola* Kirkaldy, right. (Drawn at the British Museum of Natural History by Smith.)

Nesophrosyne nuenue Kirkaldy (figs. 13, c; 19).
Nesophrosyne nuenue Kirkaldy, 1910:572. Osborn, 1935:32.

Endemic. Lanai, Hawaii (type locality: Kilauea).
Hostplant: *Dodonaea viscosa* variety *spathulata*.
Kirkaldy (1910:572) described the nymph.

Perkins said in his letter that the type "should have been amongst Kirkaldy's or Swezey's specimens," and I have located this material. The type mount now in Bishop Museum consists of two examples. Osborn said that no type material could be located in the British Museum, but he apparently did examine the holotype which was sent to him from Honolulu. Osborn determined a large series of Lanai specimens as this species, but he failed to list them in his text.

Nesophrosyne obliqua Osborn (fig. 19).
Nesophrosyne obliqua Osborn, 1935:23, fig. 9.

Endemic. Maui, Lanai (type locality: 2,300–2,400 feet).
Hostplants: *Coprosma montana, Sadleria* fern.
Holotype and allotype in the Bishop Museum.

In my opinion, the "last ventral segment" of the female is longer than is indicated by Osborn. The species is remarkably similar to *angulifera* from Molokai and Maui, but the vertex is shorter and less pointed and is not conspicuously subapically impressed as in that species.

Nesophrosyne oneanea Kirkaldy (fig. 19).
Nesophrosyne oneanea Kirkaldy, 1910:566. Osborn, 1935:35.

Endemic. Lanai (type locality: 3,000 feet).
The type was examined at the British Museum by Osborn. It is evidently a close ally of the Oahu *bobeae* and the Hawaii *silvicola*. A cotype (?) from the *Fauna Hawaiiensis* collection in Bishop Museum does not agree with the example compared with the holotype by Osborn. See also the notes under *cinerea*.

Nesophrosyne opalescens Kirkaldy (fig. 18).
Nesophrosyne opalescens Kirkaldy, 1910:561. Osborn, 1935:28.

Endemic. Oahu (type locality: "Waianae Mts.").
Osborn (p. 28) says, "I have not found any type. Specimens which agree with the descripiton can be referred to *N. pipturi* by recognizing the opalescent character as variable." I have seen no specimens assigned to this species. A drawing of the type, which is in the British Museum, is included herewith.

Figure 19—*Nesophrosyne* species. Top row, left to right: *N. nimbicola* Kirkaldy; *N. nimbigena* Kirkaldy; *N. notatula* Osborn, allotype; *N. nuenue* Kirkaldy. Bottom row, left to right: *N. obliqua* Osborn, paratype; *N. oneanea* Kirkaldy (compared with type by Osborn); *N. oreadis* Kirkaldy; *N. palolo* Osborn, allotype.

Nesophrosyne oreadis Kirkaldy (fig. 19).
Nesophrosyne oreadis Kirkaldy, 1910:569. Osborn, 1935:41.

Endemic. Oahu, Hawaii (type locality: Kilauea).
Hostplant: *Wikstroemia.*
Osborn stated, "Location of the type if existing is not known." Perkins said in his letter, "I could find no trace of the type of this sp. but may have overlooked it. It should bear beneath the card (or on a label, if pinned) the number 656." I have found Kirkaldy's original type in the Bishop Museum. It bears the number 656, and is labeled with Kirkaldy's manuscript name *volcanicola.* It is not surprising that it has been lost for so many years. I have labeled it as the holotype and placed it in the type collection.

It has not been recorded from Oahu before, but specimens agreeing with the type have been seen from Konahuanui and Kaumuohona. Osborn determined some specimens from "Kilauea, 29 miles," Hawaii, as *arcadiicola.*

Nesophrosyne palolo Osborn (fig. 19).
Nesophrosyne palolo Osborn, 1935:24, fig. 10.

Endemic. Oahu (type locality: Palolo Valley).
The holotype and allotype are in the Bishop Museum.

Nesophrosyne paludicola Kirkaldy (fig. 18).
Nesophrosyne paludicola Kirkaldy, 1910:564. Osborn, 1935:44.

Endemic. Molokai (type locality: 4,000 feet).
Kirkaldy had only a single example of this species, and I have not recognized it among the material studied. Osborn failed to find the type at the British Museum, but I include a drawing made from the type which has since been located in that institution.

Nesophrosyne palustris Kirkaldy.
Nesophrosyne palustris Kirkaldy, 1910:564. Osborn, 1935:39.

Endemic. Molokai (type locality: Kahanui).
The unique holotype of this species (now in Bishop Museum) is a teneral individual. I have seen one other example, identified by Osborn, which is closely similar to the type with which I have compared it. I am not sure that this species is really specifically distinct from *ulaula,* although the bright red coloring of its clavus, head and thorax is conspicuous. This red coloration is variable, however, and it is more distinct and extensive on the holotype than on the other example at hand.

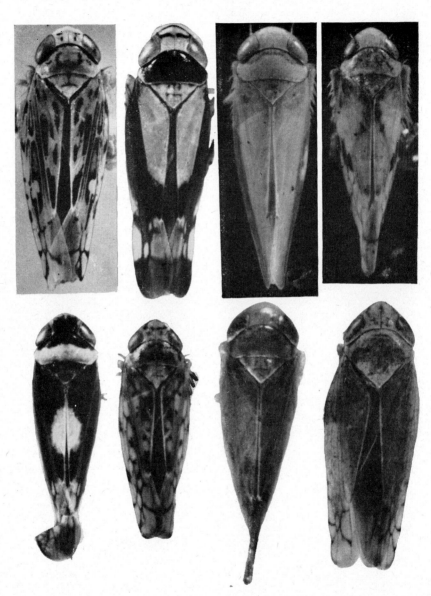

Figure 20—*Nesophrosyne* species. Top row, left to right: *N. pele* Kirkaldy; *N. peleae* Osborn, paratype; *N. perkinsi* (Kirkaldy); *N. pipturi* Kirkaldy. Bottom row, left to right: *N. pluvialis* Kirkaldy; *N. ponapona* Kirkaldy; *N. procellaris* Kirkaldy (compared with type by Osborn); *N. signatula* Osborn, allotype.

Nesophrosyne pele Kirkaldy (fig. 20).
Nesophrosyne pele Kirkaldy, 1910:570. Osborn, 1935:47.

Endemic. Hawaii (type locality: Kilauea).
The type was examined in the British Museum by Osborn. Perkins says in his letter that the type is from Kilauea, 1895, and that "Kirkaldy's label in pencil was nearly illegible." (See the note under *craterigena,* also.)

Nesophrosyne peleae Osborn (figs. 14, c; 20).
Nesophrosyne peleae Osborn, 1935:25, fig. 12.

Endemic. Oahu (type locality: Mount Kaala).
Hostplant: *Pelea.*
The holotype and allotype are in the Bishop Museum.
Osborn makes no mention in his text that he designated a series of specimens from Kilauea, Hawaii, as paratypes, but such material is in Bishop Museum. These Kilauea examples are differently colored and are apparently a different form. His figures 12, *a, b,* are of the female holotype, which, it appears, is somewhat teneral and does not have the color pattern as well defined as do more mature specimens.

Nesophrosyne perkinsi (Kirkaldy) (figs. 8, i, k; 9; 13, a, b; 20).
Eutettix perkinsi Kirkaldy, 1904:178.
Nesophrosyne perkinsi (Kirkaldy) Kirkaldy, 1907a:160; 1908:208, fig. 3. Osborn, 1935:30. Genotype.

Endemic. Oahu (type locality: Diamond Head ["Leahi"], Honolulu).
Hostplant: *Sida cordifolia* ("ilima").
Kirkaldy described the nymph. Perkins noted in his letter that the type should be in the British Museum.

Nesophrosyne pipturi Kirkaldy (figs. 8, a; 20).
Nesophrosyne pipturi Kirkaldy, 1910:560. Osborn, 1935:27.

Endemic. Oahu (type locality: Mount Tantalus, 1,300 feet).
Hostplant: *Pipturus,* abundant at times.
According to Perkins' letter the type should be in the British Museum.
See my remarks under *ponapona,* below.

Nesophrosyne pluvialis Kirkaldy (fig. 20).
Nesophrosyne pluvialis Kirkaldy, 1910:568. Osborn, 1935:43 (applies to this species ?).

Endemic. Hawaii (type locality: Olaa).

Hostplants: *Acacia koa, Broussaisia, Coprosma.*

The type was examined in the British Museum by Osborn.

Osborn's extensive series under this name is composed of several species from several islands. I have listed only the type locality.

Nesophrosyne ponapona Kirkaldy (figs. 8, j; 20).

Nesophrosyne ponapona Kirkaldy, 1910:561. Osborn, 1935:30.

Endemic. Oahu (type locality: Mount Tantalus).

Hostplant: *Pipturus.*

Osborn examined the type in the British Museum.

I have compared the type of *N. montium,* which is in Bishop Museum, with cotypes of *ponapona* and a large series of specimens determined by Osborn which apparently include both forms. Kirkaldy said that *montium* differs from *ponapona* by "the clypeus and lora being always dark piceous, except a short ferrugineous line on the clypeus, and by the dark suffused terminal subapicals" (1910: 569), whereas *ponapona* has the "clypeus and lora apically blackish brown." I cannot separate these forms satisfactorily by these characters, for there appears to be almost every gradation in color of the face from immaculate and pale to almost entirely black. The species appears to be highly variable. However, I believe that it would be unwise to place *montium* with it without first making a careful study of the entire series. There may be more than two species involved, or there may be a series of color forms. On a single card of Kirkaldy's cotypes of *ponapona* (from Mount Tantalus, Oahu, in Perkins' collection), containing six specimens, three examples have the face immaculate, and three have dark marks at the apices of the clypeus and lora. The male and female types of *montium* also have more extensive dark coloring on the tegmina as outlined in the key. This latter difference is the more conspicuous one.

There is a discrepancy between Kirkaldy's description of *ponapona* and the series of his which I have examined. He says that there are "two nodal veins, one from the middle, one from the base of the exterior subapical cell, suffused." In none of the cotype specimens examined is there more than one nodal from the exterior subapical cell. The type needs reexamination.

Osborn's *touchardii* belongs in this group and is not always easily separable from *ponapona.* However, I have found *ponapona* and *pipturi* to be more closely allied and difficult to separate. The ventral surface of *pipturi* appears to be quite stable in its entirely pale color, whereas *ponapona* is usually dark, but pale specimens do occur. The hind wings of *ponapona* appear usually to be more transparent with dark veins, whereas they may be more opaque milky-white with pale veins in *pipturi.*

This is a complex, involved and most confusing group, and a proper understanding of it can only be had by more detailed study than can be afforded here.

Nesophrosyne procellaris Kirkaldy (fig. 20).

Nesophrosyne procellaris Kirkaldy, 1910:565. Osborn, 1935:33.

Endemic. Molokai (type locality: Kalae).
Osborn examined the type in the British Museum.

Nesophrosyne signatula Osborn (figs. 8, g; 20).

Nesophrosyne signatula Osborn, 1935:48, fig. 18.

Endemic. Oahu (type locality: Mount Kaala, 2,000 feet).
Hostplant: *Alyxia olivaeformis.*
The holotype and allotype are in the Bishop Museum.

Nesophrosyne silvicola Kirkaldy (fig. 21).

Nesophrosyne silvicola Kirkaldy, 1910:570. Osborn, 1935:36.

Endemic. Hawaii (type locality: Kilauea), Lanai.
Hostplants: *Metrosideros, Straussia hawaiiensis.*
Osborn examined the type in the British Museum collection and noted that it
"has no locality record except 'Sandwich Ids. no. 656'." The number 656 is
Perkins' field number meaning "Kilauea, Hawaii, August, 1896." An example
with similar data is in the Bishop Museum. Kirkaldy noted that he selected a Kilauea
specimen as the type. Perkins says in his letter, "The specimens variable, and I
could see none from Kona nor from Lanai; there were two of Swezey's from
Hamakua, according to my note." Osborn determined a series of specimens from
Oahu as this species, but I have not accepted his determination.

Nesophrosyne silvigena Kirkaldy (fig. 22).

Nesophrosyne silvigena Kirkaldy, 1910:559. Osborn, 1935:37 (applicable to
this species ?).

Endemic. Kauai (type locality: Kaholuamano).
Perkins stated in his letter that the type should be in the British Museum, but
Osborn said that he could not find it there. However, the type is there, and a
drawing of it is presented herein. I do not know the species. A note sent in by
Perkins stated that "This has pronotum nearly all whitish, as well as a roundish
spot near the middle of the tegminal suture."
The series of eight specimens labeled as this species and returned to the Bishop
Museum after study by Osborn includes possibly five species, probably none of
which is this species, from four different islands.

Figure 21—*Nesophrosyne* species. Top row, left to right: *N. silvicola* Kirkaldy, cotype (compare bottom figure); *N. sinuata* Osborn; *N. touchardii* Osborn, paratype; *N. ulaula* Kirkaldy. Bottom: lateral view of specimen at left top, *N. silvicola* Kirkaldy.

Nesophrosyne sinuata Osborn (fig. 21).
Nesophrosyne sinuata Osborn, 1935:34, fig. 15.

Endemic. Hawaii (type locality: Olaa, 29 miles, 3,800 feet).
Hostplant: *Metrosideros*.
The holotype is in the Bishop Museum.
This species resembles a pale form of what Osborn identified as *pluvialis*. In fact, examples which agree with his holotype were placed by him under *pluvialis*, and others from the same lot were placed with *silvicola*. I have seen only one male in a series of 15 or more examples.

Nesophrosyne touchardii Osborn (fig. 21).
Nesophrosyne touchardii Osborn, 1935:18, fig. 4.

Endemic. Oahu (type locality: Manoa), Hawaii (?).
Hostplant: *Touchardia*.
The type mount is in the Bishop Museum and consists of three examples on the same pin.
Osborn stated in the original description that the tegmina had "a fuscous patch at nodus and apex," but there is also a dark patch basad of the nodus. His male type has terminal appendages on the genital valves, but these are not indicated in his drawing. Osborn's type series appears to me to include more than one form. The paratypes from Hawaii may be distinct and are more like the Hawaii *montium* than typical *touchardii* from Oahu.

Nesophrosyne ulaula Kirkaldy (fig. 21).
Nesophrosyne ulaula Kirkaldy, 1910:563. Osborn, 1935:33.

Endemic. Oahu (type locality: "Honolulu Mts.," probably Mount Tantalus), Maui, Hawaii.
Hostplant: *Myrsine (Suttonia) lessertiana*.
Osborn examined the type at the British Museum. W. E. China has informed me that the holotype is damaged and lacks tegmina. It bears Perkins' collecting number 888 and was taken in July, 1900.
This species is closely allied to, if truly specifically distinct from, *palustris*.
Kirkaldy said that he had only two females. A female specimen labeled by him as *"Nephotettix ula"* in the Bishop Museum appears to be a cotype. However, it bears Perkins' number 601 which refers to "Haleakala, Maui, 4,800+ ft. V '96," but Kirkaldy did not list Maui as a locality.

Nesophrosyne ulaula nigrolineata Kirkaldy.
Nesophrosyne ulaula variety *nigrolineata* Kirkaldy, 1910:563.

Endemic. Oahu (type locality: Moanalua, 2,000 feet; erroneously cited as "Maunaloa" by Kirkaldy).

The original specimen of this form is in the Bishop Museum and is labeled as "*Nesophryne ula* Kirk. Cotype." Beneath that label is one written in indelible pencil (by Osborn ?) which reads, "This specimen is described as *N. ulaula* var. *nigrolineata.*" It was the only specimen Kirkaldy had of this form, and it is thus the holotype of *nigrolineata*. I have so labeled it and placed it in the type collection at the Bishop Museum. The collecting data labels read "Maunaloa 2000 ft. Oahu" and "W. M. Giffard Coll. 31, XII, '05," as noted by Kirkaldy in his original description. This variety was overlooked by Osborn in his 1935 report. Perkins' letter noted that the type was in the Giffard collection, where I found it. It is doubtful that this is a good "variety."

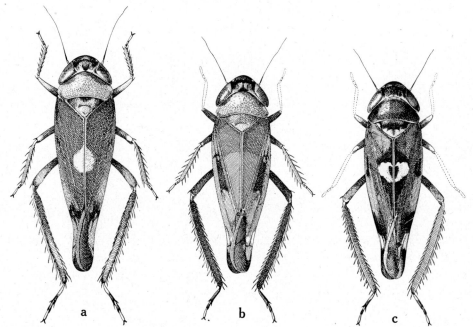

Figure 22—Holotypes of some *Nesophrosyne*: **a,** *N. silvigena* Kirkaldy; **b,** *N. umbricola* Kirkaldy; **c,** *N. umbrigena* Kirkaldy. (Drawn at the British Museum of Natural History by Smith.)

Nesophrosyne umbratilis Kirkaldy.

Nesophrosyne umbratilis Kirkaldy, 1910:588. Osborn, 1935:17.

Endemic. Kauai (type locality: Kalihiwai, 400 feet).
Hostplant: *Microlepia strigosa* (?).
The holotype is in the Bishop Museum.
Osborn identified specimens from Hawaii as this species, but I believe them to be distinct from *umbratilis*.

Nesophrosyne umbricola Kirkaldy (fig. 22).

Nesophrosyne umbricola Kirkaldy, 1910:565. Osborn, 1935:45.

Endemic. Lanai (type locality: 2,000 feet).

Osborn says, "I have not found any specimens that could be separated from *N. nimbicola* that would seem to fit this description and I have not seen any type." I do not know it, but a drawing of the type in the British Museum has been made for this text.

Nesophrosyne umbrigena Kirkaldy (fig. 22).

Nesophrosyne umbrigena Kirkaldy, 1910:571. Osborn, 1935:40.

Endemic. Hawaii (type locality: Kilauea).

I have not recognized this species in the material I have seen, but a drawing of the type is included here. The type is in the British Museum, in spite of the fact that Osborn stated that he could not locate it there.

Subgenus **Nesoreias** Kirkaldy, 1910:558

Kirkaldy separated *N. insularis* and *N. oceanides* from the remainder of the *Nesophrosyne* known to him and established the subgenus *Nesoreias* for them because they have lost the outer anteapical cell from each tegmen. This is, in my opinion, not a natural, monophyletic subgenus, but it is a group of species descendant from more than one stock, some of which have lost their outer anteapical cells independently. It is retained here because the grouping is of aid in the identification of several species of a taxonomically difficult assemblage.

There is considerable variation in the size of the outer anteapical cell in the various species of *Nesophrosyne*. In some of them it is large and in others very small. In a male specimen, determined by Osborn as *Nesophrosyne craterigena*, the outer anteapical cell is present in the left wing, but it is absent in the right. Thus, the right side is *Nesophrosyne*, the left side *Nesoreias!* I have seen other specimens of other species with a similar arrangement. Other species have the outer anteapical cell much reduced. Kirkaldy (1910:572) records an individual of *Nesophrosyne nuenue* in which upon "one tegmen there is only one subapical, the exterior, both discoidals being undivided." In specimens of *Nesophrosyne furculata* the outer anteapical cell may be stylate at each end, or the posterior end may be joined to the apical cell directly and lack a single connecting vein, or one wing may be one way and the other wing the other. Further observations of the venation would reveal, I am sure, other "abnormalities." Most specimens examined have only three apical cells, but some have four.

Key to the Species of Nesoreias

1.   Clavi almost entirely yellow, at most dark only at outer
     base and apex, but without a common saddle mark well
     isolated from base and apex......................... 2
     Clavi with a distinct, common saddle mark well isolated
     from base.. 3

2(1). Tegmina broadly black or dark next to clavus; face pale
     ....**oceanides** Kirkaldy.
     Tegmina without such a dark band, apical cells dark, but
     elsewhere largely pale with veins partly or mostly dark
     and conspicuous; face with extensive dark coloring...
     ....**insularis** Kirkaldy.

3(1). Clavus with inner margin dark along saddle mark so as
     to isolate the latter from claval margin which thus may
     be in form of a yellow comma, tegmen elsewhere mostly
     dark but with conspicuous white or subhyaline spots or
     areas, especially laterad where costal area may be largely
     pale ....**comma** Osborn.
     Not so colored, saddle mark not isolated from inner claval
     margin by any dark coloring......................... 4

4(3). Saddle mark broad, extending to claval suture, at most
     dark at base and apex; tegminal veins usually orange
     or conspicuously red; more or less orange or brownish-
     orange species 5
     Saddle mark not extending to claval suture, mostly or en-
     tirely bordered with black; tegminal veins yellowish or
     dark, or if saddle mark does reach claval suture, then
     head is as broad or slightly broader than pronotum...... 6

5(4). Saddle mark collectively subovate; veins of tegmina almost
     entirely blood-red; "last" ventral segment of female ab-
     domen notched in middle..............**sanguinea** Osborn.
     Saddle mark collectively elongate-subtriangular, tegminal
     veins mostly orange or yellowish; "last" ventrite of
     female not notched at middle...........**eburneola** Osborn.

6(4). Pronotum slightly but distinctly broader than head across
     eyes; face extensively dark...........**marginalis** Osborn.
     Head fully as broad or slightly broader across eyes than
     pronotum; face pale..................**koleae** (Kirkaldy).

Nesophrosyne (Nesoreias) comma Osborn (fig. 23).
Nesophrosyne (Nesoreias) comma Osborn,. 1935:52, fig. 21.

Endemic. Hawaii (type locality: Kilauea).
The holotype is in the Bishop Museum.

Nesophrosyne (Nesoreias) eburneola Osborn (fig. 23).
Nesophrosyne (Nesoreias) eburneola Osborn, 1935:54, fig. 23.

Endemic. Hawaii (type locality: Glenwood, Olaa, 2,300 feet).

Figure 23—The species of *Nesoreias*. Top row, left to right: *N. comma* Osborn, allotype; *N. eburneola* Osborn, paratype; *N. insularis* Kirkaldy, cotype; *N. koleae* (Kirkaldy). Bottom row, left to right: *N. marginalis* Osborn; *N. oceanides* Kirkaldy; *N. sanguinea* Osborn, holotype.

Hostplants: *Antidesma platyphyllum, Myoporum sandwicense, Straussia hille-brandii.*

The holotype is in the Bishop Museum.

Nesophrosyne (Nesoreias) insularis Kirkaldy (figs. 9, 23).
   Nesophrosyne (Nesoreias) insularis Kirkaldy, 1910:573. Osborn, 1935:51. Type
   of subgenus *Nesoreias.*

   Endemic. Hawaii (type locality: Kilauea).
   Hostplant: *Straussia hillebrandii.*
   According to Perkins' letter, the type should be in the British Museum, but
Osborn does not mention having seen it among the British Museum material.
The cotypes from Hamakua are in the Bishop Museum.

Nesophrosyne (Nesoreias) koleae (Kirkaldy), new combination (fig. 23).
   Nesophrosyne koleae Kirkaldy, 1910:562. Osborn, 1935:42.

   Endemic. Oahu (type locality: Mount Tantalus, 1,300 feet).
   Hostplants: *Eugenia sandwicensis* ("ohia ha"), *Myrsine lessertiana, Straussia.*
   Osborn noted that no type material was seen by him at the British Museum.
Perkins stated in his letter that the type was in the Giffard collection. I have found
one of Kirkaldy's cotypes in the Giffard collection at the Bishop Museum and
have designated this specimen as the holotype (Mount Tantalus, 1,300 feet, April
9, 1905, W. M. Giffard, collector). This example does not agree with every statement made in Kirkaldy's description, but other specimens of the series before me
fill in the gaps.

   Considerable confusion exists in regard to this species. Osborn's series determined as this species was mixed, and the specimens from Hawaii and Kauai as
well as the example from Wahiawa, Oahu, belong to different species. Neither
Kirkaldy nor Osborn noted that the outer anteapical cell was lacking and that
the species belonged in *Nesoreias* instead of *Nesophrosyne.* There are six examples
before me, and all of them have typical *Nesoreias* tegmina, and the species cannot
remain in *Nesophrosyne* if *Nesoreias* is to be maintained.

Nesophrosyne (Nesoreias) marginalis Osborn (fig. 23).
   Nesophrosyne (Nesoreias) marginalis Osborn, 1935:51, fig. 20.

   Endemic. Hawaii (type locality: Kilauea, dry forest, 4,000 feet).
   The holotype is in the Bishop Museum.

Nesophrosyne (Nesoreias) oceanides Kirkaldy (fig. 23).
   Nesophrosyne (Nesoreias) oceanides Kirkaldy, 1910:573. Osborn, 1935:50.

Endemic. Hawaii (type locality: Olaa, 18 miles).

Hostplant: *Straussia hawaiiensis.*

The holotype is now in the Bishop Museum and the type nymph is mounted on the same card. Kirkaldy described the pretty nymph (1910:573).

Nesophrosyne (Nesoreias) sanguinea Osborn (fig. 23).

Nesophrosyne (Nesoreias) sanguinea Osborn, 1935:53, fig. 22.

Endemic. Lanai (type locality).

The holotype is in the Bishop Museum.

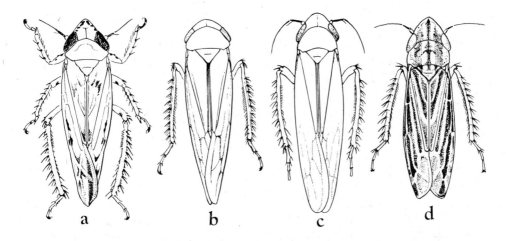

Figure 24—Some cicadellids. **a,** *Deltocephalus hospes* Kirkaldy; **b,** *Balclutha hospes* (Kirkaldy); **c,** *Balclutha timberlakei* (Osborn); **d,** *Nesolina lineata* Osborn. (Abernathy drawings.)

Genus **DELTOCEPHALUS** Burmeister, 1838

This is a widespread genus whose single immigrant representative in our fauna somewhat resembles certain of our pointed-headed *Nesophrosyne* and *Kirkaldiella.* Its non-stylate, outer anteapical cell will readily distinguish it from *Nesophrosyne,* and its more strongly produced, sharply pointed head will separate it from *Kirkaldiella,* although the differences between it and the latter genus are rather difficult to express in writing.

A single nymph examined has conspicuous, erect bristles on the entire dorsum including the wing pads.

Deltocephalus hospes Kirkaldy (figs. 24, a; 25, a–e).

Deltocephalus hospes Kirkaldy, 1904:177.

Phrynomorphus (Conosanus) hospes (Kirkaldy) Kirkaldy, 1907:60, pl. 1, figs. 13–17.

Conosanus hospes (Kirkaldy) Kirkaldy, 1907a:160.

Stirellus hospes (Kirkaldy) Osborn, 1935:55.

Kauai, Oahu (type locality: Honolulu, at light), Molokai, Hawaii.

Immigrant. Described from specimens taken in Honolulu, March, 1904, but now known to be a widespread species at least in eastern Australia and in the Marianas and Fiji.

Hostplants: *Cynodon dactylon* (Bermuda grass), *Digitaria henryi*.

The last nymphal instar has been described and figured by Kirkaldy (1907:60, pl. 1, fig. 13). The eggs are inserted in the leaves of the hostplant. The long- and short-winged adults, together with a wing of each, are also figured by Kirkaldy (1907: pl. 1, figs. 14–17).

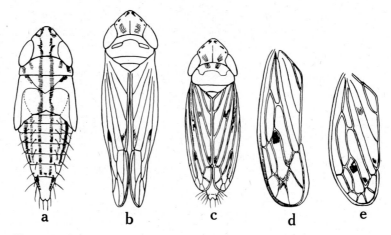

Figure 25—*Deltocephalus hospes* Kirkaldy: **a**, nymph; **b**, long-winged adult; **c**, brachypterous adult; **d**, tegmen of macropterous form; **e**, tegmen of brachypterous form. (Redrawn from Kirkaldy, 1907.)

The adult tegmina are typically hyaline or subhyaline with a yellowish or milky tinge, the middle anteapical cell has a dark spot at the base, there is a scattering of dark color on the membrane along some of the veins, and the outer and next to outer apical cells are usually at least partly infuscated. The vertex is conspicuously pointed. The adults have been collected at lights.

I have seen the species swarming by thousands on lawns at Punaluu, Oahu, but because of their habits and quick movements they might easily go unnoticed.

The type from Perkins' collection is now in the Bishop Museum.

Genus **OPSIUS** Fieber, 1866

A single immigrant species represents this genus in our fauna. The following combination of characters will serve to distinguish *Opsius* from its associates now known to occur in our Territory: vertex short, broadly rounded and broad (about three times as broad as long), tegmina with three anteapical cells, the outer one of which is not stylate at the apex. The nymphs do not have long, erect dorsal bristles.

Figure 26—*Opsius stactogalus* (Amyot).

Opsius stactogalus (Amyot) (fig. 26).

"*Stactogale*" *stactogala* Amyot, 1847:217.

Opsius stactogalus (Amyot) Fieber, Verh. zool.-bot. Ges. Wien 16:505, 1866. (Not seen.)

See Osborn, 1935:56, for synonymy.

The tamarix jassid.

Kauai, Oahu, Molokai, Lanai.

Immigrant. A widespread European species; common in North America. First found in Hawaii by H. L. Lyon at Honolulu in 1928 injuring *Tamarix aphylla*.

Hostplants: *Tamarix aphylla, Tamarix aestivalis, Tamarix indica, Tamarix africana.*

Parasite: *Polynema saga* (Girault) (Hymenoptera: Mymaridae), in the eggs.

"The eggs are laid singly just under the epidermis of the woody growth, usually transversely with reference to the axis of the branch." (Van Zwaluwenburg, *Proc. Hawaiian Ent. Soc.* 7(2):224, 1929, under the name *Euscelis stactogalus*.)

This species retains its green coloring after death and can almost be distinguished from our other euscelids because of its color alone. The tegmina each have several white spots and the apices are tinged with yellowish or brown.

Genus **BALCLUTHA** Kirkaldy, 1900

Gnathodus Fieber, 1806, preoccupied.
Nesosteles Kirkaldy, 1906:343.

This is a widespread genus containing a number of Pacific species from Indonesia to the Marquesas and Hawaii.

The head is slightly to distinctly broader than the pronotum in most species, but at least in one (*kilaueae*), the pronotum is broader than the head. The tegmina have an obsolescent vein which arises from the outer sector toward the base and rejoins the sector shortly beyond the fork as shown in the illustration. This vein is often almost impossible to detect, and, it must be admitted, one sometimes needs some imagination to distinguish it. In some examples, however, it is fairly obvious, but perhaps it is wanting in others. A close study of the wing under various light conditions and a comparison with the illustrations will be necessary. (Traces of this vein are difficult to see even when best developed; look for a slight inward angulation of the sector basad of the fork at which place the vein arises, and the sector is usually very slightly angulate beyond the fork where the obsolescent vein rejoins the sector.) However, the species form a rather distinct group in our fauna, and as a genus they should not be difficult to place on their general facies alone.

The genus is a taxonomically difficult assemblage of small, slender leafhoppers. They are poorly known. They occur throughout the main islands; there are more Hawaiian species than have been described, and a critical review of the specimens assembled in collections is needed.

Perkins, in a letter to Swezey dated June 15, 1945, includes the following notes: "The species of this which was common at Honolulu was found containing gonatopine larvae by Kirkaldy himself. He found several thus parasitized but killed them without noticing this till they were dead. No doubt living pupae of gonatopines in their cocoons on grass stems were occasionally brought to Honolulu when hay was imported. No gonatopines on Jassids were ever liberated by Koebele or myself in the islands."

Kirkaldy (1910:574) and Osborn (1935:57) each gave a key to the species. I have drawn up a new key with the aid of the types of each species, but a more careful survey of the group should reveal other, and perhaps better, characters to use for the separation of the species.

The nymphs have no erect bristles on the dorsum. The adults of at least some of the species have been collected in numbers at lights.

Key to the Hawaiian Balclutha

1. Pronotum broader than head (9:8); vertex along median
    line half as long as distance between eyes; length 4 mm.
    .... **kilaueae** (Kirkaldy).
    Head broader than pronotum.......................... 2

2(1). Vertex along median line hardly longer than one-fourth
    distance between eyes, or shorter, and subequal in length
    along median line and at inner edges of eyes or very
    slightly shorter; length 3.5–4.0 mm..... **hospes** (Kirkaldy).
    Vertex about one-third or distinctly more than one-third
    as long as interocular breadth, its median length slightly
    to distinctly longer than length at fore edge of an eye as
    seen from above; length 2 to 4 mm..................... 3

3(2). Vertex comparatively long and pointed (fig. 24, c), slightly
    more than one-half as long as interocular breadth.....
    .... **timberlakei** (Osborn).
    Vertex shorter and more rounded...................... 4

4(3). Vertex, pronotum and scutellum with pale-brown vittae
    and/or maculae, grill on front fairly conspicuous for
    this group; length 2.5–3.0 mm...... **volcanicola** (Kirkaldy).
    Without such a distinct color pattern, grill faint or absent... 5

5(4). Length less than 3 mm.; front with a faint grill; clypeus
    parallel-sided, its apex completely rounded....................
    .... **peregrina** (Kirkaldy).
    Length 3 mm. or more; grill on front usually indistin-
    guishable; clypeus slightly but distinctly expanded dis-
    tad, its apex rounded but blunted or almost slightly con-
    cave at tip........................ **plutonis** (Kirkaldy).

Balclutha hospes (Kirkaldy), new combination (fig. 24, b).

Nesosteles hebe variety *hospes* Kirkaldy, 1910:574.

Nesosteles hospes (Kirkaldy) Timberlake, 1918:381.

Osborn, 1935:57, figs. 24, *a, b,* male internal genitalia.

Endemic. Kauai, Oahu, Maui, Hawaii (type locality: Kilauea).

Hostplant: "coarse grass."

Timberlake (1918:381) noted that the specimens from Fiji, Australia and Hawaii lumped by Kirkaldy under the name for the Fijian form, *hebe,* each represented a distinct species and gave notes on the male genitalia.

There has never been a type selected for this species. There is in Perkins' collection at the Bishop Museum a single specimen bearing Kirkaldy's label "hebe ?" written in pencil on a torn bit of paper. It was collected by Perkins at Kilauea, July, 1906. I have designated this example from Kirkaldy's original series as the type and have so labeled it and stored it in the Bishop Museum.

This species has been taken abundantly in light traps near Pearl Harbor.

Balclutha kilaueae (Kirkaldy), new combination (figs. 7, a; 11, d–f).

Macrosteles kilaueae Kirkaldy, 1910:575.

Cicadula kilaueae (Kirkaldy) Osborn, 1935:55.

Endemic. Hawaii (type locality: Kilauea).

Hostplant: *Cibotium chamissoi.*

This species has been a puzzle to us ever since it was described. The unique female holotype which Osborn supposed was in the British Museum is in the Bishop Museum. Osborn confused *Balclutha timberlakei* with this species (at least some material he identified when he worked over the Hawaiian Cicadellidae was confused), and he assigned it to *Cicadula.* On the eve of going to press, I fortunately discovered a series of topotypic specimens collected by Dr. Swezey and have been able to clarify the confused situation.

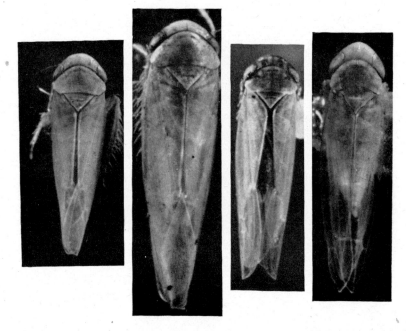

Figure 27—Some cicadellids. Left to right: *Balclutha peregrina* (Kirkaldy); *Balclutha plutonis* (Kirkaldy); *Balclutha volcanicola* (Kirkaldy); *Empoasca solana* DeLong. (Not to same scale.)

Balclutha peregrina (Kirkaldy), new combination (fig. 27).

Nesosteles peregrina Kirkaldy, 1910:575. Osborn, 1935:59, fig. 24, *c,* male internal genitalia.

Endemic. Oahu, Hawaii (type locality: Kilauea).

Kirkaldy considered this species as a probable immigrant; perhaps some of the specimens he examined were taken at lights in Honolulu.

The type, from Perkins' collection, is in the Bishop Museum.

Balclutha plutonis (Kirkaldy), new combination (fig. 27).

Nesosteles plutonis Kirkaldy, 1910:574. Osborn, 1935:57, fig. 24, *d,* internal male genitalia.

Endemic. Oahu, Molokai, Hawaii (type locality: Kilauea).

The type is now in the Bishop Museum. The mount originally held two specimens and bears the following labels written by Perkins: "*N. ignigena* MS–*plutonis* type, Kilauea, VII-06" and "The other specimen was possibly removed by K[irkaldy] for examination of wings. I did not find it."

Balclutha timberlakei (Osborn), new combination (figs. 7, e; 24, c).

Nesosteles timberlakei Osborn, 1935:59, figs. 25, *a–e.*

Endemic. Oahu (type locality: Palolo Valley).

Hostplant: *Eragrostis variabilis.*

Osborn evidently confused this species, in part, with *kilaueae* (Kirkaldy).

The type is in the Bishop Museum.

Balclutha volcanicola (Kirkaldy), new combination (fig. 27).

Nesosteles volcanicola Kirkaldy, 1910:574. Osborn, 1935:58, fig. 24, *e,* internal male genitalia.

Endemic. Maui, Hawaii (type locality: Kilauea).

Hostplant: *Eragrostis.*

The type from Perkins' collection is in the Bishop Museum.

Genus **NESOLINA** Osborn, 1935:60

Osborn's original description of the genus reads, "Similar to *Cicadula* in venation but with the head more deltocephaloid. Vertex, produced, angular; front flattened, tapering to clypeus which is narrow, nearly twice as long as wide; elytra narrow, two anteapical, four apical areoles." Osborn failed to call attention to the fact that as on *Balclutha* the "first sector of the elytra fuses with the second near the fork," thus forming a cell. But in this case the vein and the cell are distinctly developed and conspicuous. Therefore, it appears that the venation is more like that of *Balclutha* than it is like that of *Cicadula.* The illustrations show this clearly.

The prolonged and pointed head together with the wing venation will serve to distinguish this genus readily from our other cicadellids.

Nesolina lineata Osborn (figs. 7, d; 8, e, f; 24, d).

Nesolina lineata Osborn, 1935:60, figs. 26, a–c. Genotype.

Endemic (?). Oahu (type locality: Diamond Head, Honolulu), Hawaii.

Hostplant: *Eragrostis variabilis*.

This is a striking species. The dorsum including the head, pronotum and tegmina is conspicuously vittate. The veins of the tegmina are white, and the cells bear the brown coloring of the vittae.

The head of the nymph is conspicuously different from that of the adult, as the illustration on page 30 shows. It recalls the form of the heads of certain Mallophaga, and is characteristic. The nymphs do not have long erect bristles on the abdominal tergites.

The type is in the Bishop Museum.

Family **MEMBRACIDAE** Germar, 1821

The Treehoppers

This large, widespread family is represented in our Territory by only two immi-grant species. They may be readily distinguished from all of the associated groups in Hawaii because of the greatly enlarged pronotum which is produced back over the abdomen into a long point, the scutellum is concealed and the vertex and front of the head are continuous and vertical. Both adults and nymphs are agile jumpers. The eggs are inserted in slits cut into plant tissue.

Funkhouser (1927) has published a catalogue of the Membracidae of the world.

KEY TO THE GENERA OF MEMBRACIDAE FOUND IN HAWAII

1. Sides of pronotum not produced into horns; green or yellowish species, not conspicuously hirsute above......**Stictocephala** Stål.
2. Each side of the pronotum produced into an outstanding pointed horn; dark-colored species, conspicuously hirsute above.....................................**Tricentrus** Stål.

Subfamily SMILIINAE (Stål, 1866)

Tribe CERESINI Goding, 1892

Genus **STICTOCEPHALA** Stål, 1869

This is an American genus, and most of the species are recorded from the United States.

Stictocephala festina (Say) (fig. 28).
Membracis festina Say, 1830:243.

Oahu, Molokai, Maui, Lanai.

Immigrant. A widespread species in the United States; described from Florida. First found in Hawaii at Honolulu by Hadden in 1925.

Hostplants: alfalfa, *Crotalaria,* garden beans (occasionally heavy infestations), grasses, *Leucaena,* potato, *Tribulus cistoides.*

Parasite: *Gonatocerus ornatus* Gahan (Hymenoptera: Mymaridae), in the eggs.

This species has been reported as a pest of alfalfa in the United States; in Hawaii it is a minor bean pest. In life it is bright green, but it changes to brownish-yellow when stored in collections. For an illustrated discussion of the species on the United States mainland, see V. L. Wildermuth, 1915:343.

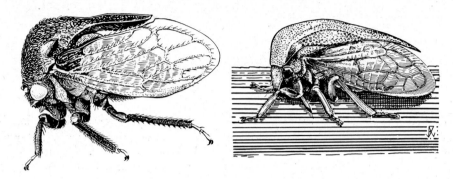

Figure 28—*Tricentrus albomaculatus* Distant, left (Abernathy drawing); *Stictocephala festina* (Say), right (Williams drawing, 1931).

Subfamily CENTROTINAE (Spinola, 1850)

Genus TRICENTRUS Stål, 1866

This is a large Indo-Pacific genus.

Tricentrus albomaculatus Distant (fig. 28).
Tricentrus albomaculatus Distant, 1908:56.

Oahu.

Immigrant. A widespread species described from India and ranging to Singapore. First found in Hawaii by Swezey in 1912 on the lower slopes of Mount Tantalus, Honolulu.

Hostplants: *Cajanus indicus* (pigeon pea), *Canangium odoratum* (ylang-ylang or ilang-ilang), *Cassia bicapsularis, Eucalyptus, Sesbania.*

This species is easily recognized because of its prothoracic horns. Kershaw (1913:186) published an account of the alimentary canal.

Superfamily FULGOROIDEA Kirkaldy, 1907

The Fulgoroid Leafhoppers

See Muir, 1923:205, for detailed discussion.

KEY TO THE FAMILIES FOUND IN HAWAII

1. Hind tibiae each with a very large movable apical spur or
   calcar ....**Delphacidae.**
   Hind tibiae with variable spines but never with such a spur.... 2
2. Body greatly compressed laterally; wings held vertically with
   the apices contiguous or nearly so; clavi with distinct
   granules .... **Flatidae.**
   Body not laterally compressed; apices of wings strongly divergent dorso-ventrally at apices; clavus not granulate... **Cixiidae.**

Family CIXIIDAE (Spinola, 1839)

The Cixiids

This world-wide family contained 84 genera and 786 species in 1936, according to Metcalf's (1936) world catalogue, and is thus one of the larger fulgoroid families. It is represented in the autochthonous Hawaiian fauna by two genera containing 84 forms. The group contains the largest (up to a centimeter or more in length) and most conspicuous of all of the native Hawaiian leafhoppers. Also, many of the species are fairly abundant and conspicuous in the native forests.

Their large size together with the absence of a large, specialized, movable tibial spur, and the wings held broadly ∧-like over the abdomen will readily serve to distinguish them from all other Hawaiian fulgoroids.

The most primitive of living fulgoroids belong to this family. Most of the species of the two genera found in Hawaii have three ocelli, although the median ocellus is obscure in some.

The native *Nesomimesa* wasps include these homopterans in their list of provisions for their nests.

[91]

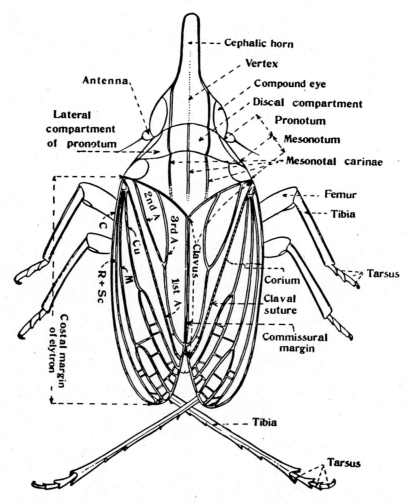

Figure 29—Diagram illustrating characters of a fulgorid leafhopper. (After Van Duzee, 1923.)

Subfamily CIXIINAE Muir, 1923:222

Tribe CIXIINI Muir, 1923:222

KEY TO THE CIXIID GENERA OF HAWAII

1. Mesonotum with five longitudinal carinae.........**Oliarus** Stål.
2. Mesonotum with only three longitudinal carinae...........
.... **Iolania** Kirkaldy.

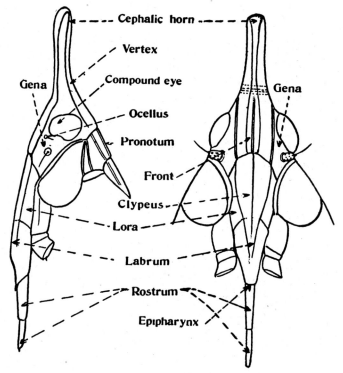

Figure 30—Diagrams of fulgorid head characters. (After Van Duzee, 1923.)

Genus **OLIARUS** Stål, 1862

Nesoliarus Kirkaldy, 1909:76. New synonym.
See Metcalf, 1936:44, for synonymy and world catalogue.

This genus contains about 295 forms and is the largest of the family. The 78 forms found in Hawaii make this the richest single faunal unit. The genus is most abundantly developed in the Indo-Pacific regions, is well represented in the Holarctic region, but few species have been recorded from Africa or South America.

Kirkaldy (1909:76) erected the subgenus *Nesoliarus* for the Hawaiian species. His reasons for separating the Hawaiian forms into a group by themselves are as follows:

So far as concerns the structure of the legs, the Hawaiian forms all belong to the typical subgenus, but I separate them off under the name *Nesoliarus,* on account of the great plasticity of those characters which are of specific value in the exotic forms, and on account of the sexual dimorphism, which is more or less apparent—mostly considerably so—in the pattern and colouring of the tegmina. As it would not be possible to include these Hawaiian forms in a general table of species, owing to the above-mentioned plasticity, it is convenient to group them under a special subgeneric name (type *tamehameha*). (1909:76.)

Muir (1925:161) said that *Nesoliarus* "is purely a geographical subgenus and is of great convenience, as it segregates a number of species, varieties and forms, which are closely allied and monophylatic[*sic*] ; among them we find some forms that could go into the typical subgenus *Oliarus* and others into *Nesopompe*."

I feel, however, that the use of *Nesoliarus* serves no good purpose, and it is not used in this text. A subgeneric name should have something more substantial than mere "convenience" to back it up.

There is a considerable range of variability of various structural characters in the Hawaiian species. Kirkaldy (1909:76) said, "The venation, which in the Australian and Fijian species I found so characteristic, is highly variable in the Hawaiian forms. The place of forking of the radial and brachial veins, and the place of union of the two claval veins, which characters seem to be of specific value in exotic forms, are inconstant and of no value here." Giffard (1925) noted great individual variation in the number of spines on the hind tibiae, a character found useful for specific segregation elsewhere, and he outlined other variations.

Thus, this group shares with the other large Hawaiian genera the great plasticity of form and structure that is so typical of this insular fauna.

Little is known of the biology of these insects. Nymphs have been found in Hawaii beneath stones, in rotting tree fern stumps and fronds, in tree fern ground litter, in rotting wood and under the bark of trees. It is thought that they feed upon fungi or rotting vegetation or plant sap, but nothing certain is known of their food habits. Hacker (1925:113) reported upon the life history of the Australian species *O. felis* Kirkaldy, which he found in cracks in soil about *Sporobolus* bunch grass, and published some excellent photographs of the eggs, nymphs and adults.

Swezey has made some observations on the nymphs of what he considered to be *Oliarus koanoa* (1907:83), and many of his data are worthy of quotation. He found the nymphs, which were reared to maturity, "among the decaying leaf-bases and fibrous material of tree-fern trunks."

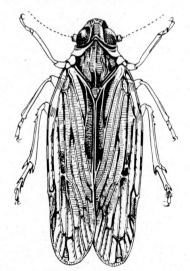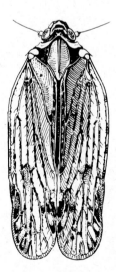

Figure 31—*Oliarus tamehameha* Kirkaldy, female, left; *Iolania perkinsi* Kirkaldy, female, right. (Drawings by Abernathy.)

The nymphs were in cavities or tunnels lined with a white fibrous material which resembled mold, or spider's web, and which is an excretion from the terminal abdominal segments of the nymph. Each nymph had a tuft or brush of straight fibers of this material, extending backward and slightly upwards, and spread somewhat fan-shaped. It is probably rubbed off accidentally in the movements of the insects, and serves to aid in hiding or protecting it. It is rapidly replaced. A specimen from which it was entirely removed, had it completely produced again within 24 hours.

The full-growth nymph is about 5 mm. long, and 2 mm. wide, about even width throughout; the tuft is from 2 to 5 mm. Whole insect whitish, with pale greyish markings on the thorax, and 5 dorsal bands on the abdomen in front of the cottony tuft. Eyes dark brown, partially hidden behind projecting margins of the frons. Rostrum extends beyond 2nd abdominal segment. Sensory pits are very numerous; a row near the margin of frons, many on dorsal part of thorax and wing cases, a transverse dorsal row on abdominal segments 2, 3 and 4. The abdomen is obliquely truncated behind the 4th segment, so that the dorsal surfaces of segments 5, 6 and 7 are directed nearly posteriorly. These contain the numerous pores from which the fibers of the tuft are extruded.

The nymphs probably feed upon the fern roots in the fibrous mass of the outside of the fern trunks, or on juices of the decaying material. The largest nymphs collected transformed to adults in a few days. (1907:83–84.)

The adult females have the end of the abdomen greatly modified into a broad, concave plate-like area (see fig. 34, a), from which a flocculent white wax is exuded in myriads of filaments to form a great white mass. The eggs, which are deposited in clusters, are enclosed and concealed by a mass of the white wax. Swezey found a clutch of eggs on a bracket fungus on a koa log, and he reported (*Proc. Hawaiian Ent. Soc.* 5(3):365–366) that "There were about a dozen of the oval white eggs loosely enclosed beneath what had the appearance of a small bit of lichen. The inner edge of this was composed of white, waxy material usually found at the apex of the abdomen of the female *Oliarus;* the outside was greenish as if covered by a minute growth of lichen."

This is a difficult genus containing many variable and confusing forms. Although Giffard spent much time studying the group and had the guidance of the experienced hemipterist, F. A. G. Muir, the present arrangement of the genus is not satisfactory. I have deemed it outside the scope of my present experience to attempt any detailed revisionary work here, and I leave the problem for some future monographer skilled in the study of the fulgorids to present a revised classification. However, certain obvious points permit or require statements of opinion herewith.

Giffard sorted out various forms from certain variable species and designated them as varieties. He did not name them, but gave them *a, b, c,* etc., designations and selected types for some of them. For example, he listed varieties *a* to *f* of his *Oliarus instabilis,* a highly variable species. However, he was inconsistent, for he described varieties of certain other species without giving them any alphabetical designations, although the sum of their variation appears to be of equal rank to those to which he applied indicating letters. I do not believe that Giffard fully understood the limits of individual variation among the species, and it appears that in at least some of his cases, the species normally include, within their populations, individual variables which should not be named. Perhaps the situation can be likened to litters of cats, no two individuals of which may be identical. Metcalf, unfortunately, has made matters worse, for, in his catalogue of the Cixiidae, he has chosen to erect names for Giffard's varieties, although he did not examine Giffard's material and thus could not evaluate properly the various problems. I believe that it would perhaps be best to relegate these varietal designations to synonymy. However, as above stated, I feel that such revisional work is really outside the scope of my present problem, and inasmuch as my studies in this genus can hardly be termed more than cursory, I feel that it is best to leave the names in *status quo* until the genus can be revised in detail.

The following six Kirkaldy species were unknown to Giffard, and I, too, have not seen them; they are not included in the following tables: *O. procellaris, O. pluvialis, O. monticola, O. paludicola, O. nemoricola, O. orono*. Three of these species are, however, illustrated here from drawings made from the holotypes at the British Museum. Giffard gives notes on these forms (1925:147–149), and it is probable that he has unknowingly redescribed some of Kirkaldy's species.

The divisions erected by Giffard on the basis of the characters of the vertex are not satisfactory because of intergradation or obscurity of the parts involved.

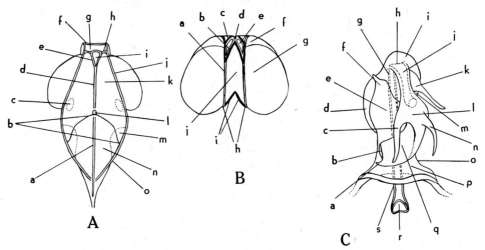

Figure 32—Details of *Oliarus*. **A,** frontal view of frons and clypeus of head of *Oliarus euphorbiae* Giffard: **a,** median carina of clypeus; **b,** fronto-clypeal suture (apex of frons and base of clypeus); **c,** fenestra; **d,** medio-frontal suture; **e,** fork of medio-frontal suture; **f,** transverse carina of vertex; **g,** fossette of vertex; **h,** apex of vertex; **i,** areolet of fork of medio-frontal suture; **j,** lateral carina of frons; **k,** frons; **l,** median ocellus; **m,** macula; **n,** clypeus; **o,** lateral carina of clypeus.
B. Dorsal view of head of *Oliarus swezeyi* Giffard: **a,** lateral carina of vertex; **b,** transverse carina of vertex; **c,** apical carina of vertex; **d,** median longitudinal carina of vertex; **e,** areolet (divided fossette); **f,** upper part of gena; **g,** eye; **h,** basal angles of vertex; **i,** base of vertex; **j,** vertex (including fossette).
C. Dorsal view of aedeagus of *Oliarus acaciae* Kirkaldy: **a,** right apical spur; **b,** functional orifice; **c,** right median spur; **d,** membranous part of periandrium; **e,** periandrium; **f,** apex of periandrium; **g,** apodeme of phallus; **h,** conjunctiva; **i,** membranous part of periandrium; **j,** basal part of phallus; **k,** basal spur of phallus attached to membrane (behind); **l,** phallus; **m,** membranous part of periandrium; **n,** left median spur; **o,** side margin of periandrium; **p,** base of periandrium; **q,** apical part of phallus; **r,** entrance of ejaculatory duct; **s,** apodeme of phallus. (Redrawn from Giffard, 1925.)

Some future monographer should find a more satisfactory method of dividing the species. As it stands, the key may be found confusing and misleading. On some examples the characters of the vertex are difficult to make out, whereas on other examples they may be clear-cut and can fit comparatively easily into their proper places in the keys.

Giffard's divisions are, in my opinion, largely meaningless phylogenetically. Obviously closely related species have been placed by him in different divisions and widely separated in his text. *O. agnatus* and *O. koele* are herein synonymized, after a study of the holotypes, yet Giffard made no mention in his text that the "species" were allied, and he placed *agnatus* in division "E" and *koele* in division "C."

The following key is a recast and somewhat revised version of Giffard's key to the species. Following this key is a set of new keys which may be found more easily used. The substance of Giffard's key (1925) is given here for the sake of completeness and to follow the only revision of the group. I have not included the

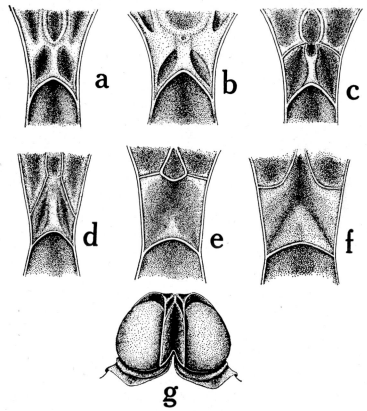

Figure 33—Details of fossettes and bases of frons of *Oliarus* to show key characters. **a,** *O. tantalus* Giffard (Division B); **b,** *O. koanoa* Kirkaldy (Division B); **c,** *O. nubigenus* Kirkaldy (Division C); **d,** *O. immaculatus* Giffard (Division D); **e,** *O. hevaheva* Kirkaldy (Division E); **f,** *O. kulanus* Giffard (Division E); **g,** *O. swezeyi* Giffard, head from above (Division A). (Rearranged from Giffard, 1925.)

various "varieties" in the keys; Giffard's original descriptions should be consulted for notes regarding them.

KEY TO THE DIVISIONS OF HAWIIAN OLIARUS

1.   Fossette of vertex completely divided by a median longi-
        tudinal carina, thus forming two areolets............ 2
        Fossette of vertex either not divided or else incompletely
        divided by a median longitudinal carina.............. 4

2(1).   Areolets of vertex very acutely angulate posteriorly, much
        longer at sides than at middle............... **Division A.**
        Areolets much less acutely angular posteriorly, length at
        sides not much greater than in middle................ 3

3(2).   Areolets sub-ovate, and either base of frons or else edges
        of areolets (or both) more or less tumescent and largely
        obscuring apical carinae of vertex............. **Division B.**
        Areolets usually somewhat subquadrate and/or base of
        frons and carinae not or but slightly tumescent so that
        apical carinae are distinct (Note: This dichotomy is not
        very satisfactory and you may have to try each section.)
        .... **Division C.**

4(1).   Fossette incompletely divided, basal part of dividing carina
        more or less evident, but never reaching apical carinae
        of vertex.................................. **Division D.**
        Fossette of vertex entirely undivided or with only a rudi-
        mentary basal part of dividing carinae........ **Division E.**

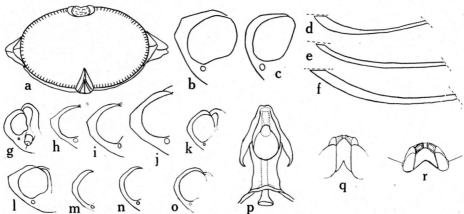

Figure 34—Details of *Oliarus*: **a,** end view of apex of abdomen of a female of *O. waialeale* Giffard to show the greatly modified plate from which wax is extruded (anus at top, ovipositor at bottom, concave plate between); **b,** profile of head of male of *O. similis* Giffard to show outline of gena and vertex; **c,** the same of *O. koele* Giffard, male; **d,** costa of *O. hevaheva* Kirkaldy to show basal expansion on convexity of lateral margin; **e,** the same of *O. kauaiensis* Kirkaldy; **f,** the same of *O. niger* Giffard; **g,** lateral view of head of female of *O. discrepans* Giffard; **h,** the same of *O. instabilis* Giffard; **i,** the same of *O. olympus* Giffard; **j,** the same of *O. tamehameha* Kirkaldy; **k,** the same of *O. muiri* Giffard; **l,** the same of *O. silvestris* Kirkaldy; **m,** the same of *O. filicicola* Kirkaldy; **n,** the same of *O. koele* Giffard; **o,** the same of *O. swezeyi* Giffard; **p,** male genitalia of *Iolania perkinsi* Kirkaldy; **q,** dorsal view of head of *Oliarus kirkaldyi* Giffard; **r,** the same of *O. discrepans* Giffard, female. (a–f, original; g–r, after Giffard, 1925.)

These divisions are not as clear-cut as one might expect them to be. In fact, there appears to be a blending among them. It is often difficult to decide the category to which one's examples should be assigned. Some individuals have the characters obscurely developed, but on others they are clearly defined.

DIVISION A

Fossette of vertex completely divided by a median longitudinal carina which forms two areolets. Areolets elongated and very acutely angulate caudad, much longer at sides than at middle. Kauai species (fig. 33, g).

1. Vertex broader at extreme base than breadth of an eye at same
    level; tegmina clear or yellowish hyaline.........**muiri** Giffard.
2. Vertex only about two-thirds or less as wide at extreme base
    as breadth of an eye; tegmina milky hyaline....**swezeyi** Giffard.

DIVISION B

Fossette of vertex completely divided by a median longitudinal carina forming sub-ovate areolets. Areolets much more obtusely angular posteriorly than in division A, length at sides of areolets not much greater than along the median carina. Base of frons or edges of areolets, or both, more or less tumescent and in great measure obscuring apical carinae of vertex. Excavate area small (fig. 33, a, b).

1.   Vertex very broad, almost twice as broad at base as median
         length to transverse carina...........**discrepans** Giffard.
         Vertex much narrower............................... 2
2(1).   Costa particolored; length: male, 6–7 mm.; female, 7–8
         mm.; Oahu..........................**kaiulani** Giffard.
         Costa unicolored..................................... 3
3(2).   Tegminal veins particolored........................... 4
         Tegminal veins not particolored....................... 7
4(3).   Breadth of extreme base of vertex greater than breadth of
         an eye.......................female **kirkaldyi** Giffard.
         Base of vertex narrower.............................. 5
5(4).   Mesonotum pale castaneous; length: male, 6 mm.; female,
         7 mm.; Oahu (and female *wailupensis* Giffard ?)......
         ....**kaumuahona** Giffard.
         Mesonotum dark castaneous........................... 6
6(5).   Cross-veins seldom suffused; tegmina clear hyaline or not
         very distinctly milky, males always maculate; length:
         6–8 mm.; Hawaii.....................**koanoa** Kirkaldy.
         Cross-veins always suffused; tegmina milky hyaline; males
         immaculate, females maculate; length: male, 4.5–5.25;
         female, 6 mm.; Oahu...............**myoporicola** Giffard.
7(3).   Tegminal veins dark; tegmina immaculate cloudy or
         bronzy hyaline; length: male, 6.75–7 mm.; female,
         7.5–8 mm.; Oahu.....................**tantalus** Giffard.
         Tegminal veins comparatively pale..................... 8

8(7).   Extreme breadth across base of vertex distinctly more than
        one-half as great as median distance from a line drawn
        across base to transverse carinae........**kirkaldyi** Giffard.
        Extreme breadth of vertex at base less than one-half as
        long as median length from a line drawn across extreme
        base to transverse carinae.......................... 9
9(8).   Length 4.5–5.5 mm.; tegmina of male and female clear
        hyaline, immaculate; Oahu............**wailupensis** Giffard.
        Length 6–7 mm.; tegmina of male clear hyaline, immacu-
        late; female maculate; Hawaii...........**koanoa** Kirkaldy.

DIVISION C

Fossette of vertex completely divided by a median longitudinal carina (this carina forked or minutely annulate anteriorly in some species) forming sub-quadrate areolets. Base of frons and carinae not tumescent as in division B, or only slightly so and the excavate area larger and more distinct than in that group (fig. 33, c).

1.   Basal and apical third of tegmina darkly fuliginous, mid-
        dle third clear or milky hyaline; length: male, 5–5.5
        mm.; Oahu..........................**neotarai** Giffard.
        Usually larger species; tegmina not so colored, not di-
        vided into three color areas.......................... 2
2(1).   Tegmina of males and females clear or milky hyaline,
        without any yellowish tinge (none from Lanai)........ 3
        Tegmina of males yellowish, ochraceous, or tawny hya-
        line; females with tegmina darker yellowish to fuligi-
        nous, immaculate.................................. 9
3(2).   Mesonotal carinae dark.............................. 4
        Mesonotal carinae pale.............................. 5
4(3).   Kauai species.......................**nubigenus** Kirkaldy.
        Hawaii species.......................**filicicola** Kirkaldy.
5(3).   Kauai or Hawaii species............................. 6
        Oahu or Maui species............................... 7
6(5).   Kauai species; tegmina of male immaculate, of female
        maculate; length: 10.5–11 mm.....**tamehameha** Kirkaldy.
        Hawaii species; both sexes immaculate; length: male,
        5–6.5 mm.; female, 7–7.25 mm.........**filicicola** Kirkaldy.
7(5).   Cross-veins distinctly suffused; length: male, 5.25 mm.;
        Oahu.............................**makaala** Giffard.
        Cross-veins not or only slightly suffused............... 8
8(7).   Length: male, 6.5–7.5 mm.; female, 7–9 mm.; particol-
        oration of veins comparatively pale........**pele** Kirkaldy.
        Length: male, 5.5–6 mm.; female, 7 mm.; particolora-
        tion of veins comparatively dark.........**likelike** Giffard.
9(2).   Oahu species; mesonotum pale to dark castaneous......
        ....**kaonohi** Kirkaldy.
        Not so 10

10(9). Lanai species; mesonotum flavous to dark castaneous..
....**koele** Giffard.
Not so..11

11(10). Maui species; mesonotum flavous to fusco-piceous.....
.... **halehaku** Giffard.
Hawaii species; mesonotum flavous to dark castaneous
..............................**filicicola** Kirkaldy.

DIVISION D

Fossette of vertex incompletely divided by a median longitudinal carina, the basal part of the dividing carina more or less evident, but never reaching the apical carinae of the vertex (fig. 33, d).

1.   Discal tegminal veins dark............................ 2
Discal tegminal veins pale............................ 6
2(1).   Tegmina with about basal and apical thirds darkly fuliginous, middle third largely clear or milky hyaline...... 3
Tegmina not so colored and not divided into three colored
areas 4
3(2).   Small species, length: males, 5–5.5 mm.; females, 6–6.5
mm. ....**neotarai** Giffard.
Larger, males, 6.5–7.25 mm.; females, 7.5–8 mm.........
....**tarai** Kirkaldy.
4(2).   Tegmina yellowish or tawny, with apical third more or
less fuliginous.................female **neomorai** Giffard.
Tegmina entirely dark fuliginous, opaque............... 5
5(4).   Molokai species; length: male, 7.25–7.75 mm.; female,
8.5–9 mm...........................**morai** (Kirkaldy).
Kauai species; length: female, 8 mm.................
......................variety of **immaculatus** Giffard.
6(1).   Base of fork of medio-frontal carina open (obsolete); tegmina immaculately dark yellowish, semi-opaque; length:
male, 7 mm.; female, 8 mm.; Kauai only............
.... **immaculatus** Giffard.
Base of fork of medio-frontal carina closed; tegmina yellowish or tawny hyaline, with apical third or less fuliginous; length: male, 7.5 mm.; female, 9 mm.; on all
islands.............................**neomorai** Giffard.

DIVISION E

Fossette of vertex entirely undivided by a median longitudinal carina, or, at most, the basal part of the carina when present is rudimentary or obscure (fig. 33, e, f).

1.   Costa, as seen from above or from side (not from below)
obviously much expanded toward base, sometimes
nearly flange-like (fig. 34, d, f), distinctly much

          broader than at middle and in some species strongly
             convex in tegminal outline............................ 2
          Costa not or but slightly broadened toward base, only
             slightly broader at base than at middle, never strongly
             convex basad (fig. 34, e)............................ 7
2(1).   Costa not conspicuously arched basad, more flatly arcuate
             (fig. 34, f)... 3
          Costa distinctly and comparatively strongly arched basad
             (fig. 34, d)... 4
3(2).   Tegmina milky hyaline; wings hyaline; costa not so thick
             at base as in some other species; tegminal veins very
             dark; length: males, 6.5–7 mm.; females, 7.5–7.75 mm.;
             Hawaii...............................**niger** Giffard.
          Tegmina dark yellowish or tawny hyaline, maculate;
             wings apically fuliginous; length: male, 9.25 mm.;
             Maui...........................**haleakalae** Kirkaldy.
4(2).   Mesonotal carinae black or dark castaneous............. 5
          Mesonotal carinae comparatively pale castaneous......... 6
5(4).   Kauai species...........................**montanus** Giffard.
          Oahu species............................**olympus** Giffard.
          Lanai and Hawaii species..............**hevaheva** Kirkaldy.
6(4).   Oahu species............................**olympus** Giffard.
          Maui species..........................**mauiensis** Giffard.
          Hawaii species.......................**hevaheva** Kirkaldy.
7(1).   Tegminal veins particolored (comparatively large species,
             7–12 mm. in length).............................. 8
          Tegminal veins not particolored (usually smaller species,
             length of males seldom more than 7 mm.)..............12
8(7).   Oahu species........................**kaohinani** Kirkaldy.
          Hawaii species.....................**kanakanus** Kirkaldy.
          Not so.. 9
9(8).   Kauai species...10
          Maui or Molokai species...............................11
10(9).   Sides of vertex only slightly expanded basad (apex di-
             vided into breadth across basal angles in holotype male
             equals 1.18); length: male, 7 mm.; female, 9 mm.....
             ....**consimilis** Giffard.
          Sides of vertex obviously divergent basad (apex divided
             into breadth between basal angles equals 1.41 in male
             holotype); length: male, 8 mm.; female, 10 mm....
             ....**intermedius** Giffard.
11(9).   Fossette of vertex a little longer than wide; base of fork
             of median frontal carina closed; length: 8 mm.......
             ....**kahavalu** Kirkaldy.
          Fossette of vertex a little broader than long; base of fork
             of median frontal carina open; length: male, 10 mm.;
             female, 11.5–12 mm....................**kulanus Giffard.**
12(7).   Tegmina maculate......................................13
          Tegmina immaculate 17
13(12).   Mesonotal carinae dark................................14
          Mesonotal carinae pale 16

14(13). Basal two-thirds of tegminal veins mostly pale; darkly
        fuliginous over basal third of tegmina.......**lihue** Giffard.
        Basal two-thirds of tegminal veins dark and pale, but not
        particolored; not darkly fuliginous over basal third of
        tegmina...15

15(14). **O. waialeale** Giffard, and **kauaiensis** Kirkaldy. The holo-
        type and lectotype of these two species are so closely
        similar that I cannot separate them. I do not now feel
        that they are distinct species, but consult Giffard's text.

16(13). Kauai species............................**koae** Giffard.
        Oahu species...........................**acaciae** Kirkaldy.
        Maui species.......................**euphorbiae** Giffard.
        Hawaii species........................**opuna** Kirkaldy.
        Note: The above forms all have the fossette broader
        than long. They may only be forms of a single species.

17(12). Mesonotum pale (tegmina broad, veins lightly particol-
        ored and medianly pallid; length: male, 5.25 mm.;
        Kauai)............................ **halemanu** Giffard.
        Mesonotum dark...................................18

18(17). Tegmina and wings conspicuously and unusually milky
        white; at least outer mesonotal carinae pale; Oahu
        ....**albatus** Giffard.
        Not so..19

19(18). Kauai species (yellowish macula at lateral margins of
        frons near clypeal suture distinct and elongate; teg-
        mina hyaline, veins dark)...........**silvestris** Kirkaldy.
        Not Kauai species................................20

20(19). Oahu species.......................**instabilis** Giffard.
        Not so..21

21(20). Maui or Lanai species....................**similis** Giffard.
        Hawaii species.....**inaequalis** Giffard and **inconstans** Giffard.
        I do not understand why Giffard separated these last
        two forms as distinct species. I have been unable to
        find specific differences between them, and Giffard did
        not give characters to separate them in his key.

Inasmuch as Giffard's keys, even as herein altered and recast, are difficult to use and may greatly confuse the student unfamiliar with the group, especially if he does not have an adequate, carefully named collection for comparative purposes, I have felt it desirable to draw up tentative supplementary keys. These have been prepared using distribution as a primary divisional character, for most of the species are known from single islands only. These keys will have to be altered in the future when more data are available regarding distribution, but in the meantime they may aid in the identification of localized collections of these difficult and confusing forms. The keys are based upon the males and have been drawn up from the type specimens of most of the species.

Island Keys to the Male Oliarus

KAUAI SPECIES

(Excepting *orono* and *pluvialis,* but see figure 35, c, d of the latter)

1.   Areolets of vertex unusually prolonged caudad into slen-
          der points as in figure 33, g, much longer at sides than
          along median line.................................. 2
          Areolets not so formed, never so prolonged backward..... 3

2(1).   Vertex broader across basal angles than breadth of an
          eye at same level; tegmina clear or yellowish hyaline
          ....**muiri** Giffard.
          Vertex only about two-thirds or less as broad across basal
          angles as breadth of an eye; tegmina milky hyaline..
          ....**swezeyi** Giffard.

3(1).   Costa of tegmina, as seen from side or above, strongly
          expanded toward base and there about three or four
          times as broad as at middle and strongly arched
          (fig. 34, d)..........................**montanus** Giffard,
          Costa not so expanded, usually not much broader sub-
          basally than at middle, never more than twice as broad
          and not strongly arched............................. 4

4(3).   Basal color of mesonotum brown....................... 5
          Basal color of mesonotum black or nearly so............ 7

5(4).   Lateral margin of front of head as viewed from side form-
          ing a very definite and conspicuous angle with sides of
          fossette; distance between eye and side of fossette
          greater than breadth of second antennal segment; a
          large species, 7.5–12.5 mm. in length...............
          ....**tamehameha** Kirkaldy.
          Lateral margin of front forming nearly an even curve
          with side of fossette and never so angulate as *tameha-
          meha;* distance between an eye and side of fossette less
          than breadth of second antennal segment; length:
          5.5–8.0 mm.. 6

6(5).   A short, stumpy species with tegmina only about two and
          one-half times as long as broad; veins partly particol-
          ored, granules darker than veins and conspicuous....
          ....**halemanu** Giffard.
          A comparatively slender species with tegmina about three
          times as long as broad or longer; tegmina conspicu-
          ously yellowish; veins pallid, not particolored, granules
          pale and inconspicuous.............**immaculatus** Giffard.

7(4).   Mesonotal carinae largely pale...............**koae** Giffard.
          Mesonotal carinae mostly or entirely dark.............. 8

8(7).   Tegminal membrane immaculate, veins not or only slight-
          ly particolored...................................... 9
          Tegmina maculate, or veins particolored, or both.........10

9(8).   Lateral margins of fossette and vertex, as seen from side
          forming a very conspicuous nearly right angle; dis-

tance between an eye and above-mentioned angle greater than breadth of a second antennal segment........
...................................**silvestris** Kirkaldy.
Lateral margins of fossette and vertex more nearly rounded into one another; distance between an eye and hind angle of fossette less than breadth of a second antennal segment..................**nubigenus** Kirkaldy.

10(8). About the basal third of tegminal membrane fuliginous
....**lihue** Giffard.
Tegminal membrane not so colored..................11

11(10). Tegminal veins conspicuously particolored, their granules mostly inconspicuous.............................12
Tegminal veins not or inconspicuously particolored, granules mostly conspicuous...........................13

12(11). Sides of vertex subparallel, hardly expanded caudad, extreme breadth between basal angles obviously much narrower than breadth of an eye..................
...................................**consimilis** Giffard.
Sides of vertex obviously divergent caudad, distance across basal angles nearly, but not quite, as broad as an eye...........................**intermedius** Giffard.

13(12). **O. kauaiensis** Kirkaldy and **waialeale** Giffard. I have been unable to find adequate characters to separate these supposed species on the basis of available material.

OAHU SPECIES

(Excepting *procellaris*)

1. Costa of tegmina, as seen from side or above, strongly expanded basad and there about three or four times as broad as at middle (fig. 34, d)..........**olympus** Giffard.
Costa not so expanded, usually not much broader sub-basally than at middle, never more than twice as broad... 2

2(1). Vertex unusually broad and short, breadth across basal angles much greater than breadth of an eye, nearly twice as broad; a peculiar small (4.5 mm.), stubby, lowland species with a predominantly pale mesonotum
...................................**discrepans** Giffard.
Not such species..................................... 3

3(2). Basal color of mesonotum brown or pale brown, or keels pale or both...................................... 4
Basal color of mesonotum, including keels, black or nearly so..15

4(3). Tegmina and wings appearing unusually and conspicuously milky white to the unaided eyes, without numerous maculae and veins pallid except at apex.....
...................................**albatus** Giffard.
Not such white species, tegmina either hyaline, milky hyaline or maculate or both, but never unusually white.. 5

5(4).   Fossette of vertex appearing conspicuously transverse, or
         the depression continuous transversely and median line
         not elevated except at base to divide fossette into two
         areolets, or both............................... 6
         Fossette of vertex with median line elevated to a greater
         or lesser extent and dividing or partially dividing fos-
         sette into two areolets........................... 7

6(5).   Tegmina maculate.....................**acaciae** Kirkaldy.
         Tegmina not maculate..................**instabilis** Giffard.

7(5).   Tegminal veins particolored but mostly conspicuously
         dark brown and outstanding over most of tegmina...... 8
         Tegminal veins particolored or not, but mostly pale or
         pale brown, never dark and prominent over most of
         wing 10

8(7).   Median line of fossette of vertex distinct only at base
         and not separating areolets which are thus broadly
         coalescent........................ **kaohinani** Kirkaldy.
         Median line of fossette swollen and elevated throughout
         nearly all of its length thus separating areolets........ 9

9(8).   Fossette dark, V-shaped anteriorly.........**likelike** Giffard.
         Fossette apically rounded or subtruncate, usually mostly
         pale.....................................**pele** Kirkaldy.

10(7).   Vertex comparatively narrow, median length about two
         and one-half times as long as broad across basal angles
         from a line drawn between basal angles to base of fos-
         sette...11
         Vertex less than or hardly more than twice as long as
         broad across basal angles..........................12

11(10). Tegminal veins particolored.........**kaumuahona** Giffard.
         Tegminal veins not particolored........**wailupensis** Giffard.
         (Note: I am not satisfied that these names represent
         two distinct species.)

12(10). Foveate or depressed area at top of median facial carina
         and between its divergent arms well removed from level
         of areolets of fossette.................**kirkaldyi** Giffard.
         This foveate area closely approaching level of areolets
         of fossette, at most only shortly separated from level
         of areolets.....................................13

13(12). Tegmina milky.....................**myoporicola** Giffard.
         Tegmina hyaline or yellowish hyaline, not milky........14

14(13). Cross-veins of apical parts of tegmina distinctly suffused;
         face with pale maculae at sides..........**makaala** Giffard.
         Cross-veins not suffused; face without pale maculae at
         sides............................... **kaonohi** Kirkaldy.

15(3).   Basal and apical thirds of tegmina conspicuously fuli-
         ginous, middle third mostly hyaline, colored zones con-
         spicuous to unaided eyes..........................16
         Tegmina without three color zones...................17

16(15). The fuliginous color on tegmina broadly, conspicuously
         extending entirely along claval area, thus joining basal
         and apical fuliginous areas..............**neotarai** Giffard.

The fuliginous color on tegmina not extending along claval area at middle, or only indistinctly so, and not connecting basal and apical fuliginous areas.........
...................................**tarai** Kirkaldy.

17(15).   Tegminal veins particolored..............**kaiulani** Giffard.
Tegminal veins not particolored..........**tantalus** Giffard.

MOLOKAI SPECIES

(Excepting *paludicola,* but see figure 35, e, f)

1.   Vertex very broad, broader across basal angles than breadth of an eye, and about as broad as long; tegmina in part or largely fuliginous........................ 2
Vertex narrower, longer than broad, tegmina not fuliginous...3

2(1).   Tegmina entirely dark fuliginous, veins dark.........
...................................**morai** (Kirkaldy).
Tegmina mostly pale fuliginous, veins mostly pale.....
...........................**neomorai** Giffard.

3(1).   Tegmina clear, veins particolored, membrane maculate
...............................**kahavalu** Kirkaldy.
Tegmina yellowish hyaline, veins not particolored, membrane immaculate in basal two-thirds at least.......
...................................**similis** Giffard.

LANAI SPECIES

1.   Costa broadly expanded and strongly curved basad (fig. 34, d), three or more times as broad subbasally as near stigma...........................**hevaheva** Kirkaldy.
Costa not so broadened and strongly arched basad, at most twice as broad subbasally as near stigma......... 2

2(1).   Mesonotum broad or pale; rather small slender species
.....................................**koele** Giffard.
Mesonotum black; medium-sized, broad species.......... 3

3(2).   Tegmina clear, veins particolored, membrane maculate
...............................**kahavalu** Kirkaldy.
Tegmina yellowish hyaline, veins not particolored, membrane immaculate in basal two-thirds at least.........
...................................**similis** Giffard.

MAUI SPECIES

(Excepting *monticola*)

1.   Tegmina fuliginous at base and apex, hyaline in middle section, thus with three conspicuous color zones.....
...................................**tarai** Kirkaldy.
Tegmina without three such colored bands............... 2

2(1).   Costa strongly convex in longitudinal outline basad, and thickened and three times as broad near base as nar-

rowest breadth before stigma (a large species with tegmina largely yellowish, but fuliginous on about apical
third)............................... **mauiensis** Giffard.

Costa not so expanded and arched, not more than twice
as broad subbasally as before stigma and more flatly
arcuate than arched basad (some species have costa
expanded basad, but not so much as in *mauiensis* and
without such colored tegmina in combination with a
much-thickened costa)............................... 3

3(2).   Mesonotum and keels black........................... 4
Mesonotum and/or keels pale or brown................. 6

4(3).   Tegminal membrane conspicuously spotted; veins conspicuously particolored (a large spotted species).....
.... **kulanus** Giffard.
Tegminal membrane inconspicuously spotted or immaculate in basal two-thirds; veins not particolored......... 5

5(4).   Length about 9 mm. or more; rostrum surpassing hind
coxae for a distance about as great as length of an eye
.... **haleakalae** Kirkaldy.
Length not over 8 mm.; rostrum extending but little behind hind coxae...................... **similis** Giffard.

6(3).   Tegminal membrane spotted, costal cell spotted........
.... **euphorbiae** Giffard.
Tegminal membrane not spotted in basal two-thirds,
costal cell not spotted............................... 7

7(6).   Wings appearing opaque white through tegmina......
.... **halehaku** Giffard.
Wings clear............................... **pele** Kirkaldy.

HAWAII SPECIES

(Excepting *nemoricola*, but see figure 35, a, b)

1.   Tegmina fuliginous at base and apex, hyaline between,
thus with three colored zones............. **tarai** Kirkaldy.
Tegmina not so colored............................... 2

2(1).   Costa three times as broad near base as at its narrowest
point near stigma.................. **hevaheva** Kirkaldy.
Costa not more than twice as broad subbasally as near
stigma... 3

3(2).   Fossette of vertex with median line for most part or entirely swollen or cariniform and dividing fossette into
two areolets, fossette never continuously and evenly
excavate transversely............................... 4

Fossette of vertex nearly or quite continuously excavate
transversely and with median line traceable only shortly
at base, fossette usually, not always, transverse, sometimes strongly so................................. 5

4(3).   Areolet-like depression between basal arms of median
carina of frons large, about twice as long as median
line of fossette...................... **filicicola** Kirkaldy.

The above-described depression much smaller, more
nearly size of an areolet of fossette and not much longer
than median line of fossette, area between areolets and
arms of median carina of frons tumescent and carinae
coalescent..........................**koanoa** Kirkaldy.

5(3).   Keels of mesonotum pale; vertex unusually broad......
....**opuna** Kirkaldy.
Keels of mesonotum dark; vertex not unusually broad.... 6

6(5).   Veins of tegmina mostly uniformly dark overall; membrane whitish..........................**niger** Giffard.
Veins particolored, partly pale or mostly pale, never
dark overall...................................... 7

7(6).   Veins over basal two-thirds of tegmina all pale, yellowish,
membrane immaculate................**inaequalis** Giffard.
Veins at least partially particolored; membrane maculate or not....................................... 8

8(7).   Length 8–9 mm.; veins mostly conspicuously dark, particoloration sharply marked, membrane usually conspicuously maculate...................**kanakanus** Kirkaldy.
Length 6–7.5 mm.; veins mostly pale, particoloration
feeble, maculae of membrane pale if present........
...................................**inconstans** Giffard.

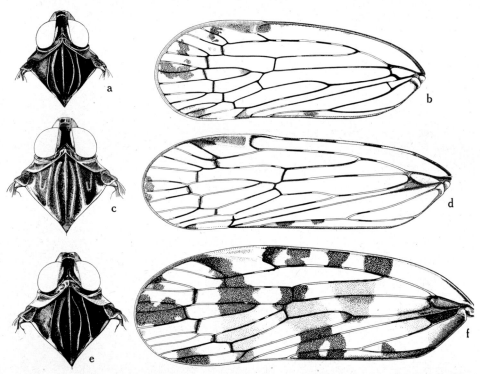

Figure 35—Holotypes of some *Oliarus*: **a, b,** *O. nemoricola* Kirkaldy; **c, d,** *O. pluvialis* Kirkaldy; **e, f,** *O. paludicola* Kirkaldy. (Drawn at the British Museum of Natural History by
Smith. The tegmina are not drawn to same scale as the head figures.)

Oliarus acaciae Kirkaldy (figs. 32, C; 36).
   Oliarus acaciae Kirkaldy, 1909:78. Giffard, 1925:129, pl. 1, fig. 9; pl. 2, fig. 14.

   Endemic. Oahu (type locality: Mount Kaala, 3,500 feet).
   Hostplant: *Acacia koa.*
   This species is a close ally of *euphorbiae, opuna* and *koae.*

Oliarus albatus Giffard (fig. 36).
   Oliarus albatus Giffard, 1925:135, pl. 6, figs. 104, 105.

   Endemic. Oahu (type locality: Hillebrand Glen, Nuuanu Valley, Honolulu).
   The unusually milky tegmina are distinctive.

Oliarus consimilis Giffard (fig. 36).
   Oliarus consimilis Giffard, 1925:123, pl. 7, figs. 123, 124.

   Endemic. Kauai (type locality: "lower forest above Lihue, at 800 feet elevation").

Oliarus discrepans Giffard (figs. 34, g, r; 36).
   Oliarus discrepans Giffard, 1925:79, pl. 3, figs. 41, 48.

   Endemic. Oahu (type locality: Ewa Mill).
   Hostplant: *Gossypium tomentosum.*
   This is a peculiar little species. It so differs from the other Hawaiian *Oliarus* that Giffard thought that it might possibly prove to be an immigrant. However, it appears more likely that it is a remnant of the now nearly extinct lowland fauna of Oahu. I have collected usually single specimens here and there about Honolulu and elsewhere in the lowlands. Most of the examples taken by me were seen sitting on the sides of buildings or on posts or have been swept from vegetation. A specimen flew onto my desk at the Bishop Museum while I was writing this volume. Dr. Swezey has taken series of examples from the native cotton, *Gossypium tomentosum,* and has found the nymphs and adults under stones. Giffard did not know the males, but male examples are now in our collections.

Oliarus euphorbiae Giffard (figs. 32, A; 36).
   Oliarus euphorbiae Giffard, 1925:128, pl. 2, fig. 16; pl. 6, fig. 102.

   Endemic. Maui (type locality: Iao Valley).
   Hostplant: *Euphorbia.*

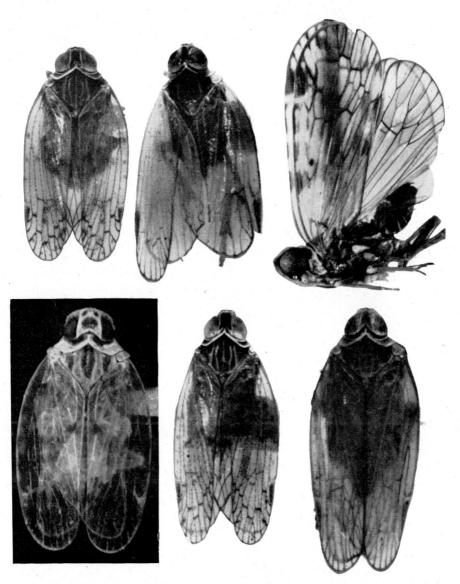

Figure 36—*Oliarus* species. Top row, left to right: *O. acaciae* Kirkaldy, paratype female; *O. albatus* Giffard, paratype male; *O. consimilis* Giffard, paratype male. Bottom row, left to right: *O. discrepans* Giffard, paratype female; *O. euphorbiae* Giffard, paratype male; *O. filicicola* Giffard, paratype male.

Oliarus filicicola Kirkaldy (figs. 34, m; 36).

    Oliarus filicicola Kirkaldy, 1909:77. Giffard, 1925:88, pl. 4, figs. 63, 64; pl. 8, fig. 140.

    Oliarus montivagus Kirkaldy, 1909:78; synonymy by Giffard, 1925:88.

    Oliarus kaonohi variety *volcanicola* Kirkaldy, 1909:78, footnote; synonymy by Giffard, 1925:88.

Endemic. Hawaii (type locality: Naalehu).

Hostplant: *Cibotium* tree ferns (nymphs found amongst decaying fronds).

Oliarus haleakalae Kirkaldy (fig. 37).

    Oliarus haleakalae Kirkaldy, 1909:78.

Endemic. Maui (type locality: Haleakala, 5,000 feet).

Hostplants: *Cibotium chamissoi* (tree fern), *Cyrtandra.*

Oliarus halehaku Giffard (fig. 37).

    Oliarus halehaku Giffard, 1925:94, pl. 4, figs. 68, 69.

Endemic. Maui (type locality: Nahiku).

Hostplants: *Cibotium, Sadleria,* rotten tree fern fronds, *Pipturus.*
It may be that this is really *kaonohi.*

Oliarus halemanu Giffard.

    Oliarus halemanu Giffard, 1925:133, pl. 6, figs. 99, 100.

Endemic. Kauai (type locality: Halemanu).

Oliarus hevaheva Kirkaldy (figs. 33, e; 34, d; 37).

    Oliarus hevaheva Kirkaldy, 1902:122, pl. 4, fig. 6. Giffard, 1925:104, pl. 1, fig. 5; pl. 5, figs. 84, 85.

    Oliarus lanaiensis Giffard, 1925:106, pl. 5, figs. 80, 81 (type locality: Lanai, 2,000 feet). New synonym.

Endemic. Lanai, Hawaii (type locality: Kona).

There are several species which have the costa distinctly expanded basad which are associated with this form. The drawings illustrate the character. I cannot accept Giffard's *lanaiensis,* for I can find no reason to separate his holotype from typical *hevaheva.*

Oliarus immaculatus Giffard (figs. 33, d; 37).

    Oliarus immaculatus Giffard, 1925:96, pl. 1, fig. 4; pl. 4, figs. 60, 65; pl. 6, fig. 106.

Figure 37—*Oliarus* species. Top row, left to right: *O. haleakalae* Kirkaldy, male; *O. halehaku* Giffard, paratype male; *O. halehaku* Giffard, paratype female. Bottom row, left to right: *O. hevaheva* Kirkaldy, male; *O. inaequalis* Giffard, paratype male; *O. immaculatus* Giffard, paratype male.

Endemic. Kauai (type locality: Kokee).
Hostplants: "ferns."

Oliarus inaequalis Giffard (fig. 37).
Oliarus inaequalis Giffard, 1925:136, pl. 6, figs. 110, 111.

Endemic. Hawaii (type locality: South Kona Road, 1,600 feet).
This species is closely allied to, and forms a group with, *similis, instabilis* and *inconstans*. The group may be a species or a "superspecies." The typical form has pale, yellowish-clouded, immaculate tegmina. Giffard noted (1925:139) that "There is apparently but little difference in the structure or characters of the aedeagus of this species and of its varieties, and these indicate very close affinities to *similis* of Maui, as well as *inconstans* of Hawaii. Both of these species are undoubtedly extreme forms of *inaequalis*."

Oliarus inaequalis koebelei Metcalf.
Oliarus inaequalis variety *b* Giffard, 1925:137.
Oliarus inaequalis variety *koebelei* Metcalf, 1936:69.

Endemic. Hawaii (type locality: above Dowsett Ranch, Kona, 7,000 feet).

Oliarus inaequalis kohala Metcalf.
Oliarus inaequalis variety *c* Giffard, 1925:138.
Oliarus inaequalis variety *kohala* Metcalf, 1936:69.

Endemic. Hawaii (type locality: Upper Hamakua Ditch Trail, Kohala Mountains).

Oliarus inaequalis konana Metcalf.
Oliarus inaequalis variety *a* Giffard, 1925:137.
Oliarus inaequalis variety *konana* Metcalf, 1936:69.

Endemic. Hawaii (type locality: Puuwaawaa, North Kona, 3,800 feet).

Oliarus inconstans Giffard (fig. 38).
Oliarus inconstans Giffard, 1925:145, pl. 8, figs. 132, 133.

Endemic. Hawaii (type locality: Kilauea).
Giffard noted varieties with maculate and immaculate tegmina, and said (p. 147) "The aedeagus indicates that this species is merely another form of *inaequalis* and its insular allies, and is equally as variable as these."

Oliarus instabilis Giffard (figs. 34, h ; 38).

Oliarus instabilis Giffard, 1925 :142, pl. 8, figs. 129–131, 137.

Endemic. Oahu (type locality: Wailupe).

Giffard (p. 145) noted that "This is a very variable species and no doubt represents the Oahu form of what I have called the '*inaequalis–similis*' group from Hawaii and Maui. As in that group, the structure and colorations are very unstable, the sexual dimorphism confusing, and the characters of the genitalia in a marked degree variable. Of the seven dissections made of the aedeagus, no two are quite alike as to the structural outline of the apical third of the periandrium, but all have a similarity in one aspect or another."

Although Giffard designated and labeled types of his varieties of *inaequalis*, he neglected to do so for the varieties of this species. His material of the following varieties bears no type labels, but one example of each form bears a label on which the sex and the variety name are written in red ink. I have used the localities of these forms as the typical localities.

Oliarus instabilis bryani Metcalf.

Oliarus instabilis variety *a* Giffard, 1925 :143.

Oliarus instabilis variety *bryani* Metcalf, 1936 :70.

Endemic. Oahu (type locality: Mount Kaala).

Oliarus instabilis crawi Metcalf.

Oliarus instabilis variety *b* Giffard, 1925 :144.

Oliarus instabilis variety *crawi* Metcalf, 1936 :70.

Endemic. Oahu (type locality: Mount Olympus).

Oliarus instabilis ehrhorni Metcalf.

Oliarus instabilis variety *c* Giffard, 1925 :144.

Oliarus instabilis variety *ehrhorni* Metcalf, 1936 :70.

Endemic. Oahu (type locality: Mount Kaala).

Oliarus instabilis osborni Metcalf.

Oliarus instabilis variety *d* Giffard, 1925 :144.

Oliarus instabilis variety *osborni* Metcalf, 1936 :70.

Endemic. Oahu (type locality: Waialae Nui).

Oliarus instabilis terryi Metcalf.

Oliarus instabilis variety *e* Giffard, 1925:144.

Oliarus instabilis variety *terryi* Metcalf, 1936:70.

Endemic. Oahu (type locality: Mount Kaala).

Oliarus instabilis williamsi Metcalf.

Oliarus instabilis variety *f* Giffard, 1925:144.

Oliarus instabilis variety *williamsi* Metcalf, 1936:70.

Endemic. Oahu (type locality: Punaluu).

Oliarus intermedius Giffard (fig. 38).

Oliarus intermedius Giffard, 1925:122, pl. 7, figs. 121, 126.

Endemic. Kauai (type locality: Kaholuamano).

This is perhaps a representative of the Oahu *kaohinani*.

Oliarus kahavalu Kirkaldy (fig. 38).

Oliarus kahavalu Kirkaldy, 1909:77. Giffard, 1925:116, pl. 7, figs. 116, 117.

Endemic. Molokai (type locality: 4,000 feet), Maui.

Hostplant: *Metrosideros*.

This is an ally of *kanakanus* from Hawaii.

Oliarus kaiulani Giffard (fig. 38).

Oliarus kaiulani Giffard, 1925:69, pl. 3, figs. 27–30.

Endemic. Oahu (type locality: Halawa).

Oliarus kanakanus Kirkaldy (fig. 38).

Oliarus kanakanus Kirkaldy, 1902:121, pl. 4, fig. 5. Giffard, 1925:113, pl. 7, figs. 114, 115.

Endemic. Hawaii (type locality: Kilauea).

Hostplant: *Metrosideros*.

The specimens from Maui and Oahu referred to this species by Kirkaldy in his original description belong to other species, as Giffard has shown.

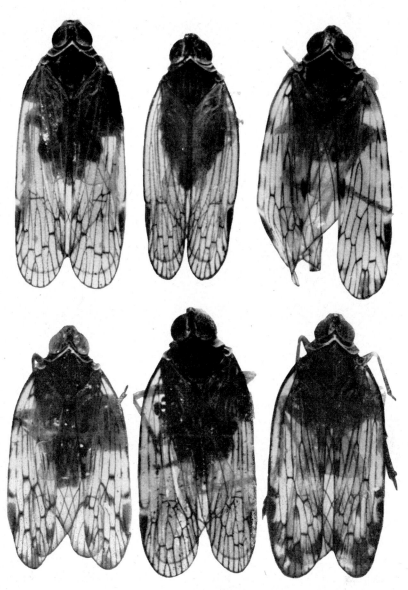

Figure 38—*Oliarus* species. Top row, left to right: *O. inconstans* Giffard, paratype female; *O. instabilis* Giffard, paratype male; *O. intermedius* Giffard, paratype male. Bottom row, left to right: *O. kahavalu* Kirkaldy, male; *O. kaiulani* Giffard, paratype male; *O. kanakanus* Kirkaldy, male.

Oliarus kanakanus punaensis Metcalf.

Oliarus kanakanus variety *a* Giffard, 1925:114.

Oliarus kanakanus variety *punaensis* Metcalf, 1936:71.

Endemic. Hawaii (type locality: Puna, 750 feet).

Oliarus kaohinani Kirkaldy (fig. 39).

Oliarus kaohinani Kirkaldy, 1909:78. Giffard, 1925:119, pl. 7, figs. 119, 120.

Endemic. Oahu (type locality: Mount Tantalus).

Oliarus kaohinani perkinsi Metcalf.

Oliarus kaohinani variety Giffard, 1925:120.

Oliarus kaohinani variety *perkinsi* Metcalf, 1936:71.

Endemic. Oahu.

Although Metcalf stated that Giffard had called this form "var. *a*," Giffard simply labeled it "var.," and did not further designate it. Giffard also listed specimens under the following subtitles: "Varieties with tegmina almost immaculate" and "Varieties with tegmina maculate."

Oliarus kaonohi Kirkaldy (fig. 39).

Oliarus kaonohi Kirkaldy, 1909:77; Giffard, 1925:91, pl. 4, figs. 61, 62.

Oliarus silvicola Kirkaldy, 1909:78 (type from Konahuanui, Oahu). Synonymy by Giffard, 1925:91.

Endemic. Oahu (type locality: "Honolulu").

Hostplants: *Broussaisia,* rotting tree fern fronds.

Kirkaldy's Hawaii record of this species applies to another.

This is an ally of *morai*. Giffard said (p. 93) that "It is suspiciously evident that either both forms are the result of cross-breeding, or that one of these is still evolving from the other."

Oliarus kauaiensis Kirkaldy (figs. 34, e; 39).

Oliarus kauaiensis Kirkaldy, 1909:79. Giffard, 1925:123, pl. 6, figs. 90, 91.

Endemic. Kauai (lectotype locality: lower forest, near Lihue, 800 feet).

The holotype is presumed to be lost, and Giffard selected male and female lectotypes.

Figure 39—*Oliarus* species. *O. kaonohi* Kirkaldy, female, top; *O. kaohinani* Kirkaldy, male, left; *O. kauaiensis* Kirkaldy, male, center; *O. kaumuahona* Giffard, paratype male, right.

Oliarus kaumuahona Giffard (fig. 39).

   Oliarus kaumuahona Giffard, 1925:77, pl. 3, figs. 42, 43.

Endemic. Oahu (type locality: Kaumuahona).
This is a close ally of *wailupensis,* and I am not sure that it is not the same species.

Oliarus kirkaldyi Giffard (figs. 34, q; 40).

   Oliarus kirkaldyi Giffard, 1925:77, pl. 3, figs. 31, 36, 45–47, 49.

Endemic. Oahu (type locality: Waianae).

Oliarus koae Giffard.

Oliarus koae Giffard, 1925:130, pl. 6, fig. 103.

Endemic. Kauai (type locality: Halemanu).

Hostplant: *Acacia koa.*

This belongs in association with *acaciae, euphorbiae* and *opuna,* and Giffard noted that it is "one extreme and *opuna* of Hawaii the other in this particular group, the intermediates being *euphorbiae* of Maui and *acaciae* of Oahu."

Oliarus koanoa Kirkaldy (figs. 33, b; 40).

Oliarus koanoa Kirkaldy, 1902:124, pl. 4, fig. 11. Giffard, 1925:72, pl. 1, fig. 2; pl. 3, figs. 34, 35.

Endemic. Hawaii (type locality: Kona).

Hostplants: *Maba sandwicensis,* tree fern.

Perhaps if Giffard had not had such a large series of this variable species before him he would have given letters of designation to various of the varietal forms. But his series was extensive enough to include intergrades, and he said (p. 74), "It would be impossible to discriminate between all these variations, because of slight differences in size and color without even larger series of each than those studied, and, so long as the structures [of the genitalia] of all are alike, it is well to lump them and save confusion."

Swezey (1907:83–84) recorded his observations on the biology of this species, and his remarks are included here in the introductory notes to this family.

Oliarus koele Giffard (figs. 34, c, n; 40).

Oliarus koele Giffard, 1925:93, pl. 4, figs. 70, 71.

Oliarus agnatus Giffard, 1925:134, pl. 6, figs. 107, 108; pl. 8, fig. 139 (type locality: Lanai, 3,000 feet). New synonym.

Endemic. Lanai (type locality: 3,000 feet).

Hostplant: ferns.

This is the Lanai representative of *kaonohi,* and closer study may show that it is identical to *kaonohi;* but as Giffard's drawings of the male genitalia show differences, I do not feel qualified to synonymize the species at this time.

Although Giffard placed *agnatus* in division E and *koele* in division C, I find from a study of the types that the two names apply to only one species. *O. agnatus* is represented by the male holotype and one male paratype. I cannot understand why Giffard separated the two forms when the holotypes so closely resemble each other, or why he did not draw some attention to this fact in his text.

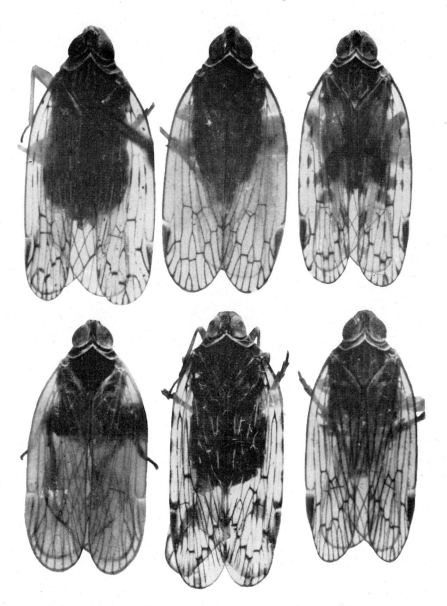

Figure 40—*Oliarus* species. Top row, left to right: *O. kirkaldyi* Giffard, paratype female; *O. koanoa* Kirkaldy, male; *O. koanoa* Kirkaldy, female. Bottom row, left to right: *O. koele* Giffard, paratype male; *O. kulanus* Giffard, paratype female; *O. likelike* Giffard, paratype male.

Oliarus kulanus Giffard (figs. 33, f; 40).
  Oliarus kulanus Giffard, 1925:117, pl. 1, fig. 6.

  Endemic. Maui (type locality: Haleakala, 5,000–5,300 feet).
  This species is an associate of *kahavalu* in the *kanakanus* group.

Oliarus lihue Giffard.
  Oliarus lihue Giffard, 1925:125, pl. 6, figs. 94, 95.

  Endemic. Kauai (type locality: near Lihue, 800 feet).

Oliarus likelike Giffard (fig. 40).
  Oliarus likelike Giffard, 1925:86, pl. 4, figs. 58, 59.

  Endemic. Oahu (type locality: Konahuanui).
  This is a close ally of *pele,* and I am not sure that it is specifically distinct.

Oliarus makaala Giffard (fig. 41).
  Oliarus makaala Giffard, 1925:87, pl. 4, figs. 54, 55.

  Endemic. Oahu (type locality: Mount Kaala).
  This species is allied to *likelike* and *pele.*

Oliarus mauiensis Giffard.
  Oliarus mauiensis Giffard, 1925:109, pl. 7, figs. 112, 113.

  Endemic. Maui (type locality: Waihee Valley).
  This is a member of the *hevaheva* group.

Oliarus montanus Giffard (fig. 41).
  Oliarus montanus Giffard, 1925:111, pl. 5, figs. 86, 87; pl. 8, fig. 125.

  Endemic. Kauai (type locality: Olokele Canyon).
  Giffard considered this to be an "intermediate form" between the *hevaheva* and *kanakanus* groups.

Oliarus monticola Kirkaldy.
  Oliarus monticola Kirkaldy, 1909:78. Giffard, 1925:148.

  Endemic. Maui (type locality: Haleakala, 5,000 feet).
  The single male type is in the British Museum, but Giffard was unable to recognize the species in the material studied by him.

Figure 41—*Oliarus* species. *O. makaala* Giffard, paratype male, left; *O. montanus* Giffard, male, center; *O. myoporicola* Giffard, paratype female, right; *O. morai* Kirkaldy, male, bottom.

Oliarus morai (Kirkaldy) (fig. 41).

Oliarus tarai variety *morai* Kirkaldy, 1902:123.

Oliarus morai (Kirkaldy) Kirkaldy, 1908:201, pl. 4, fig. 9. Giffard, 1925:101, pl. 5, figs. 76, 77.

Endemic. Molokai (type locality: 4,000 feet).

This is a close ally of *tarai,* and Giffard considered it to be "one of the transitional forms of *kaonohi.*" It does not occur on Maui as recorded by Kirkaldy.

Oliarus muiri Giffard (fig. 34, k).
Oliarus muiri Giffard, 1925:66, pl. 2, figs. 19–21.

Endemic. Kauai (type locality: Alakai Swamp).
Giffard (p. 67) noted that "This unique species and the one following (*swezeyi*) are evidently the closest relatives, so far known, of the ancestral form from which all the Hawaiian species have descended. The structure of the vertex, particularly, presents the strongest evidence that it is congeneric with the genotype *Oliarus walkeri* Stål. The aedeagus of this and the following species (*swezeyi*) is quite unlike that of any other Hawaiian forms."

Oliarus myoporicola Giffard (fig. 41).
Oliarus myoporicola Giffard, 1925:74, pl. 1, figs. 12, 13; pl. 3, figs. 37, 38, 44.

Endemic. Oahu (type locality: Barber's Point).
Hostplant: *Myoporum sandwicense.*
This is one of the few existing lowland *Oliarus.*

Oliarus neomorai Giffard (fig. 42).
Oliarus neomorai Giffard, 1925:102.

Endemic. Molokai (type locality: Kalae).
This form is closely allied to *morai* and may not be specifically distinct.

Oliarus neomorai oahuana Metcalf.
Oliarus neomorai variety *a* Giffard, 1925:103.
Oliarus neomorai variety *oahuana* Metcalf, 1936:85.

Endemic. Oahu, Hawaii (?).
The status of this form is questionable.

Oliarus nemoricola Kirkaldy (fig. 35, a, b).
Oliarus nemoricola Kirkaldy, 1909:79. Giffard, 1925:148.

Endemic. Hawaii (type locality: Hilo, 2,000 feet).
The male type (figured here) is in the British Museum, and the species was not recognized by Giffard, who considered it to be possibly "one of the varietal forms of either the *kanakanus* or *hevaheva* groups."

Oliarus neotarai Giffard (fig. 42).
Oliarus neotarai Giffard, 1925:99, pl. 4, figs. 66, 67.

Endemic. Oahu (type locality: Lanihuli).
This species is allied to *tarai.*

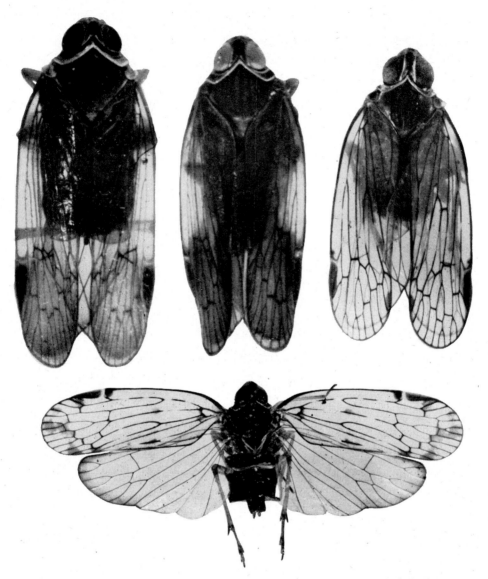

Figure 42—*Oliarus* speçies. *O. ncomorai* Giffard, female, left; *O. neotarai* Giffard, paratype male, center; *O. niger* Giffard, paratype female, right; *O. olympus* Giffard, paratype female, bottom.

Oliarus niger Giffard (figs. 34, f; 42).
  Oliarus niger Giffard, 1925:131, pl. 6, figs. 88, 89, 96.

Endemic. Hawaii (type locality: South Kona Road, 1,900 feet).

Oliarus nubigenus Kirkaldy (figs. 33, c; 43).
  Oliarus nubigenus Kirkaldy, 1909:78. Giffard, 1925:82, pl. 1, figs. 3, 8; pl. 4,
    figs. 52, 53.

  Endemic. Kauai (type locality: Halemanu, 4,000 feet).

Oliarus olympus Giffard (figs. 34, i; 42).
  Oliarus olympus Giffard, 1925:106, pl. 5, figs. 78, 79; pl. 6, fig. 109.

  Endemic. Oahu (type locality: Kuliouou).
  Hostplant: *Metrosideros.*
  This is another of the *hevaheva* group.

Oliarus olympus paliensis Metcalf.
  Oliarus olympus variety *a* Giffard, 1925:108.
  Oliarus olympus variety *paliensis* Metcalf, 1936:87.

  Endemic. Oahu.
  Giffard selected no type for this form, and I doubt that it should be named.

Oliarus opuna Kirkaldy (fig. 43).
  Oliarus opuna Kirkaldy, 1902:122, pl. 4, fig. 7. Giffard, 1925:127, pl. 1, fig. 10.
  Oliarus puna Kirkaldy, 1909:79, typographical error.

  Endemic. Hawaii (type locality: Kilauea).
  Hostplants: *Astelia, Dubautia, Nephrolepis exaltata.*
  This species belongs to the *acaciae–euphorbiae–koae* association.

Oliarus orono Kirkaldy.
  Oliarus orono Kirkaldy, 1902:124, pl. 4, fig. 10. Giffard, 1925:148.

  Endemic. Kauai (type locality: 4,000 feet).
  This is one of the species which Giffard could not recognize from Kirkaldy's
description and which remains unknown to us, as do the following "varieties."
I have received a note from the British Museum stating that the type is in the
Cambridge Museum.

Oliarus orono molokaiensis Kirkaldy.
  Oliarus orono variety *molokaiensis* Kirkaldy, 1909:79. Giffard, 1925:149.

  Endemic. Molokai.

Oliarus orono oahuensis Kirkaldy.

Oliarus orono variety *oahuensis* Kirkaldy, 1909:79. Giffard, 1925:149.

Endemic. Oahu.

It is doubtful that either of the above two "varieties" is correctly associated.

Oliarus paludicola Kirkaldy (figs. 35, e, f).

Oliarus paludicola Kirkaldy, 1909:79. Giffard, 1925:148.

Endemic. Molokai (type locality).

This form was unknown to Giffard, who thought that it might represent the Molokai form of *haleakalae*. The type is in the British Museum and is illustrated herein.

Oliarus pele Kirkaldy (fig. 43).

Oliarus pele Kirkaldy, 1909:79. Giffard, 1925:83, pl. 4, figs. 56, 57.

Endemic. Oahu (type locality unknown to me).

Hostplants: tree ferns; nymphs found in the soil about the fern roots, and Swezey reared specimens from nymphs found in rotting *Metrosideros* wood; adults have been taken from ferns and moss.

There is considerable confusion regarding this species. Kirkaldy's original series contained several species from several islands. Giffard limited it to Oahu. However, from the original description it would appear that Kirkaldy's type, if he designated one, should be a Kilauea, Hawaii, example. The name *pele* would thus apply to a different form than that selected by Giffard. The problem needs detailed study.

Oliarus pele alpha Metcalf.

Oliarus pele variety *a* Giffard, 1925:84.

Oliarus pele variety *alpha* Metcalf, 1936:95.

Endemic. Maui. No type was selected, but the typical male is from Keanae.

Oliarus pele beta Metcalf.

Oliarus pele variety *b* Giffard, 1925:85.

Oliarus pele variety *beta* Metcalf, 1936:95.

Endemic. Oahu. No type was designated, but the typical male is from Punaluu.

Oliarus pluvialis Kirkaldy (figs. 35, c, d).
Oliarus pluvialis Kirkaldy, 1909:78. Giffard, 1925:147.

Endemic. Kauai (type locality: Makaweli).
This species was not known to Giffard, and no named examples are in local collections. The type from the British Museum is figured here.

Oliarus procellaris Kirkaldy.
Oliarus procellaris Kirkaldy, 1909:77. Giffard, 1925:147.

Endemic. Oahu (type locality: Konahuanui).
Giffard reported that no examples of this species could be found in the British Museum or in Honolulu, and the species remains unknown to us. It could not be located at the British Museum in 1946 when a request to have it drawn for this text was made.

Oliarus silvestris Kirkaldy (figs. 34, 1; 43).
Oliarus silvestris Kirkaldy, 1909:78. Giffard, 1925:132, pl. 6, figs. 97, 98, 101.

Endemic. Kauai (type locality: 4,000 feet).

Oliarus similis Giffard (figs. 34, b; 43).
Oliarus similis Giffard, 1925:139, pl. 8, figs. 127, 128.

Endemic. Lanai (type locality: 2,000 feet).
Giffard noted that this is "A very variable species superficially and structurally like the preceding (*inaequalis*), to which it is very closely related." He also reported finding individual variations in the structure of the male genitalia.

Oliarus similis lanaiana Metcalf.
Oliarus similis variety *a* Giffard, 1925:140.
Oliarus similis variety *lanaiana* Metcalf, 1936:101.

Endemic. Molokai, Lanai, Maui (type locality: Wailuku).

Oliarus similis mauiana Metcalf.
Oliarus similis variety *c* Giffard, 1925:141.
Oliarus similis variety *mauiana* Metcalf, 1936:101.

Endemic. Maui (type locality: Halehaku).

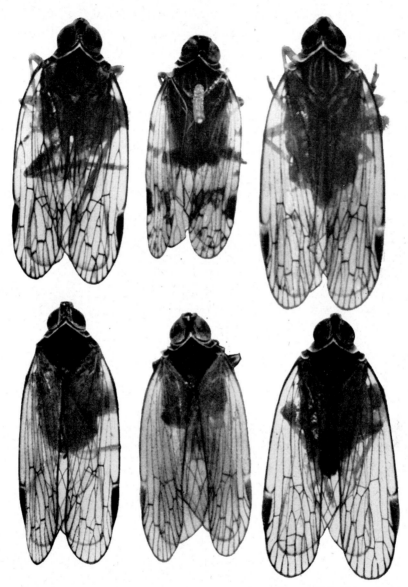

Figure 43—*Oliarus* species. Top row, left to right: *O. nubigenus* Kirkaldy, male; *O. opuna* Kirkaldy, topotype female, probably from type series; *O. pele* Kirkaldy, male. Bottom row, left to right: *O. silvestris* Kirkaldy, female; *O. similis* Giffard, paratype male; *O. tantalus* Giffard, male.

Oliarus similis molokaiana Metcalf.

Oliarus similis variety *b* Giffard, 1925:141.

Oliarus similis variety *molokaiana* Metcalf, 1936:101.

Endemic. Molokai, Maui (type locality: Olinda).

Oliarus swezeyi Giffard (figs. 32, B; 33, g; 34, o).

Oliarus swezeyi Giffard, 1925:67, pl. 1, fig. 7; pl. 2, figs. 15, 22, 23–26.

Endemic. Kauai (type locality: Olokele Canyon).
This is an ally of *muiri,* which see.

Oliarus tamehameha Kirkaldy (figs. 31; 34, j).

Oliarus tamehameha Kirkaldy, 1902:120, pl. 4, fig. 4. Giffard, 1925:81, pl. 1,
fig. 11; pl. 4, figs. 50, 51. (Type of *Nesoliarus.*)

Endemic. Kauai (type locality: Kaholuamano, 4,000 feet).

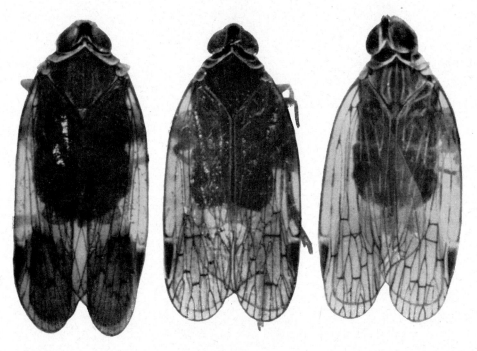

Figure 44—*Oliarus* species: *O. tarai* Kirkaldy, female, left; *O. waialeale* Giffard, female, middle; *O. wailupensis* Giffard, female, right.

Oliarus tantalus Giffard (figs. 33, a; 43).

Oliarus tantalus Giffard, 1925:71, pl. 1, fig. 1; pl. 3, figs. 32, 33.

Endemic. Oahu (type locality: Palolo Valley).
This is an associate of kaiulani, and I am not sure that it is a distinct species.

Oliarus tarai Kirkaldy (fig. 44).

Oliarus tarai Kirkaldy, 1902:123, pl. 4, figs. 6, 9. Giffard, 1925:97, pl. 5, figs. 72–75.

Endemic. Oahu (lectotype locality: Waianae).

Oliarus tarai hawaiiensis Metcalf.

Oliarus tarai variety a Kirkaldy, 1902:123.
Oliarus tarai variety hawaiiensis Metcalf, 1936:105.

Endemic. Maui (type locality: Haleakala).
Giffard did not list this form in his revision.

Oliarus tarai kohalana Metcalf.

Oliarus tarai variety a Giffard, 1925:105.
Oliarus tarai variety kohalana Metcalf, 1936:105.

Endemic. Hawaii.

Oliarus waialeale Giffard (figs. 34, a; 44).

Oliarus waialeale Giffard, 1925:125, pl. 6, figs. 92, 93.

Endemic. Kauai (type locality: Waialeale Trail, 5,000 feet).
A variable, close ally of kauaiensis.

Oliarus wailupensis Giffard (fig. 44).

Oliarus wailupensis Giffard, 1925:76, pl. 3, figs. 39, 40.

Endemic. Oahu (type locality: Wailupe).
This is an associate of kaumuahona.

Genus **IOLANIA** Kirkaldy, 1902:118

Iolania is a group which Kirkaldy, Muir and Giffard considered was an offshoot of the world-wide *Cixius*. It is easily distinguished from *Oliarus* because it has only three keels on the mesonotum instead of five. Until 1931 it was considered endemic, but Muir (1931:66–67) described two new species from Queensland and assigned them to this genus. I doubt that the Hawaiian and Australian species are monophyletic.

Giffard saw no examples from Kauai or Molokai, but specimens have since been collected from both these islands. This new material has not been examined critically and I have not included the records in this text.

Kirkaldy recognized a single species among the series of examples from several islands studied by him. However, Giffard split the group into five species on the basis of differences found in the male genitalia only, and he stated that it was practically impossible to separate the species by any other method. I am not altogether convinced that there are five full species involved here and suggest that further studies be made.

Kirkaldy gave the varietal name *notata* to the form which has "a large brown blotch at the base of the tegmina in the male." This was not recognized by Giffard, who stated that no type of this form could be located either at the British Museum or in Honolulu. Kirkaldy did not mention any locality for *notata,* and it appears that until the type can be located it will be impossible to tell whether the variety applies to *perkinsi,* or to one of Giffard's species, or whether the name applies to a similar form of each of the five "species." For the time being, I have listed it under *perkinsi* as it was first described.

These insects frequent ferns. The adults have also been collected at lights.

The "species" of this genus can be distinguished on the basis of their distribution, excepting that two forms occur together on Oahu. A study of the male genitalia and a comparison with the illustrations will be essential to separate these two latter species. I have failed to find external characters from which to assemble a key.

Iolania koolauensis Giffard.

Iolania koolauensis Giffard, 1925:154, pl. 8, figs. 141–142.

Endemic. Oahu (type locality: Waiahole).

Iolania lanaiensis Giffard (fig. 45).

Iolania lanaiensis Giffard, 1925:155, pl. 8, fig. 136.

Endemic. Lanai (type locality: 3,000 feet).

Figure 45—*Iolania oahuensis* Giffard, male, left; *Iolania lanaiensis* Giffard, female, right.

Iolania mauiensis Giffard.

Iolania mauiensis Giffard, 1925:155, pl. 8, fig. 135.

Endemic. Maui (type locality: Waialuaiki).

Iolania oahuensis Giffard (fig. 45).

Iolania oahuensis Giffard, 1925:154, pl. 8, fig. 138.

Endemic. Oahu (type locality: Palolo Valley).

Iolania perkinsi perkinsi Kirkaldy (figs. 31; 34, p).

Iolania perkinsi Kirkaldy, 1902:119, pl. 4, fig. 3. Giffard, 1925:153, pl. 8, fig. 134. Genotype.

Endemic. Hawaii (type locality: Kilauea).

Iolania perkinsi notata Kirkaldy.

Iolania perkinsi variety *notata* Kirkaldy, 1909:75.

Endemic. Hawaii (type locality unknown to me).

Family **DELPHACIDAE** (Leach, 1815)

Asiracidae (Motschulsky, 1863).
Araeopidae Metcalf, 1938:297.

Metcalf, in his paper "The Fulgorina of Barro Colorado and Other Parts of Panama" (1938), erected the family name Araeopidae to replace the old name of Delphacidae. He considered *Delphax* Fabricius, 1798, to be preoccupied by the mammalian generic name of *Delphax* Walbaum, 1792 (listed from Klein's work of 1744). However, as pointed out by Fennah (1944), Opinion 21 handed down by the International Commission of Zoological Nomenclature was overlooked, for it states that the *Delphax* of Klein and Walbaum is not available under the rules. Opinion 21 reads as follows: "Shall the Genera of Klein, 1744, Reprinted by Walbaum, 1792, be Accepted?—When Walbaum, 1792, reprinted in condensed form (but did not accept) the genera of Klein, 1744, he did not thereby give Klein's genera any nomenclatorial status, and Klein's genera do not therefore gain availability under the present Code by reason of being quoted by Walbaum." Thus, Araeopidae of Metcalf becomes a synonym of the old and well-known family name Delphacidae.

This is the largest of the fulgoroid families. In 1943, Metcalf listed 137 genera containing 1,114 species as known from the world. Of these, 14 genera and 145 species and lesser forms are known from the Hawaiian Islands. Thus, our local fauna is one of the richest in the world. Certainly for its area Hawaii has a great concentration of species, and a number of new endemic species are yet to be described.

These are usually small insects which can be distinguished readily from all our other leafhoppers because they have a large, conspicuous, movable spur or calcar on each hind tibia.

There are three types of winged forms. In some, the tegmina are fully developed, usually surpass the apex of the abdomen, have fully developed venation and these individuals are termed macropterous forms. The second group, containing the koeliopterous forms, have the venation somewhat reduced and the tegmina are somewhat shortened and do not extend beyond the abdomen and may not completely cover it. The third, or brachypterous, forms have the tegmina much reduced with greatly reduced venation and the tegmina may cover only the base of the abdomen. The hind wings are fully developed only in the macropterous forms. Some species are known to include individuals of all three forms, whereas others are known only from the macropterous or brachypterous forms.

The females have the ovipositor well developed, and the eggs are inserted into punctures made in plant tissues.

This is the largest hemipterous family in our fauna. Kirkaldy and Muir, both of whom resided in Hawaii, described nearly all of our species. Some of the genera and a large number of the species were described after *Fauna Hawaiiensis* was completed. Giffard and especially Swezey have collected the bulk of the species and have recorded a large amount of data on the hostplants and habits of the insects.

The native delphacids are attacked by a number of parasites, but our knowledge of this parasitism is meager. Pipunculid flies, the dryinid wasps *Echthrodelphax fairchildii* Perkins, *Pseudogonatopus perkinsi* (Ashmead), and the strepsipteron *Elenchus melanias* Perkins and its variety *silvestris* Perkins are known to attack various leafhoppers. "Stylopized" or pipunculid-attacked nymphs and adults are found frequently among series of specimens of many species. Certain tiny mymarid *Polynema* wasps attack the eggs. A most interesting study and worth-while contribution could be made by a keen student who would make a careful and detailed survey of the parasites of our native leafhoppers and their habits. In addition to these parasites, there are several purposely introduced parasites which have been brought in to check immigrant leafhopper pests, and these latter parasites are discussed farther on in the text. Many of the native leafhoppers have become increasingly rare in recent years. The introduction of foreign parasites to control the sugarcane leafhopper may account for this. Some species, once common, are now difficult to find. The number of extinct species is probably large.

An interesting manifestation of the parasitic attack, which I have noticed among species of *Nesosydne* particularly, is the variable amount of castration that takes place. On some males, the genitalia may be only slightly affected, or, in the extreme, the entire sexual apparatus may be aborted. Some specimens may appear to belong to species other than their own, because if a slight amount of change takes place, the genital styles, for example, may appear to be fully developed but of a decidedly different shape from normal styles. Some examples examined have the styles considerably reduced in size, other specimens have them nearly obsolete, and still others have the entire assemblage of genital processes of the pygophore obliterated with a simple concavity remaining in the pygophore. Apparently this differential castration is the result of differences in time of attack by the parasite, or at least differences in the time when the gonads have been attacked or the amount of damage done to them before the ultimate nymphal molt. It would not be surprising to learn that some partially castrated specimens form the types of "new species," but the author of such species could hardly be blamed for considering them distinct species if the series supplied him for study was inadequate. Here is another field worthy of detailed investigation. I have found that Muir (1916:210) commented upon the same phenomenon.

The native species show great host specificity and are nearly all restricted to native plants. On the other hand, the few immigrant forms include important crop pests, among them the notorious sugarcane leafhopper. In fact, it was the latter pest that gave the great impetus in Hawaii to economic entomological research that has been centered at the Experiment Station of the Hawaiian Sugar Planters' Association. The following quotations from Giffard (1922:103–104) will not be out of place here:

Because our endemic leaf-hoppers, like some others elsewhere, do not particularly affect agricultural interests, and therefore are of no special economic importance, some may wonder why so much interest is taken in their biology and morphology by our local entomologists. There are several reasons for this. First, because of several very injurious species of hoppers, not so very far from our gates, which as yet have not reached Hawaii; and, second, because the sugar cane leaf-hopper (*Perkinsiella saccharicida*), which cost this Territory losses of many millions of dollars in 1903, 1904 and subsequent years, is, as it were, the foundation-stone of economic entomology in Hawaii. Not only was this Delphacid responsible for large money losses, but it was also the cause for organizing in 1903 a large staff of entomologists for biological research and field work in the Territory, and the building up such organizations as the Experimental Station of the Hawaiian Sugar Planters' Association and the Territorial Board of Agriculture and Forestry and its Plant Quarantine and Inspection Department. It is therefore not surprising that the many families and groups of leaf-hoppers distributed through both continents are of more than passing interest to some of our systematic as well as economic workers. The systematic study of these families or groups, whether local or foreign, is quite necessary because, with Hawaii as the "Cross Roads of the Pacific" and in almost daily steamship communication with many tropical or sub-tropical regions, there is always the possibility that one or more of the several known species of hoppers or other injurious insects may be accidentally introduced. In this connection, as an instance, it might here be recorded that in 1913 Mr. J. C. Bridwell, while in Nigeria, West Africa, collected there among other material for study in Honolulu, a small Delphacid, allied to our own sugar cane leaf-hopper, which Mr. Muir later described as *Megamelus flavolineatus*. During the past year Mr. Muir has received collections of leafhoppers from Porto Rico (where insects of some sort are carrying mosaic disease in sugar cane) and among these he found this West African species of which Mr. Wolcott, the entomologist in Porto Rico, remarks: "The identification of *M. flavolineatus* was especially fortunate, as this is a cane insect which may become a serious pest." The fact, therefore, that these insects convey many plant diseases also makes their study necessary for economic work. Knowledge acquired purely from scientific studies sooner or later is the foundation of applied practices, as is well instanced in the "Fauna Hawaiiensis," without which we never could have handled our local entomological problems with the same degree of certainty.

In contrast to continental areas where so many delphacid leafhoppers are attached to grasses and sedges, not one of the 134 species of our 7 endemic genera feeds upon such plants. The five native forms of the non-endemic genus *Kelisia* are grass feeders and are our only native delphacids which are attached to grasses. All our other species feed upon trees, vines, shrubs, herbs and ferns; most of them are attached to trees.

The hostplant relationships of our delphacids have received much attention, but much remains to be done. It must be kept in mind that adults of both long- and short-winged forms often may be taken from plants upon which they happen to be resting but upon which they do not breed. Hence, the hostplant records for not a few of our species are, I believe, inaccurately recorded. Many of our species are known from only one or a few specimens, and thus their host records cannot be relied upon entirely. A number of species, however, have been observed breeding upon given plants, and such records are the only reliable ones. Some species are known to breed on several or many kinds of plants, but the majority of them are confined to one species or one genus of plants. Some of them are remarkably restricted in their food habits.

The following plant genera are fed upon by one or more species of endemic Delphacidae, insofar as is now known:

Acacia	Eragrostis	Pittosporum
Alphitonia	Eugenia	Plectranthus
Antidesma	Euphorbia	Platydesma
Argyroxiphium	Freycinetia	Polygonum
Artemisia	Geranium	Pritchardia
Astelia	Gouldia	Raillardia
Bidens	Gunnera	Rollandia
Bobea	Herpestes	Rumex
Boehmeria	Ipomoea	Sadleria
Broussaisia	Jussiaea	Scaevola
Campylotheca	Kadua	Sesbania
Charpentiera	Lipochaeta	Sida
Cheirodendron	Lobelia	Sideroxylon
Cibotium	Lythrum	Smilax
Clermontia	Metrosideros	Sporobolus
Coprosma	Mucuna	Stenogyne
Cyanea	Myoporum	Straussia
Cyrtandra	Myrsine (Suttonia)	Strongylodon
Deschampsia	Nephrolepis	Styphelia (Cyathodes)
Diospyros (Maba)	Osmanthus	Syzygium
Dodonaea	Pelea	Tetramolopium
Dolichos	Phegopteris	Touchardia
Dubautia	Phyllostegia	Urera
Elaeocarpus	Pipturus	Vincentia

It is probable that a careful search of other genera of endemic plants will reveal the presence of many new kinds of leafhoppers. New forms, moreover, will be found on the same genera of plants on islands or isolated localities other than in the places where there are known species on given hosts. Also, we do not know the hostplants of the following 18 species: *Leialoha pacifica* (Kirkaldy), *Nesothoë frigidula* Kirkaldy, *Nesothoë silvestris* Kirkaldy, *Nesosydne haleakala* Kirkaldy, *N. hamadryas* Kirkaldy, *N. hamata* Muir, *N. incommoda* Muir, *N. koebelei* Muir, *N. nephelias* Kirkaldy, *N. nesogunnerae* Muir, *N. nigriceps* Muir, *N. nubigena* Kirkaldy, *N. palustris* Kirkaldy, *N. perkinsi* Muir, *N. procellaris* Kirkaldy, *N. rocki* Muir, *N. sola* Muir and *N. swezeyi* Muir.

As noted elsewhere, many of the male specimens were dissected before being described by Muir, and not a few of these are unique. Evidently the balsam mounts of the genitalia of these species were made by Muir and Giffard, perhaps mostly by Giffard. These slides are assembled in Giffard's collection and serially numbered. A corresponding number was usually attached to the pin of the specimen from which the organs were obtained. However, these numbers have not been always understood by workers who have examined Muir's material in recent years, and it is worth while to add a note regarding them here. The labels on the specimens may be clearly understandable or may be cryptic in nature. Numbers such as "42" or "mg 61" or "gen 80" or "62 mg" refer to the slides containing the mounted parts of the male genitalia of the specimen. Some examples carry a label reading "genitalia mounted," and a search of the slide boxes is required to bring these to light. Some of the genitalia are mounted with the specimen from which they were obtained—some in balsam cells in cards and others simply dry on the points. Muir's sketches of the genitalia must be used with care, for some of them are poorly made or are inaccurate or misleading.

In the foregoing discussion following the key to the families of Cicadoidea, I drew attention to a letter from Dr. Perkins in which he included numerous notes on Kirkaldy's type material of Hawaiian leafhoppers. The notes on the delphacids have been incorporated hereinafter in their appropriate places, with reference to "Perkins' letter."

For detailed bibliographic notes, the student is referred to Metcalf's (1936) world catalogue, because only the more important references are listed under each species here, although all the descriptive papers do appear in the bibliography at the end of this volume.

Unless otherwise stated in the text, the holotypes of our delphacids are in the collection of the Experiment Station, Hawaiian Sugar Planters' Association, at Honolulu.

Subfamily DELPHACINAE Jensen-Haarup, 1915

Araeopinae Metcalf, 1938:299.

We have representatives of only one of the two recognized subfamilies in our Territory. The Asiracinae do not occur in Hawaii, but that group is present in Samoa, Fiji and westward in the Pacific.

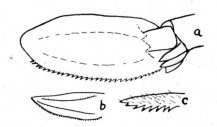

Figure 46—Hind tibial calcars of some delphacids: **a,** *Tarophagus proserpina* (Kirkaldy); **b,** *Perkinsiella saccharicida* Kirkaldy; **c,** *Aloha ipomoeae* Kirkaldy.

Key to the Tribes of Delphacinae Found in Hawaii

1. Calcar of hind tibiae solid, with both surfaces convex and distinctly dentate along hind margin, the teeth large and strongly developed (fig. 46, c) . . . .**Alohini.**

2. Calcar of hind tibiae thin or lamina-like or foliaceous or somewhat hollow sub-V-shaped in cross section because of one side being concave(not solid V-shaped, which would would be triangular), with or without teeth on hind margin, if teeth are present they are many and minute (as on our species) (fig. 46, a, b) . . . .**Delphacini.**

Tribe ALOHINI Muir, 1915:269

At one time it was thought that this tribe was restricted to the Hawaiian Islands, but further collecting and study have shown the group to be world-wide in distribution.

From the Delphacini, the only other group of delphacids found in Hawaii, this tribe is distinguished by having both sides of the posterior tibial calcar convex and with strongly developed teeth on the hind margin, as shown in the drawing. Thus the calcar resembles the blade of a pruning saw.

All our native delphacid leafhoppers with the exception of the grass-inhabiting *Kelisia* belong to this tribe.

Key to the Genera of the Alohini of Hawaii

1. First segment of antennae short, usually broader than long, or about as broad as long, never conspicuously longer than broad except in the aberrant *Nesothoë silvestris* in which it is about twice as long as broad, but the face is conspicuously pale-spotted and the tegmina are strongly compressed or constricted at the base of the apical cell area; all species macropterous; (certain species of *Nesosydne, N. cyathodis* for example, run here because of their short first antennal segments, but they have a single median frontal carina and are brachypterous) 2

    First segment of antennae distinctly longer than broad, face never pale-spotted; most species brachypterous, only a few macropterous, but if macropterous with tegmina not strongly constricted subapically 4

2(1). With two median frontal carinae, approximating at base or apex or both, or even meeting, but not forming a stalk . . . . **Leialoha** (Kirkaldy).

    With only a single median frontal carina, forked at extreme base, if at all . . . . : . 3

3(2). Male pygophore with a large, upcurved spine-like process on each lateral margin at about middle, a pair of style-like spines behind genital styles at middle of hind mar-

gin and with two anal styles; female with two anal
styles, lower one very large and protruding far behind
apex of abdomen (see illustrations)..................
...............................**Nesodryas** Kirkaldy.
Male pygophore without lateral spines and without accessory spine-like processes behind genital styles; anal
styles single and small in both sexes................
.................................**Nesothoë** Kirkaldy.

4(1). With two median frontal carinae (check your specimen
carefully, for the two carinae may seem to be one)....... 5
With only one median frontal carina (which, however,
may be furcate above apex)......................... 6

5(4). Tegmina reaching well beyond middle of abdomen......
.... **Aloha** Kirkaldy.
Tegmina short, not reaching to middle of abdomen......
...............................**Nesorestias** Kirkaldy.

6(4). Head abnormally and enormously prolonged forward to
form a long horn............**Dictyophorodelphax** Swezey.
Head normal, not produced forward.................... 7

7(6). Tegmina much abbreviated, not reaching past middle of
abdomen, veins obscured and broken down into a coarse
reticulation.........................**Nothorestias** Muir.
Tegmina usually reaching nearly to or surpassing apex
of abdomen, veins distinct, but if wings greatly abbreviated, then veins not broken down to form a coarse
reticulation.........................**Nesosydne** Kirkaldy.

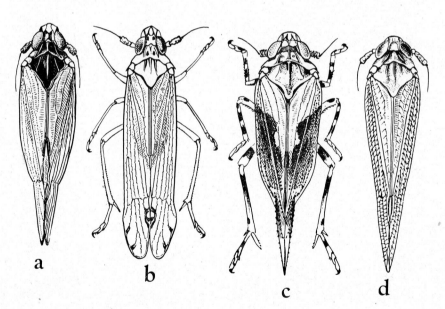

Figure 47—Some native delphacid leafhoppers: **a**, *Leialoha scaevolae* Muir; **b**, *Nesodryas freycinetiae* Kirkaldy; **c**, *Nesothoë fletus* Kirkaldy; **d**, *Nesosydne koae* Kirkaldy. (Drawings by Abernathy.)

All the genera of the Hawaiian Alohini are not as distinct from one another as a review of the literature would appear to indicate. There are certain species in several genera which cannot be placed in their assigned genera by the use of existing keys. For example, *Nesothoë silvestris* has the first antennal segment about twice as long as broad, yet this genus is assigned to a group which Muir characterized as having the first antennal segment "very short, broader than long." Some of the species of *Nesosydne* have the median frontal carina forking far down on the face so that the frons has two median carinae for much of its length. These species might be placed in *Aloha* or *Nesorestias*. In fact, Muir placed *Nesosydne wailupensis* first in *Aloha,* then later transferred it to *Nesosydne.* The close interrelationships of the local genera within the Alohini are conspicuous and evident, and most of the evolutionary story is yet to be written.

Genus **LEIALOHA** (Kirkaldy) Muir, 1915:264

Aloha subgenus *Leialoha* Kirkaldy, 1910:579.

The known species of this endemic genus are all macropterous; the first antennal segment is broader than long, or only slightly longer than broad, and the front of the head has two median carinae. It is a close associate of *Nesothoë.*

This is a confusing group, and I do not believe that it is in good taxonomic order. The assemblage of forms centering around *ohiae* and *lehuae* caused Muir considerable trouble. Much work remains to be done here. It would be advisable to collect a series of specimens from the same colony and study them to see if there is variation in the aedeagus. I do not believe that this has been done. The shape, position and size of the spines on the aedeagus differ according to the way they are oriented in the balsam mount. I do not believe Muir allowed for this apparent variation.

There is much variation in the color and color patterns of the adults, and the formulation of a key is difficult. Only use will decide the worth of the table presented here, but I feel that it is inadequate. I have failed to detect good differences to use for the separation of various of these forms.

I do not now feel that the associates of *lehuae* should be accorded full specific rank, but I am not familiar enough with the group to make a decision regarding them. Some of them were described as subspecies by Muir, who later considered them to be species. I have listed them all here as species, and leave the task of assigning them to their appropriate ranks to some future specialist who can make a concerted study of them.

Another problem that needs solution is the geographical distribution of the various forms. I have followed Muir and Giffard in recording the distribution, but I feel that if the forms are really distinct it will ultimately be shown that they have a more restricted distribution than is indicated here.

KEY TO THE SPECIES OF LEIALOHA

1.   Kauai species.. 2
      Not so... 8
2(1). "Similar to *A.* [*Leialoha*] *oceanides,* but proportionately
       slightly more robust. The whole of the tegmina basal of
       the apical cells is dark smoky except the basal fourth of
       that space, the subcostal cell in part, the apex of the
       clavus, and the tegminal granules, the latter supporting
       white hairs. Apical keels of the vertex and the middle
       keels of the pronotum and scutellum subsanguineous."
       (Kirkaldy, original description, 1910:581; this species
       has not been found since the type was collected)......
       ....**pacifica** (Kirkaldy).
       Not such species.................................. 3
3(2). Tegminal membrane mostly hyaline but with extensive
       and conspicuous dark maculations; granules of veins
       unusually conspicuous, coarse and pale.............
       ....**oceanides** (Kirkaldy).
       Tegmina without such a combination of characters....... 4
4(3). Body and appendages largely yellowish or pale brown
       (although vertex and nota are dark in males), general
       aspect pale, or, in males, comparatively pale with dark
       markings.. 5

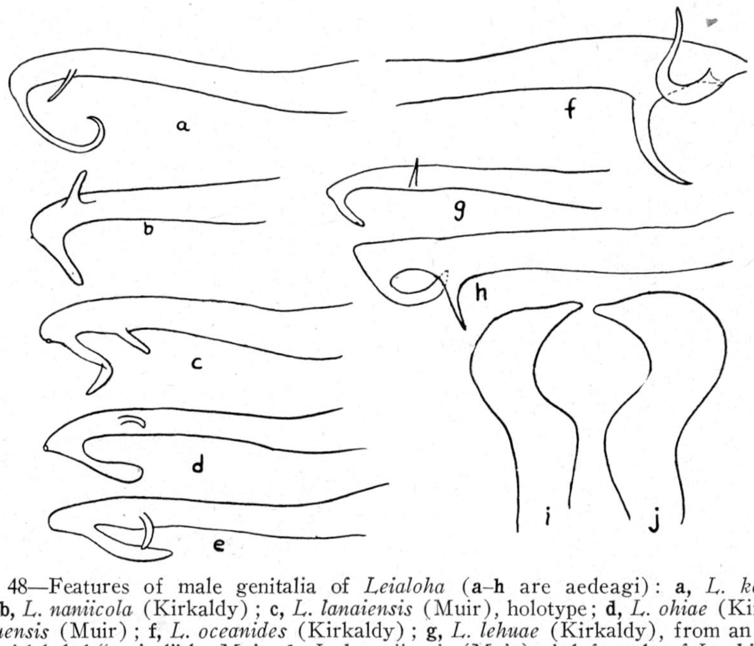

Figure 48—Features of male genitalia of *Leialoha* (a–h are aedeagi): **a,** *L. kauaiensis* (Muir); **b,** *L. naniicola* (Kirkaldy); **c,** *L. lanaiensis* (Muir), holotype; **d,** *L. ohiae* (Kirkaldy); **e,** *L. oahuensis* (Muir); **f,** *L. oceanides* (Kirkaldy); **g,** *L. lehuae* (Kirkaldy), from an example from Kauai labeled "typical" by Muir; **h,** *L. hawaiiensis* (Muir); **i,** left style of *L. ohiae* (Kirkaldy); **j,** right style of *L. oahuensis* (Muir). These drawings were made by me from dissected specimens studied by Muir and some of them are the same as those from which he made his drawings. The length, shape and position of the appendages vary according to the orientation of the specimen in the balsam mount, and these parts may appear out of place and distorted in the drawings.

Body and appendages brown to dark brown with or without a reddish tinge, general aspect of insect dark 6

5(4). Males with a fuscous band from base to apex of tegmina; on *Suttonia* . . . .**suttoniae** Muir.
Males without such a dark band, but with a dark mark at apex of clavus; on *Scaevola* . . . .**scaevolae** Muir.

6(4). Tegmina with extensive brown maculations, veins brownish; with little or no reddish coloration . . . .
. . . .**lehuae** (Kirkaldy).
Tegminal veins usually conspicuously reddish, and entire insect with considerable reddish coloration 7

7(6). Dark maculations of tegmina ill-defined or obscure; male aedeagus as in figure 48, d . . . .**ohiae** (Kirkaldy).
Dark maculations of tegmina conspicuous and extensive; male aedeagus as in figure 48, a . . . .**kauaiensis** (Muir).

8(1). Maui species . . . .**mauiensis** (Muir).
Not so 9

9(8). Lanai form, with apical hook of aedeagus curved backward, as in figure 48, c . . . .**lanaiensis** (Muir).
Not from Lanai (with exception of *oahuensis*) and with apical hook of aedeagus curved forward 10

10(9). Predominantly reddish species . . . .**ohiae** (Kirkaldy).
Predominantly brownish species with conspicuously maculate tegmina 11

11(10). Very dark (sometimes nearly black) form from Hawaii; aedeagus as in figure 48, h . . . .**hawaiiensis** (Muir).
Not so 12

12(11). Comparatively pale form with fuscous maculations of tegmina small and scattered; aedeagus as in figure 48, b
. . . .**naniicola** (Kirkaldy).
Not so, infuscation of tegmina more extensive 13

13(12). Nearly all of tegmina fuscous; aedeagus as in figure 48, g
. . . .**lehuae** (Kirkaldy).
Tegmina distinctly pale and dark maculated or banded, not almost entirely dark; aedeagus as in figure 48, e
. . . .**oahuensis** (Muir).

Leialoha hawaiiensis (Muir) (fig. 48, h).
Leialoha lehuae subspecies *hawaiiensis* Muir, 1916:173, pl. 2, fig. 4.

Endemic. Hawaii (type locality: Waimea).
Hostplant: *Metrosideros* ("ohia lehua").

Leialoha kauaiensis (Muir) (fig. 48, a).
Leialoha lehuae subspecies *kauaiensis* Muir, 1916:173, pl. 2, fig. 5.
Leialoha kauaiensis (Muir) Muir, 1922:93.

Endemic. Kauai (type locality: Waimea).
Hostplant: *Metrosideros*.

Leialoha lanaiensis (Muir) (fig. 48, c).
Leialoha lehuae subspecies *lanaiensis* Muir, 1917:299, pl. 5, fig. 1.

Endemic. Lanai (type locality: Kaiholena).
Hostplant: *Metrosideros.*
The distal spine on the aedeagus is curved backward on the holotype slide, but I feel that this might be an artificial condition brought about during the mounting of the genitalia. More material should be examined.

Leialoha lehuae (Kirkaldy) (fig. 48, g).
Aloha (*Leialoha*) *lehuae* Kirkaldy, 1910:581.
Leialoha lehuae (Kirkaldy) Muir, 1916:172–173, pl. 2, fig. 2.

Endemic. Oahu (type locality: Mount Tantalus), Lanai.
Hostplant: *Metrosideros.*
This is a variable and confusing form. Kirkaldy considered it close to the original type of ancestral immigrant which gave rise to our endemic Alohini.
The holotype is in the Bishop Museum.

Leialoha mauiensis (Muir).
Leialoha lehuae variety *mauiensis* Muir, 1919:87.

Endemic. Maui (type locality: Olinda, 4,200 feet).
Hostplant: *Metrosideros.*
This species has been credited as feeding on *Coprosma montana,* but I believe that this is in error and that its true host is *Metrosideros.* I have seen topotypic material collected by Swezey from *Metrosideros,* and on one of the paratypes dissected by Giffard there appears the note *"Coprosma montana* and ohia mixed" (the "ohia" refers to *Metrosideros*).

Leialoha naniicola (Kirkaldy) (fig. 48, b).
Aloha (*Leialoha*) *naniicola* Kirkaldy, 1910:580.
Leialoha naniicola (Kirkaldy) Muir, 1916:172, pl. 2, fig. 1; pl. 4, fig. 75. Genotype.

Endemic. Oahu (type locality: "Waianae Mts., not from Kilauea as given in F. H."; Perkins, *in litteris*), Hawaii.
Hostplant: *Metrosideros.*
"I could find in K's boxes no specimens from Kilauea (Perkins and Kirk.); nor any Swezey and Kirk. from Tantalus; but there were one or two Giffardian exx. thence. The specific name *'olopana'* was on the 'type' but *naniicola* was beneath the specimens" (Perkins' letter). The type should be in the British Museum.

Leialoha oahuensis (Muir) (fig. 48, e, j).
Leialoha lehuae subspecies *oahuensis* Muir, 1916:173, pl. 2, fig. 3.

Endemic. Oahu (type locality: Kalihi), Lanai.
Hostplant: *Metrosideros*.

Leialoha oceanides (Kirkaldy) (fig. 48, f).
Aloha (*Leialoha*) *oceanides* Kirkaldy, 1910:580.
Leialoha oceanides (Kirkaldy) Muir, 1916:174; 1922:92, pl. 3, fig. 1.

Endemic. Kauai (type locality: 4,000 feet).
Hostplant: *Osmanthus sandwicensis*.
The type is supposedly in the British Museum. Perkins notes that one of the original specimens in his collection was labeled by Kirkaldy as *"honiala,"* a manuscript name.

Leialoha ohiae (Kirkaldy) (fig. 48, d, i).
Aloha (*Leialoha*) *ohiae* Kirkaldy, 1910:581.
Leialoha ohiae (Kirkaldy) Muir, 1916:174, pl. 2, fig. 6.

Endemic. Kauai, Oahu (type locality: Waialua), Hawaii.
Hostplant: *Metrosideros* ("ohia").
Perkins notes in his letter that the type should be in the British Museum and that some of the type lot were labeled with the manuscript name *"kahavalu."*

Leialoha pacifica (Kirkaldy).
Aloha (*Leialoha*) *pacifica* Kirkaldy, 1910:581.
Leialoha pacifica (Kirkaldy) Muir, 1916:174.

Endemic. The type locality was given as "Kauai ? Molokai ?." I have considered it more probable that the species is from Kauai. No *Leialoha* have as yet been found on Molokai, but they probably occur there. To my knowledge, this form has not been rediscovered since the type was collected, and that specimen should be in the British Museum.

Leialoha scaevolae Muir (fig. 47, a).
Leialoha scaevolae Muir, 1922:93, pl. 3, fig. 3.

Endemic. Kauai (type locality: "Kumuwela" [Kumuweia]).
Hostplants: *Scaevola chamissoniana* (*Osmanthus* and *Coprosma,* accidental ?).

Leialoha suttoniae Muir.

Leialoha suttoniae Muir, 1922:92, pl. 3, figs. 2, 2a.

Endemic. Kauai (type locality: Kalalau).
Hostplant: *Myrsine* (*Suttonia*) *sandwicensis*.

Genus **NESOTHOË** Kirkaldy, 1908:203

Subgenus *Nesothoë* (of *Nesodryas*) (Kirkaldy) Muir, 1916:174.

The discussion of this genus should be read with the notes under *Nesodryas*.

The members of *Nesothoë* were originally separated from *Nesodryas* because of the stout form of some of the species. However, they are separated here on the basis of their terminalia. The terminalia of *Nesothoë* are the same basic type as those of *Leialoha*. The pygophore of the male is simple and has no spines on the side margins as on *Nesodryas;* there is no accessory anal style in addition to the usual single style; the genital styles are as illustrated and they are not followed by an additional pair of slender style-like spines; the aedeagus is basically a rather straight or slightly curved, rod-like structure with various types of spines and processes near the apex as the illustrations show. There appears to be no basic difference between the terminalia of the typical stout members of *Nesathoë* and the slender species which were formerly placed in *Nesodryas* (see the aedeagus of *eugeniae* which is a slender species and compare the aedeagus of *munroi* which is a stout species).

Nesothoë may be defined as those species of our Alohini which have the first segment of the antennae transverse with but few known exceptions such as *silvestris* whose first segment is twice as long as broad and *perkinsi* with this segment as long as broad (the former species would run to *Nesosydne* in the generic key if it were not for its pale-spotted face and long, constricted tegmina; this fact is not apparent from the literature), and which have a single median frontal carina and the terminalia as described and figured. All the species are macropterous. The genus is derived from *Leialoha*.

It is noteworthy that the pygophore and its appendages are of relatively similar pattern in this genus as they are in *Leialoha,* whereas in *Nesosydne,* the same structures are remarkably diversified. The color pattern of the frons is striking and beautiful in some of the species.

When using the aedeagus sketches, one should keep in mind that most of them have been made from old balsam mounts made for Muir's studies, and that because of the different planes in which the appendages are situated they cannot be drawn very successfully in flat lines. Allowance should be made for optical distortion and distortion caused by compression in the thin mounts. New drawings made from new dissections mounted dry or in fluid are needed.

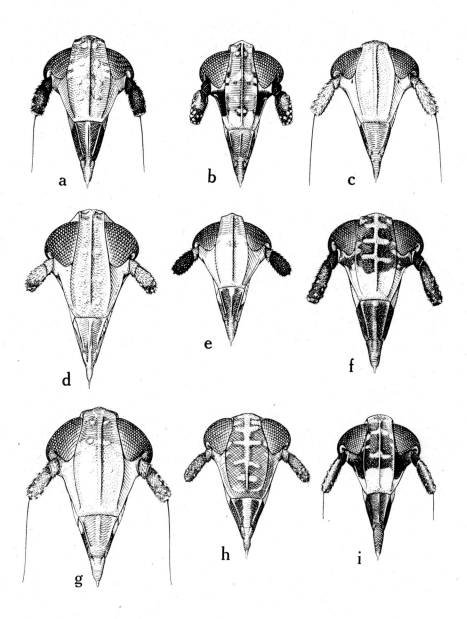

Figure 49—Faces of holotypes of *Nesothoë*: **a,** *N. fletus* Kirkaldy, female; **b,** *N. bobeae* Kirkaldy, male; **c,** *N. terryi* Kirkaldy, female; **d,** *N. laka* Kirkaldy, female; **e,** *N. frigidula* Kirkaldy, female; **f,** *N. perkinsi* Kirkaldy, female; **g,** *N. piilani* Kirkaldy, female; **h,** *N. pluvialis* Kirkaldy, female; **i,** *N. hula* Kirkaldy, male. (Drawn at the British Museum of Natural History by Smith.)

KEY TO THE SPECIES OF NESOTHOË

(Excepting *laka,* which I have not seen; see the notes under that species heading below.)

Because there are two groups of species which in most instances may be distinguished rather easily by their form, the genus may be separated into two sections as an aid to determination.

A. Elongate, slender forms; tegmina usually only comparatively slightly constricted at about level of base of anal cells, as viewed from above..............................**Section A.**

B. Stout, robust forms whose tegmina are strongly constricted at about base of anal cells (fig. 47, c)..............**Section B.**

SECTION A

1. Vertex and anterior part of pronotum black...........
...................................**dryope** (Kirkaldy).
Vertex and anterior part of pronotum not black.......... 2

2(1). First antennal segment, front of head and genae between eyes black or nearly so; on *Antidesma* on Oahu......
...................................**antidesmae** (Muir).
First antennal segment and head not so marked, usually entirely pale 3

3(2). Not pallid species, but a brownish, comparatively dark form from Kauai...................**dodonaeae** (Muir).
Largely pallid species which, in spite of fuscous markings, do not appear predominantly dark colored........ 4

4(3). Pronotum and mesonotum dark between keels.........
.... **elaeocarpi** (Kirkaldy).
Pronotum pale, mesonotum not dark in middle........... 5

5(4). Tegmina and wings milky.............**giffardi** (Kirkaldy).
Tegmina and wings hyaline or yellowish hyaline, but not milky........................**eugeniae** (Kirkaldy).

SECTION B

1. First antennal segment about twice as long as broad; Lanai..............................**silvestris** Kirkaldy.
First antennal segment broader than long to as long as broad, or slightly longer, but never approaching twice as long as broad................................... 2

2(1). First antennal segment, measured carefully in full view on its longest side, as long as or slightly longer than broad (face brown with pale spots to lower level of pronotum, thence pale to the dark clypeus); Oahu...
...................................**perkinsi** Kirkaldy.
First antennal segment shorter, usually distinctly transverse 3

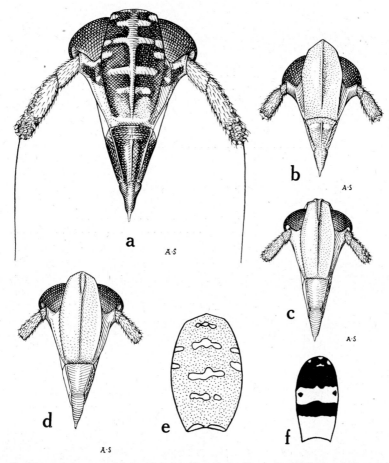

Figure 50—Faces of some delphacids: **a,** *Nesothoë silvestris* Kirkaldy, holotype female; **b,** *Nesodryas freycinetiae* Kirkaldy, holotype female; **c,** *Nesothoë giffardi* (Kirkaldy), holotype female; **d,** *Nesothoë eugeniae* (Kirkaldy), holotype female; **e,** diagram of color pattern on frons of *Nesothoë maculata* (Muir), stippled area is brown; **f,** the same of *Nesothoë munroi* (Muir). (Figures **a–d** drawn at the British Museum of Natural History by Smith.)

3(2).   First or second antennal segment, or both, largely dark,
      nearly or quite black............................... 4
    Antennae entirely pale or brown, first segment never
      much darker than second and second never very dark...14

4(3).   Frons dark or black between eyes and with a conspicu-
      ous, dark, transverse band between lower edges of
      sides of pronotum, elsewhere nearly all yellow, frons
      thus with two dark and two pale fasciae conspicuously
      contrasting (fig. 50, f); antennae entirely black; Ha-
      waii ....**munroi** (Muir).
    Face without such a striking color pattern, at least not as
      in figure 50, f.. 5

5(4).   Mesonotum, pronotum, vertex, frons, genae and clypeus
         almost or entirely dark or black; tegmina largely
         brown from base to middle, but with white maculae
         and with apical half white and sharply contrasted with
         darker basal half (at least on the unique holotype);
         Kauai ....**semialba** (Muir).
         Not such species................................... 6

6(5).   Vertex and anterior part of pronotum black, frons, cly-
         peus and genae pale yellow; tegmina mostly hyaline
         with some infuscation in basal half only............
         ....**dryope** (Kirkaldy).
         Vertex and pronotum pale or brown, but not very dark
         and otherwise not as above........................ 7

7(6).   Vertex and disc of pronotum white or creamy white,
         mesonotum mostly black; tegmina largely immaculate
         hyaline................................**hula** Kirkaldy.
         Not such species................................... 8

8(7).   Frons brown or black from lower level of sides of pro-
         notum upward with some pale spots on interocular
         area, but white or creamy from lower level of prono-
         tum to clypeus which is largely dark; tegmina with
         brown maculae 9
         Without such a combination of characters..............10

9(8).   Oahu form ....**perkinsi** Kirkaldy.
         Kauai form ....**seminigrofrons** (Muir).

10(8).   Tegmina mostly hyaline tinged with yellowish or pale
         fuscous basad, but without any dark maculae distad..
         ....**frigidula** Kirkaldy.
         Tegmina conspicuously dark maculate..................11

11(10). Vertex and frons almost entirely yellow; tegmina with a
         striking color pattern consisting of a broad, oblique,
         milky-white band extending from entire base diagon-
         ally to include much of clavus, a similarly colored,
         large crescent basad on costa and extending from about
         middle to about apex and extending about half way
         across tegmen at its broadest part; tegmina otherwise
         almost uniformly brown, the brown area itself assum-
         ing a more or less crescent-like shape......**fletus** Kirkaldy.
         Not such species....................................12

12(11). Disc of mesonotum dark brown; frons with dark ground
         color extending to apex and without a broad pale apical
         band (but pale spotted)...............**maculata** (Muir).
         Disc of mesonotum pale brown; frons broadly pale or
         white from level of inflexed sides of pronotum distad...13

13(12). Oahu species; granules on tegmina very conspicuous with
         membrane suffused around their bases over entire teg-
         mina ....**bobeae** Kirkaldy.
         Hawaii species; granules distinct but not outstanding and
         membrane not suffused around their bases, few, obscure
         or partly absent in pale subcostal area outward from
         apical cells................................**haa** (Muir).

14(3). Tegmina conspicuously milky-white with some restricted pale-brown maculae; disc of mesonotum darker than sides, frons and genae pale yellow below level of eyes; Molokai, (Lanai ?)....................**piilani** Kirkaldy.
Not such species....................................15

15(14). Tegmina almost entirely hyaline, with little or no distinct maculation ....**terryi** Kirkaldy.
Tegmina conspicuously blotched with brown or fuscous...16

16(15). Tegmina distinctly milky-white where not brown; granules along veins dark; apices of femora yellowish or brownish; median frontal carina sharply and strongly elevated throughout and distinctly protuberant over fronto-vertex angle as seen from above; Hawaii......
.... **gulicki** (Muir).
Tegmina not conspicuously milky-white where not brown; granules along veins pale; apices of femora partly red, or the color of boiled lobster; median frontal carina comparatively low, not sharply elevated, especially low at angle between frons and vertex; Kauai...........
.... **pluvialis** Kirkaldy.

Nesothoë antidesmae (Muir), new combination (fig. 51, i).
Nesodryas antidesmae Muir, 1917:300, pl. 5, fig. 2, 2a.

Endemic. Oahu (type locality: Nuuanu Pali).
Hostplant: *Antidesma platyphyllum.*

Nesothoë bobeae Kirkaldy (fig. 49, b).
Nesothoë bobeae Kirkaldy, 1908:204, fig. 2; 1910:593.
Nesodryas (Nesothoë) bobeae (Kirkaldy) Muir, 1916:177, pl. 2, fig. 14; pl. 3, fig. 61.

Endemic. Oahu (type locality: Mount Tantalus).
Hostplant: *Bobea.*
Perkins says in his letter that "Only one S.I.C. [Sandwich Islands Committee] example was found and it was labeled *'giffardi.'* Specimens of my own were labeled *bobeicola."* The holotype male is now in the British Museum.

Nesothoë dodonaeae (Muir), new combination (fig. 51, d).
Nesodryas dodonaeae Muir, 1916:176, pl. 2, fig. 10; 1922:95.

Endemic. Kauai (type locality: Waimea).
Hostplants: *Alphitonia, Dodonaea, Myrsine (Suttonia).*
The carinae at the apex of the vertex and top of the face are obsolete.

Nesothoë dryope (Kirkaldy), new combination (fig. 51, b).

> *Nesodryas dryope* Kirkaldy, 1910:597. Muir, 1916:176, pl. 2, fig. 11; pl. 3, fig.
> 62 (applies to this species ?).
> *Nesodryas* (*Nesothoë*) *dryope* (Kirkaldy) Muir, 1917:301, misidentification.

Endemic. Kauai, Oahu (type locality: Mount Tantalus, 1,500 feet), (Hawaii?).
Hostplant: *Antidesma platyphyllum.*
I have examined two of the original examples from the type locality in Perkins'
collection. These appear to me to belong to the group of slender species where Kirkaldy placed them, rather than to the stout *Nesothoë* group where the species was
transferred by Muir. The female holotype is now in the Bishop Museum.
The specimens recorded by Muir under this name (1917:301) from *Antidesma
platyphyllum* from Hawaii represent another species and were misidentified, in my
opinion. Muir's figures must be checked with topotypical material, for it is possible that they represent another form.

Nesothoë elaeocarpi (Kirkaldy), new combination (fig. 51, c).

> *Nesodryas elaeocarpi* Kirkaldy, 1908:103; 1910:596. Muir, 1916:175, pl. 2, fig.
> 8; pl. 3, fig. 57.

Endemic. Oahu (type locality: Mount Tantalus, 1,500 feet).
Hostplants: *Cyrtandra paludosa, Elaeocarpus bifidus, Scaevola mollis.*
The holotype female is now in the Bishop Museum.

Nesothoë eugeniae (Kirkaldy), new combination (figs. 50, d; 51, l, p).

> *Nesodryas eugeniae* Kirkaldy, 1908:203; 1910:597. Muir, 1916:175, pl. 2, fig. 9;
> pl. 3, fig. 60.

Endemic. Oahu (type locality: "Honolulu Mts. 1500 ft." [Mount Tantalus ?]),
Lanai.
Hostplants: *Eugenia sandwicensis, Straussia kaduana.*
The female holotype is in the British Museum.

Nesothoë fletus Kirkaldy (figs. 47, c; 49, a).

> *Nesothoë fletus* Kirkaldy, 1908:204; 1910:592.
> *Nesodryas* (*Nesothoë*) *fletus* (Kirkaldy) Muir, 1916:176, pl. 2, fig. 12; pl. 3,
> fig. 58; 1917:302; 1919:87. Genotype.

Endemic. Lanai, Maui (type locality: Iao Valley).
Hostplants: *Antidesma platyphyllum, Myrsine* (*Suttonia*).
This is a large, strikingly marked species whose tegminal color pattern is clearly
apparent to the unaided eyes.
The holotype female is in the British Museum.

Nesothoë frigidula Kirkaldy (fig. 49, e).

Nesothoë frigidula Kirkaldy, 1908:204; 1910:593.

Nesodryas (Nesothoë) frigidula (Kirkaldy) Muir, 1916:178.

Endemic. Hawaii (type locality: Kona, 2,000 feet).

Perkins, in his letter, states of the type: "the specimen was labeled *'konae'* but was determined by the locality, date and description. Of the two specimens one was much broken." The female holotype is in the British Museum.

Nesothoë giffardi (Kirkaldy), new combination (figs. 50, c; 51, e).

Nesodryas giffardi Kirkaldy, 1908:203; 1910:597. Muir, 1916:175, pl. 2, fig. 7; pl. 3, fig. 59.

Endemic. Oahu (type locality: "Honolulu Mts. 1500 ft." [Mount Tantalus ?]).

Hostplants: *Cyrtandra grandiflora, Touchardia latifolia* ("olona").

This form and *eugeniae* and *elaeocarpi* are all closely allied. The female type is in the British Museum.

Nesothoë gulicki (Muir), new combination (fig. 51, f–h).

Nesodryas (Nesothoë) gulicki Muir, 1916:177, pl. 2, fig. 13; 1917:301; 1919: 87–88.

Endemic. Oahu, Lanai (?), Hawaii (type locality: Kahuku lava flows, Kau, 1,800 feet).

Hostplants: *Euphorbia, Metrosideros, Osmanthus sandwicensis.*

Muir (1919:88) emended his original description of the aedeagus as follows: "The orifice is at the apex, from the left edge of the orifice arises a small spine, a little basad and slightly more ventrad is a larger spine expanded at the apex with some small projections on the expanded portion, basad of this and on the right side is a small spine curved distad and with a minute spine about the middle."

Nesothoë haa (Muir), new combination.

Nesodryas (Nesothoë) haa Muir, 1921:509, pl. 8, fig. 1.

Endemic. Hawaii (type locality: Olaa, 29 miles, 2,300 feet).

Hostplant: *Antidesma platyphyllum* ("haa").

Nesothoë hula Kirkaldy (fig. 49, i).

Nesothoë hula Kirkaldy, 1908:204; 1910:592.

Nesodryas (Nesothoë) hula (Kirkaldy), Muir, 1916:178; 1922:93, pl. 3, fig. 4.

Endemic. Kauai (type locality: "high plateau," 4,000 feet).

Hostplants: *Osmanthus sandwicensis, Pelea, Phyllostegia, Sideroxylon, Myrsine (Suttonia).*

The holotype male is in the British Museum.

Nesothoë laka Kirkaldy (figs. 49, d; 59, a, b).
  Nesothoë laka Kirkaldy, 1908:204; 1910:594.
  Nesodryas (Nesothoë) laka (Kirkaldy) Muir, 1916:178; 1919:87.

Endemic. Maui (type locality: Iao Valley).
Hostplant: *Sida.*
Perkins states in his letter that he has "no note against this; the type should be in the B.M." [British Museum]. Muir (1919:87) said that he had studied "One male, three females and two nymphs from ridge south of Iao Valley, Maui, 800 feet elevation (Bridwell, August, 1918) on *Sida.* These conform fairly well to Kirkaldy's description which was made from one female, and are the only specimens taken since the type." I have been unable to locate these specimens in Honolulu, but the slide containing the genitalia of the above-mentioned male is in Giffard's collection. I have sketched the aedeagus and a genital style from this slide. The holotype female is in the British Museum.

Nesothoë maculata (Muir), new combination (figs. 50, e; 51, j).
  Nesodryas (Nesothoë) maculata Muir, 1916:177, pl. 2, fig. 15; 1917:302.

Endemic. Oahu, Lanai, Hawaii (type locality: although the text gives the Kahuku lava flows, Kau, 1,800 feet, as the locality, the holotype bears a "Kilauea" label).
Hostplants: *Diospyros (Maba) sandwicensis, D. hillebrandii, Metrosideros* (?), *Osmanthus sandwicensis.*

Nesothoë munroi (Muir), new combination (figs. 50, f; 51, n).
  Nesodryas (Nesothoë) munroi Muir, 1917:303, pl. 5, fig. 6; 1919:87.

Endemic. Lanai (type locality: 2,000 feet), Hawaii.
Hostplant: *Dodonaea.*

Nesothoë perkinsi Kirkaldy (fig. 49, f).
  Nesothoë perkinsi Kirkaldy, 1908:204; 1910:593.
  Nesodryas (Nesothoë) perkinsi (Kirkaldy) Muir, 1916:178; 1922:94, pl. 3, fig. 6.

Endemic. Oahu (type locality: "Honolulu 2000 feet 31-X-1892" [Mount Tantalus region]).
Hostplants: *Clermontia kakeana, Metrosideros, Myrsine (Suttonia).*
The holotype female is in the British Museum.

Nesothoë piilani Kirkaldy (figs. 49, g; 51, k).
  Nesothoë piilani Kirkaldy, 1908:204; 1910:594.
  Nesodryas (Nesothoë) piilani (Kirkaldy) Muir, 1916:178, misspelled *pulani;* 1917:301, pl. 5, fig. 4.

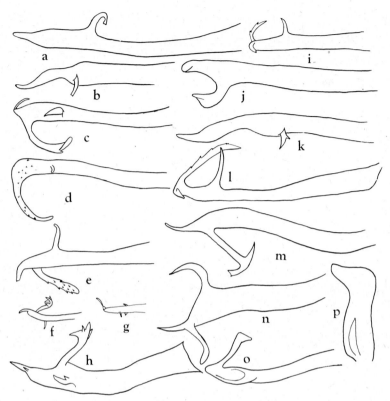

Figure 51—Genitalia of *Nesothoë* species (p, is a right style, the other figures are aedeagi; all except f and g are from balsam mounts) : **a,** *N. terryi* Kirkaldy; **b,** *N. dryope* (Kirkaldy); **c,** *N. elaeocarpi* (Kirkaldy) ; **d,** *N. dodonaeae* (Muir) ; **e,** *N. giffardi* (Kirkaldy) ; **f, g,** two different views of the dry-mounted aedeagus of holotype of *N. gulicki* (Muir) to show differences of appearance when viewed from different angles; **h,** *N. gulicki* (Muir) ; **i,** *N. antidesmae* (Muir) ; **j,** *N. maculata* (Muir) ; **k,** *N. piilani* Kirkaldy; **l,** *N. eugeniae* (Kirkaldy) ; **m,** *N. seminigrofrons* (Muir), holotype (the anchor-like appendage may be broken at the tip); **n,** *N. munroi* (Muir), holotype; **o,** *N. pluvialis* Kirkaldy (from the type of *alboguttata* Muir) ; **p,** *N. eugeniae* (Kirkaldy), right style as seen from behind.

Endemic. Molokai (type locality: 3,000 feet), Lanai(?).

Hostplant: *Osmanthus sandwicensis* (Lanai examples).

Perkins gave no information in his letter regarding this species. The female holotype is in the British Museum.

The material used for this text came from Lanai. The unique female type has not been checked with this material and there may be two species involved here. See Muir's note (1917:302).

Nesothoë pluvialis Kirkaldy (figs. 49, h; 51, o).

Nesothoë pluvialis Kirkaldy, 1908:204; 1910:595.

Nesodryas (Nesothoë) pluvialis (Kirkaldy) Muir, 1916:178.

Nesodryas (Nesothoë) alboguttata Muir, 1922:94, pl. 3, fig. 7. New synonym.

Endemic. Kauai (type locality: Halemanu, 4,000 feet).

Hostplant: *Antidesma.*

The female holotype is in the British Museum. It was the only specimen of the species studied by Kirkaldy. Additional specimens collected by Perkins near Lihue were not seen by Kirkaldy, but the material was compared with the type by Perkins. It has been from the study of the latter examples and the unique holotype of Muir's *alboguttata* that I have established the above synonymy. Muir had never seen specimens which had been determined as *pluvialis,* and he did not know the species.

Nesothoë semialba (Muir), new combination.

Nesodryas (Nesothoë) semialba Muir, 1922:95, pl. 3, fig. 8.

Endemic. Kauai (type locality: Kalalau).

Hostplant: *Osmanthus sandwicensis.*

Nesothoë seminigrofrons (Muir), new combination (fig. 51, m).

Nesodryas (Nesothoë) seminigrofrons Muir, 1922:94, pl. 3, fig. 5.

Endemic. Kauai (type locality: "Kumuwela" [Kumuweia]).

Hostplant: *Campylotheca.*

This species is closely similar to *perkinsi,* and, if they are fully distinct species, the differences between them are not conspicuous.

Nesothoë silvestris Kirkaldy (fig. 50, a).

Nesothoë silvestris Kirkaldy, 1908:204; 1910:595.

Nesodryas (Nesothoë) silvestris (Kirkaldy) Muir, 1916:178.

Endemic. Lanai (type locality: Koele Mountains, 2,000 feet), Maui.

I have identified a single female from Waikamoi, Maui, taken at 4,500 feet by Muir, January 14, 1926, as this species—a new record for that island. The specimen is 6 mm. long and is one of the largest native Hawaiian delphacids I have seen. An example from Perkins' collection now before me was compared with the type by Perkins. The holotype female is in the British Museum. The elongate first antennal segment is unusual in this group.

Nesothoë terryi Kirkaldy (figs. 49, c; 51, a).

Nesothoë terryi Kirkaldy, 1908:204; 1910:594.

Nesodryas (Nesothoë) terryi (Kirkaldy) Muir, 1916:178; 1917:301, pl. 5, fig. 3.

Endemic. Oahu (type locality: Waialua district).

Hostplant: *Osmanthus sandwicensis.*

"Only two examples were found [in Kirkaldy's collection], one of these belonging to the S.I.C. [Sandwich Islands Committee] was labeled '*solitudinis,*' the other of later date captured by me." (Perkins' letter.) The female holotype is now in the British Museum.

Genus **NESODRYAS** Kirkaldy, 1908:203

Subgenus *Nesodryas* (Kirkaldy) Muir, 1916:170.

This genus was originally separated from *Nesothoë* because the included forms are "very slender, frail species," whereas those of *Nesothoë* are "robust forms." Muir (1916:170) stated that "The difference between *Nesodryas* and *Nesothoë* is, at most, only of sub-generic value; the type of the former (*N. freycinetiae*) is not typical of the other species, but is an extreme form, either divergent or convergent."

I had followed Muir's arrangement until the eve of going to press, when the study of a new species of *Nesodryas* taken by Dr. Swezey led me to examine the genitalia of the group in more detail. This examination has brought me to the conclusion that the types of *Nesodryas* and *Nesothoë* belong to different genera.

Typical *Nesothoë* are robust species with the wings conspicuously constricted at the base of the apical cells, as figure 47, c, of the genotype *N. fletus* plainly shows. However, there is a series of species which are slender, delicate forms rather superficially similar to the type of *Nesodryas* (*freycinetiae*) or approaching it more than *fletus*. All of these slender species have typical *Nesothoë* genitalia. On the other hand, *Nesodryas freycinetiae* has terminalia basically unlike those of any other described Hawaiian leafhopper genus. Therefore, I propose to place all of the slender forms now included in *Nesodryas* (excepting its type *freycinetiae*) in *Nesothoë* and retain *Nesodryas* for the species whose terminalia fit the basic pattern of *freycinetiae*. The discovery of a second species of the *freycinetiae* type gives weight to this decision.

The terminalia of both male and female *Nesodryas* are distinctive. Both are remarkable because they appear to have two anal styles instead of the normal one. The diagrams show this plainly. The lower anal style of the female is very large and conspicuous (about 0.5 mm. on the species at hand). The females of the genera in question can be separated easily on the basis of this character. The male pygophore of *Nesodryas* has a long upcurved spine at about the middle of each side margin and there is a pair of long, slender, spine-like processes arising behind the genital styles (thus forming what appear to be four genital styles). The aedeagus is a rather stout, decurved organ quite unlike the long, more or less rod-like aedeagus of *Nesothoë*. These characters may best be appreciated by examining the drawings.

Nesodryas, as here redefined, will include our Alohini which have the first antennal segment transverse, a single median frontal carina and terminalia of the basic type just described. The species are macropterous. The genus is a divergent development of the *Leialoha–Nesothoë* complex.

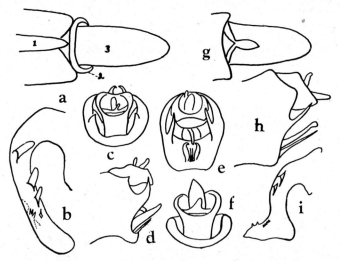

Figure 52—Details of genitalia of *Nesodryas*. **a–e,** *N. freycinetiae* Kirkaldy: **(a)** apex of female abdomen as seen from below, **(1)** ovipositor, **(2)** anal segment, **(3)** anal style; **(b)** aedeagus; **(c)** pygophore as seen from directly above; **(d)** side view of pygophore; **(e)** rear view of pygophore. **f–i,** *N. swezeyi* Zimmerman, new species: **(f, g)** dorsal views of apex of abdomen of male and female as seen from above, note the two anal styles; **(h)** side view of pygophore; **(i)** aedeagus.

KEY TO THE SPECIES OF NESODRYAS

1. Oahu species from *Freycinetia;* vertex of head and pronotum each with two conspicuous black spots; tegmina not striped with brown; male pygophore and genitalia as in figure 52, a–e ....**freycinetiae** Kirkaldy.
2. Hawaii species from *Pritchardia* palm; head and pronotum immaculate; tegmina with conspicuous brown vittae; male pygophore and genitalia as in figure 52, f–i............. .... **swezeyi** Zimmerman.

Nesodryas freycinetiae Kirkaldy (figs. 47, b; 50, b; 52, a–e).

Nesodryas freycinetiae Kirkaldy, 1908:203; 1910:596. Muir, 1916:175, pl. 2, fig. 16. Genotype.

Endemic. Oahu (type locality: Pacific Heights Ridge, Honolulu).

Hostplant: *Freycinetia arborea.*

Muir (1916:175) said when he included this species with those now placed in *Nesothoë*, "Unfortunately Kirkaldy chose this extreme form as the type of the genus; both in general build and in genitalia it departs from the other species very considerably." One might wonder why he did not separate the genera at that time.

The small but outstanding spots on the vertex and pronotum are rather surprising distinctive marks.

Swezey (1908:13–14) has reported on the life history of this interesting leaf-hopper. He notes that

This is a delicate pale green little leaf-hopper living on the "ieie" vine.... The eggs are inserted in the younger leaves at the crown of the growing vine, parallel with the fibers of the leaves, one or two together. The young nymphs are very flat, adapted to crawling between the leaves in the crown of the plant. They also may be found exposed on the surfaces of the outer parts of the leaves, where they might not be recognized as young leaf-hoppers at first sight, on account of their flatness; and their coloration... allows them to be mistaken for a bit of dirt or debris.

His paper should be consulted for a description of the nymphs.

The female type is in the British Museum.

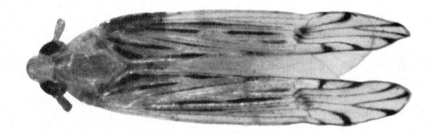

Figure 53—*Nesodryas swezeyi* Zimmerman, male paratype.

Nesodryas swezeyi, new species (figs. 52, f–i; 53).

Pale green or yellowish-green throughout except for the brown ovipositor and the following brown marks on fore wings: conspicuous narrow brown vittae down each membrane between veins of clavus and corium excepting the costal cell, and the mark may be pale or absent in the cell made by the forking of the vein above the costa; a short fascia across bases of anal cells just beyond apex of corium; veins of anal cell-complex each darkened distad and the membrane darkened along them in such a way as to make it appear that the veins expand apically, thus forming six dark lines in the apical cell area; veins in both pairs of wings otherwise pale; membrane of both pairs clear or only faintly tinged milky, but fore pair more yellowish or green basad; granules on fore-wing veins pale, giving rise to long, fine, pale hairs.

Face pale, unmarked and without callosities, derm appearing thin and transluscent; vertex obtusely pointed in front as seen from above, but median carina not protuberant.

Pygophore, its appendages and aedeagus as in figure 52, f–i.

Length: 5–6 mm. from front of head to apex of tegmina; breadth across hind margin of pronotum: 0.8–0.9 mm.

Endemic. Hawaii. Holotype male, allotype female and one female paratype taken from the leaves of *Pritchardia* palm on the Kulani Prison road, May 29, 1947, by O. H. Swezey. The types are in the Bishop Museum.

This species is closely allied to *freycinetiae,* but there are excellent characters to separate the two species. The vittae on the basal part of the tegmina are conspicuous and can be seen with the naked eyes or under low magnification. The male terminalia are closely similar in general type to those of *freycinetiae,* but they display good specific characters. The aedeagus is quite different, the spines below the anal styles are nearly as long as the styles, but they are only about one-half as long on *freycinetiae.* The sketches reveal these and other differences. Neither this species nor *freycinetiae* has anal spines.

It gives me the greatest of pleasure to dedicate this fine species to my close friend and colleague, Dr. O. H. Swezey, who collected it during a field trip on the eve of his seventy-eighth birthday.

Genus **ALOHA** Kirkaldy, 1904:177

This endemic genus is distinguished from its associated genera as follows: first antennal segment longer than broad; frons with two median carinae (sometimes low, poorly developed and obscure); tegmina extending beyond the middle of the abdomen, but macropterous in only a few known females.

The species originally assigned by Kirkaldy to the subgenus *Leialoha* of *Aloha* have been subsequently assigned to the full genus *Leialoha,* and some of the species described under *Nesopleias* have been included in *Aloha.*

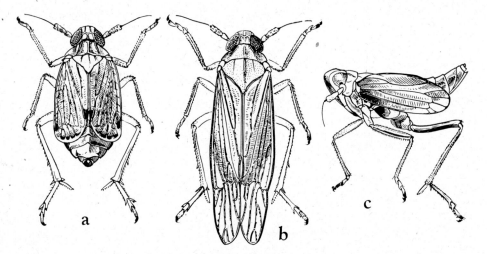

Figure 54—a, *Aloha ipomoeae* Kirkaldy, brachypterous female; b, the same, macropterous female; c, *Aloha flavocollaris* Muir, brachypterous female. (Drawn to same scale by Abernathy.)

Key to the Species of Aloha
(Male specimens)

1.　　Frons almost entirely black, with a yellow apical band and usually with a variable amount of brown from about middle of eyes dorsad, but pronotum not strikingly pale and tegmina not extensively dark.................
..................................**myoporicola** Kirkaldy.
Frons either largely pale, or if dark, then pronotum markedly pale and tegmina with extensive dark areas......... 2

2(1).　Face very dark but apically pale; pronotum sharply contrasting pale (yellow) with the dark mesonotum (nearly black); tegmina extensively dark........**flavocollaris** Muir.
Not so, face pale..................................... 3

3(2).　Tegmina each with a large, extensive, continuous dark macula... 4
Tegmina largely pale, with at most small or restricted dark areas... 7

4(3).　Pronotum and mesonotum dark brown or black; vertex comparatively short and broad, entire visible part of head as seen from directly above with median length from base to front slightly broader than long; tegmina reaching only to base of last abdominal segment.......
.... **plectranthi** Muir.
At least pronotum pale; vertex longer than broad; tegmina reaching nearly to or beyond apex of abdomen..... 5

5(4).　Dark maculae of tegmina smaller, usually distinctly shorter than median length from mesonotum to front of head and widely separated from base of tegmina...........
.............................**campylothecae** Muir.
Dark maculae of tegmina each longer than median length of body from apex of mesonotum to front of head, extending forward nearly to humerus at sides............ 6

6(5).　Dark coloring of tegmina extending over apical cells to apex, tegmina thus pale only at base...............
................................**artemisiae** (Kirkaldy).
Tegmina pale at base and apex, dark coloring not extending over apical cells.................**dubautiae** (Kirkaldy).

7(3).　Head with interocular area appearing subquadrate or comparatively short and broad when viewed from directly above, its median length about one-tenth shorter than breadth of base of vertex..............**ipomoeae** Kirkaldy.
Interocular area, as seen from above, longer than basal breadth of vertex................................... 8

8(7).　Tegmina with a dark mark at apex of clavus and apex of costal cell only; median facial keels fairly distinct and closer to each other than to lateral margins...........
....**swezeyi** Muir.
Tegmina with dark maculae in apical cells and an irregular, dark, oblique fascia running from apex of clavus to reach costa at basal one-third; median facial keels obscure and separated from one another by a distance equal to or greater than that between one of them and lateral margin..........................**kirkaldyi** Muir.

Aloha artemisiae (Kirkaldy).
Nesopleias artemisiae Kirkaldy, 1910:118.
Aloha artemisiae (Kirkaldy) Muir, 1916:182, pl. 2, fig. 27.

Endemic. Oahu (type locality: Waianae Mountains, 2,000 feet).
Hostplant: *Artemisia australis.*

Aloha campylothecae Muir.
Aloha campylothecae Muir, 1916:183, pl. 2, fig. 25; pl. 4, fig. 64.
Aloha kaalensis Muir, 1916:183, pl. 2, fig. 24 (type locality: Mount Kaala, Oahu).
    Synonymy by Muir, 1917:303.

Endemic. Oahu (type locality: Wailupe).
Hostplant: *Campylotheca.*

Aloha dubautiae (Kirkaldy).
Nesopleias dubautiae Kirkaldy, 1910:583.
Aloha dubautiae (Kirkaldy) Muir, 1916:182, pl. 2, fig. 26.

Endemic. Oahu (type locality: Mount Tantalus region).
Hostplants: *Dubautia laxa, Dubautia plantaginea.*
Perkins' notes regarding this species in his letter are as follows: "K[irkaldy] had no 1907 exx. of mine, unless they were destroyed when in his hands, but he may have read 1907 for 1902, here and elsewhere. I have no note of the type of this, but I certainly collected the sp. for the S.I.C., it being numerous in the Mts. behind Honolulu on the way up Konahuanui. The latest date I appear to have collected the sp. was early in 1906; in fact after this I only had one or two days collecting with Kershaw in Palolo and beyond on Olympus."

Aloha flavocollaris Muir (figs. 54, c; 56, h).
Aloha flavocollaris Muir, 1916:181, pl. 2, fig. 23.

Endemic. Oahu (type locality: Mount Kaala).
Hostplants: *Dubautia laxa, Dubautia plantaginea.*

Aloha ipomoeae Kirkaldy (figs. 46, c; 54, a, b).
Aloha ipomoeae Kirkaldy, 1904:177; 1908:205, pl. 4, fig. 9; 1910:581. Muir, 1916:178, pl. 2, fig. 17. Genotype.

Endemic. Kauai, Oahu (type locality: Mount Tantalus), Molokai, Lanai, Maui, Hawaii.
Hostplants: *Ipomoea batatas, I. bona-nox, I. insularis, I. pes-caprae, I. pentaphylla, I. tuberculata, Sesbania tomentosa* (accidental ?), *Scaevola coriacea* (accidental, I believe).

Parasite: *Paranagrus perforator* Perkins (Hymenoptera: Mymaridae; a purposely introduced species, although not brought in against this species) attacks the eggs.

An occasional macropterous female has been found.

The note in Perkins' letter regarding this species reads, "My note (when I corrected the proofs of K's paper in F. H. [*Fauna Hawaiiensis*]) says 'the original type of this species was in my specimens which are now in England. One card of these bears K's label *A. ipomoeae* but the word "type" is not used on any'."

Aloha kirkaldyi Muir.
  Aloha kirkaldyi Muir, 1916:180, pl. 2, fig. 20; pl. 3, fig. 63.

  Endemic. Oahu (type locality: Punaluu).
  Hostplant: *Euphorbia hillebrandi.*

Aloha myoporicola Kirkaldy.
  Aloha (?) *myoporicola* Kirkaldy, 1910:581.
  Aloha myoporicola Kirkaldy, Muir, 1916: 179, pl. 2, fig. 18; 1917:303; 1921:510,
    pl. 8, fig. 8, corrected illustration.

  Endemic. Lanai (?), Hawaii (type locality: Kilauea).
  Hostplants: *Myoporum sandwicense, Pelea volcanicola, Phyllostegia racemosa* (accidental ?), *Acacia koa* (accidental ?).
  The type should be in the British Museum, according to Perkins' letter.

Aloha plectranthi Muir.
  Aloha plectranthi Muir, 1916:179, pl. 2, fig. 19.

  Endemic. Oahu (type locality: Koko Crater).
  Hostplant: *Plectranthus parviflorus* (series of examples have been reared from eggs inserted in the plants).

Aloha swezeyi Muir.
  Aloha swezeyi Muir, 1916:180, pl. 2, fig. 21 (this figure erroneous ?; corrected
    by Muir, 1922:96, pl. 3, fig. 9); 1917:303.

  Endemic. Kauai, Oahu (type locality: Palolo Valley), Hawaii.
  Hostplants: *Bidens pilosa, Campylotheca macrocarpa, Cheirodendron gaudichaudii, Lipochaeta, Lythrum.*
  This species was originally described and figured from Oahu specimens, but in his 1922 paper Muir reported on a series of examples from Kauai and stated that "The former figure of the aedeagus was incorrect, so a more correct one is given herewith." Could it be that his Kauai examples represent a form distinct from his Oahu specimens and that both figures are correct? This problem requires study.
  Macropterous females have been found on Hawaii.

Genus **NESORESTIAS** Kirkaldy, 1908:205

Nesopleias Kirkaldy, 1910:582. Muir, 1915:265.

The Hawaiian Alohini having an elongate first antennal segment, two frontal carinae and abbreviated tegmina which do not reach beyond the middle of the abdomen are assigned to *Nesorestias*, a purely endemic group. The species resemble those of *Nothorestias*, but the presence of two frontal carinae will separate the two groups.

Muir (1916:184) considered *fiilicicola* to be an offshoot of the *ipomoeae* group of *Aloha* and *nimbata* an offshoot of the *kirkaldyi* group. As the genus is now constituted, it appears to be biphyletic. No long-winged forms are known.

KEY TO THE SPECIES OF NESORESTIAS

1. Median frontal keels strongly elevated, continued dorsad onto vertex and causing profile of front of head, as seen from directly above, to have a median protuberance consisting of two keels and their interspace (as illustrated); tegmina with a black mark at apex of clavus and a fuscous streak extending from there obliquely to humerus. .**nimbata** (Kirkaldy).

2. Median frontal keels low and obscure, front of head as seen in profile from directly above convex and without such a protuberance (as illustrated); tegmina not so maculate. . . . . **filicicola** Kirkaldy.

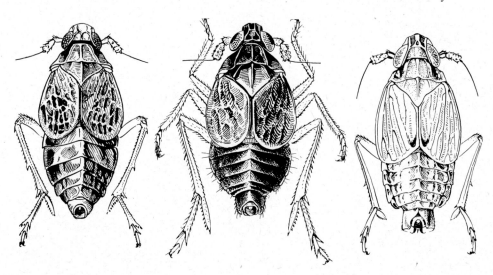

Figure 55—*Nesorestias filicicola* Kirkaldy, female, left; *Nothorestias swezeyi* Muir, male, center; *Kelisia eragrosticola* Muir, male, right. (Abernathy drawings; not to same scale.)

Nesorestias filicicola Kirkaldy (figs. 55; 56, e).

Nesorestias filicicola Kirkaldy, 1908:205; 1910:583. Muir, 1916:184, pl. 2, fig. 28; pl. 4, fig. 76. Genotype.

Endemic. Oahu (type locality: Mount Tantalus, 2,000 feet).

Hostplants: *Cibotium, Elaphoglossum gorgonum,* "ferns."

The type mount is now in the Bishop Museum and consists of a male and a female taken on fern in the "winter months" of 1902.

Nesorestias nimbata (Kirkaldy) (fig. 56, f).

Nesopleias nimbata Kirkaldy, 1910:582.

Nesorestias nimbata (Kirkaldy) Muir, 1916:184, pl. 2, fig. 29; pl. 4, fig. 77. (Genotype of *Nesopleias*).

Endemic. Oahu (type locality: Mount Tantalus, 1,500 feet).

Hostplant: *Phegopteris.*

Perkins notes in his letter that "The type must be the one in my coll. . . . labeled '*Aloha nephais*' (and without red label) and was taken in 1902 not 1907 (F.H.). If I afterward lent him [Kirkaldy] a 1907 specimen, I could not find it in his collection. . . . In the proofs of the F.H. at the end of the descript[ion] of genus the type of this is cited as *N. nephais,* but the species (1) is *N. nimbata,* (2) *dubautiae.* Consequently I deleted the 'Type *N. nephais*' as I could not find the species before the proofs had to be returned." The type is now in the Bishop Museum.

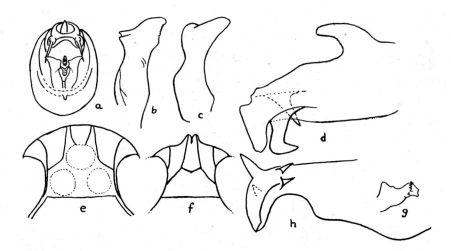

Figure 56—Features of Delphacidae: **a,** *Nothorestias swezeyi* Muir, pygophore as seen from behind (redrawn from Muir, 1922:87); **b,** right style of paratype of *Nothorestias swezeyi* Muir; **c,** *Nothorestias badia* Muir, right style of holotype; **d,** *Nothorestias badia* Muir, aedeagus of holotype; **e,** *Nesorestias filicicola* Kirkaldy, vertex from directly above to show frontal keels; **f,** the same of *Nesorestias nimbata* (Kirkaldy); **g,** *Nothorestias swezeyi* Muir, aedeagus (redrawn from Muir, 1922:87); **h,** *Aloha flavocollaris* Muir, aedeagus.

Genus **NOTHORESTIAS** Muir, 1917:304

This endemic segregate group has an elongate first antennal segment, a single frontal carina (which, on the two described species, forks at about or below the lower level of the eyes), and the tegmina are somewhat coriaceous, with the veins forming more or less of a reticulate pattern, and so abbreviated that they do not reach the middle of the abdomen.

As in *Nesorestias,* this genus is not monophyletic, but each of its species has been derived from a different species group. It is close to *Nesorestias.* Only two species have been described, and these from Oahu, but I have studied a single female of a new species from Maui.

Key to the Species of Nothorestias

(Males)

1. Underside of anal segment broadly arch-like, and with a long spine at each lateral corner; genital styles and aedeagus as in figure 56, a, b, g; lower apical margin of pygophore produced at the middle to form a triangular process (as seen obliquely from above).......................**swezeyi** Muir.
2. Anal segment without spines; aedeagus and genital styles as in figure 56, c, d. (Note: I have seen only the dissected holotype which is inadequate to supply more structural details of the pygophore for use here.)............**badia** Muir.

Nothorestias badia Muir (fig. 56, c, d).

Nothorestias badia Muir, 1917:304, pl. 5, fig. 6. Genotype.

Endemic. Oahu (type locality: Kuliouou).

Hostplant: ferns.

The holotype is the only specimen known. It was taken in a different mountain range and at the opposite end of Oahu from the following species.

Nothorestias swezeyi Muir (figs. 55; 56, a, b, g).

Nothorestias swezeyi Muir, 1922:87, figs. 1, 2.

Endemic. Oahu (type locality: Makaha Valley).

Hostplant: *Aspidium* fern.

This species lives in the vicinity of leeward Mount Kaala and has been collected rarely in that area by sweeping ferns.

Genus **DICTYOPHORODELPHAX** Swezey, 1907:104

Of all of the remarkable endemic insect genera of Hawaii, this is one of the most extraordinary. It is fitting that it should have been discovered and described by one of the most eminent of all Hawaiian entomologists.

The species of this group have the front of the head tremendously prolonged into a great process which is longer than the remainder of the body in some species. This unique character causes the species to resemble such fulgorids as *Scolops,* rather than most delphacids. The genus is a peculiar local segregate of one of the *Nesorestias-* or *Nesosydne*-like groups. *Nesosydne leahi* shows a tendency toward the development of the cephalic horn. The genus has an elongate first antennal segment, a single, median frontal carina, and the tegmina extend only about to the middle, or to beyond the middle, or about to the apex of the abdomen. No macropterous forms are known. The frons of each species is pale, and the clypeus of each is black or nearly so. The head is prolonged in the nymphs, but not nearly to the extent that it is in the adults. The species feed on *Euphorbia.*

Kershaw (1913:185), who studied the internal anatomy of *D. mirabilis,* notes that the food reservoir of the alimentary canal "enters the head capsule and continues to the tip of the greatly produced epicranium. The malpighian tubes are forked distally for a moderate length, the forked part being lobulate, the rest smooth. They are pale brown."

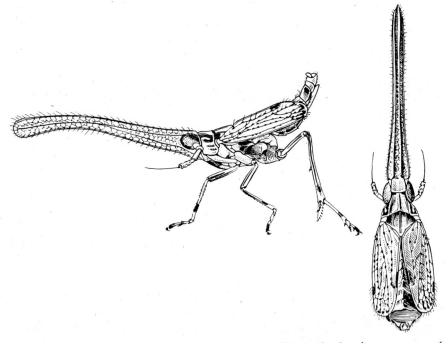

Figure 57—*Dictyophorodelphax mirabilis* Swezey, female. (Abernathy drawings to same scale.)

Figure 58—*Dictyophorodelphax* species: *D. swezeyi* Bridwell, male (Oahu), top; *D. usingeri* Swezey, paratype female (Lanai), center; *D. praedicta* Bridwell, female (Maui), bottom.

KEY TO THE SPECIES OF DICTYOPHORODELPHAX

(Revised from Swezey, 1937:431)

1. Horn of head curved continuously upward from base to apex, its longitudinal dorsal outline concave; lateral carinae confluent at about middle; veins of tegmina with dark setigerous granules; Oahu.....**swezeyi** Bridwell.
   Horn of head curved forward or down apically, thus the longitudinal dorsal contour is convex.................. 2

2(1). Horn longer than remainder of body, not laterally compressed distad; lateral carinae confluent somewhat beyond middle; tegminal veins with dark setigerous granules; Oahu..........................**mirabilis** Swezey.
   Horn not longer than remainder of body and laterally compressed distad.................................... 3

3(2). Tegmina with dark setigerous granules; length of horn from anterior margin of an eye, as seen from side, equivalent to distance from hind edge of an eye to third abdominal tergite, or only slightly beyond apices of tegmina; Lanai..........................**usingeri** Swezey.
   Tegmina without dark setigerous granules; length of horn from anterior margin of an eye, as seen from side, equal to distance between hind margin of an eye and almost to, to, or slightly beyond apex of abdomen and far beyond apices of tegmina; Maui..............**praedicta** Bridwell.

Dictyophorodelphax mirabilis Swezey (fig. 57).
   Dictyophorodelphax mirabilis Swezey, 1907:105; 1908:2, figs. 1–5. Muir, 1916: 184 (genitalia). Bridwell, 1917:279–280 (foodplant). Kershaw, 1913:185, (internal anatomy). Genotype.

   Endemic. Oahu (type locality: Mount Konahuanui). It has been found on both mountain ranges on Oahu.
   Hostplants: *Euphorbia clusiaefolia, Euphorbia hillebrandi,* (*Pittosporum glabratum,* accidental capture).
   Parasite: an unidentified dryinid wasp.
   The hairs on the sides of the horn are longer and more conspicuous on this than on the other species. Also, the horn is longer on this species.

Dictyophorodelphax praedicta Bridwell (figs. 58; 59, d, e).
   Dictyophorodelphax praedicta Bridwell, 1919:72, fig. 1 (aedeagus).

   Endemic. Maui (type locality: Iao Valley, 600–800 feet).
   Hostplant: *Euphorbia hookeri integrifolia.*

Dictyophorodelphax swezeyi Bridwell (figs. 58; 59, c).
   Dictyophorodelphax swezeyi Bridwell, 1918:386.

Endemic. Oahu (type locality: Wailupe).

Hostplant: *Euphorbia celastroides.*

The upcurved cephalic horn alone distinguishes this species from all the other known forms.

Dictyophorodelphax usingeri Swezey (fig. 58).

Dictyophorodelphax usingeri Swezey, 1937:431.

Endemic. Lanai (type locality: "trail to Lanaihale, 2000–3000 ft."):

Hostplant: *Euphorbia.*

This species most closely resembles *praedicta* from the adjacent island of Maui. It differs, however, by its shorter horn, dark setigerous granules on the tegmina and other characters. No males have been found.

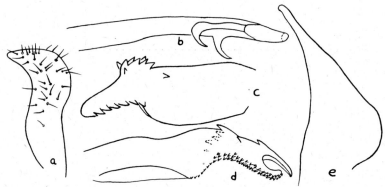

Figure 59—Some delphacid male genitalia: **a,** right style of *Nesothoë laka* Kirkaldy (?); **b,** apical part of aedeagus of *N. laka* Kirkaldy (?); **c,** aedeagus of *Dictyophorodelphax swezeyi* Bridwell; **d,** *Dictyophorodelphax praedicta* Bridwell, aedeagus; **e,** style of *D. praedicta* Bridwell.

Genus **NESOSYDNE** Kirkaldy, 1907:161

Ilburnia, in the sense of Muir, not of White, 1878.

This is the largest known genus of the Delphacidae of the world. It contains 82 described forms, all of them confined to the Hawaiian Islands. The next largest delphacid genus is the widespread, and probably composite, *Liburnia* which contains about 60 forms.

In the preliminary drafts of this work, I had followed Muir (1919:6; 1919:48) and subsequent workers in including our Hawaiian material in *Ilburnia.* This arrangement appeared to me unsatisfactory, because it was so unnatural. Further study has led me to consider Muir's sinking of *Nesosydne* under *Ilburnia* as untenable, and I have gone back to the use of *Nesosydne,* for the reasons outlined below.

After having worked on the Hawaiian delphacids for some time, Muir visited the British Museum to study the collection of Delphacidae there. He published his "Notes on the Delphacidae in the British Museum Collection" in January, 1919, and in that paper he stated that *"Ilburnia* White = *Nesosydne* Kirkaldy," without explanation. In June of 1919 his paper "On the Genus Ilburnia White" appeared in Honolulu, and in that paper he stated that there were no structural differences to use to separate the Hawaiian *Nesosydne* from the St. Helena genotype of *Ilburnia*. He redescribed *Ilburnia ignobilis* White (the genotype) from St. Helena (in the mid-South Atlantic), and transferred *Delphax simulans* Walker, which Darwin collected in the Galapagos, to *Ilburnia*. Later (1927:87), Muir described a species from the Marquesas and assigned it to *Ilburnia*. Thus, we came to have more than 80 species from Hawaii, one from the Marquesas, one from the Galapagos and one from St. Helena—a peculiar geographical distribution.

It is surprising to those who knew how insistent Muir was that no new delphacids be described from females alone, and how much emphasis he placed upon the male terminalia for information on relationships, to find that his assigning *Nesosydne* to *Ilburnia* was based upon only two female examples of *Ilburnia ignobilis* (one badly damaged). Muir's Marquesan species, likewise, was described from a unique female. The Galapagos species was represented by two males and a female. From this evidence I have felt that Muir was too hasty in his reduction of *Nesosydne*.

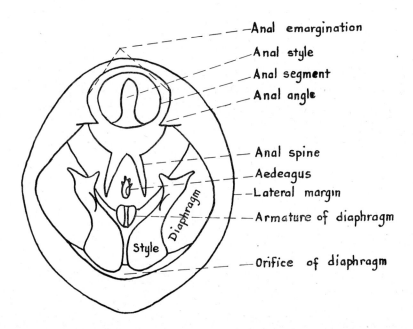

Figure 60—Diagram of rear view of pygophore of a hypothetical species of *Nesosydne* to show parts used in classification.

An outline of the problem was sent to W. E. China at the British Museum, and he has kindly examined the material at that institution. He writes that although he is not acquainted sufficiently with the group to pass final judgment on Muir's decision, "Judging by an examination of the type material of *Ilburnia* [*ig*]*nobilis* B. White from St. Helena, I should say that it is in error ..." and

We have only 3 specimens of *I.* [*ig*]*nobilis* B. White in the B. M. collection including the type and these are all females. I do not think that Muir had other material of this species as St. Helena material is not very abundant. [Muir said that he had seen only two females: "the type is in good condition but the second specimen, which is smaller and darker and represents another species, is without tegmina."] It looks therefore as though he judged from the appearance of the females in the B. M. collection. I should say that *Ilburnia* is distinct from *Nesosydne*. Unfortunately the specimens we have of *I.* [*ig*]*nobilis* are all brachypterous and it is therefore difficult to judge, but the venation seems to be quite different. The antennae too have the first joint as long as the second.

The evidence at hand is, I believe, ample for retaining *Nesosydne* as a genus distinct from the Atlantic *Ilburnia*. Muir noted that the Galapagos species "is not quite typical," and I feel that it may belong to yet another genus. I have not seen identified specimens of Muir's Marquesan species, but it may be represented in the undetermined material before me. I believe that it may prove to be allied to the Hawaiian *Nesosydne* rather than to *Ilburnia*, or it may belong to a genus distinct from either.

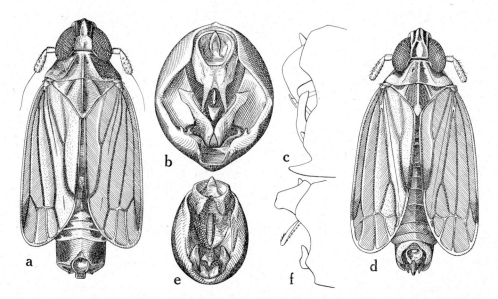

Figure 61—Holotypes of *Nesosydne*: **a**, *N. nubigena* Kirkaldy, male; **b**, rear view of pygophore of **a**; **c**, the same in lateral outline; **d**, *N. nephelias* Kirkaldy, male; **e**, rear view of pygophore of same; **f**, the same in lateral outline (the teeth on the aedeagus may not be drawn accurately, for they are hard to see and are difficult to interpret on dried specimens). (Drawn at the British Museum of Natural History by Smith.)

I have collected or examined undescribed species from southeastern Polynesia—Marquesas, Society, Austral and Mangareva Islands—which show much resemblance to the Hawaiian genera of Alohini. Some of them evidently belong to *Nesosydne,* perhaps some will be found to be isolated representatives of other Hawaiian genera, and others are localized offshoots which probably will be described as distinct new genera. Only further study will reveal the answers to these problems, but as now arranged, the geographical distribution of *Nesosydne* is more logical and falls in line with certain other genera of Polynesian organisms.

Nesosydne is separated from the other Hawaiian Alohini by the following combination of characters: first segment of antennae elongate (only slightly longer than broad in some species) ; frons with a single median carina (partly double in some forms) ; tegmina reaching nearly to, or surpassing, the apex of the abdomen in most species, but variable, the veins distinct. Most of these characters overlap one or more of the other local genera, and a combination of them may be essential to distinguish the genera which are not as clearly separated as the literature may appear to indicate. Macropterous males and/or females are known in about a dozen of the species. A few species are known only from macropterous specimens.

An adequate knowledge of this remarkable group can only be obtained by years of concentrated, careful study by a bio-systematist. Detailed field work is a prime

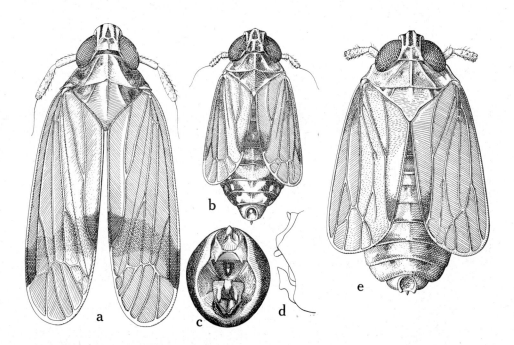

Figure 62—Holotypes of *Nesosydne*: **a,** *N. procellaris* Kirkaldy, damaged female type; **b,** *N. imbricola* Kirkaldy, male; **c,** rear view of pygophore of same; **d,** lateral outline of same; **e,** *N. haleakala* Kirkaldy, female. (Drawn at the British Museum of Natural History by Smith.)

requisite. There are a number of groups of species within the genus which, when delimited by adequate diagnoses, could be described and keyed so that identification of undetermined material would be much simplified.

The formulation of a general key to the 82 species of *Nesosydne* has been a difficult task, and the outcome of my studies is not altogether satisfactory. I have used specimens determined by Kirkaldy, Perkins, Swezey and Giffard, but most of the material studied was determined by Muir, and types of most of the species have been examined. With the exception of the four Kirkaldy species listed below, specimens representing all the other species have been studied. However, a number of the species are represented by only one or two male types, many of which are dissected, and this lack of perfect individuals in series has been a serious stumbling block. Some of the species are variable, and certain characters at first considered useful for the key have had to be discarded. I fear that study will show that some of the characters used in the key as it now stands are not stable and further modification will be necessary. The females differ so much from the males, and so few females have been associated correctly with their males, that it has been impossible for me to include the females in the keys.

A key such as this is perfected only by repeated use and revision, and it should be used by a number of individuals to make it most useful and understandable. It is obvious that the few weeks devoted to its making are inadequate for such a complex task. I hesitate to present the key now, but I feel that in spite of its shortcomings it will facilitate the work of future students and will serve as a foundation for a more accurate and complete table for identification. The perfecting of the key remains a challenge for a keen and ambitious student of the Delphacidae.

The key should not be considered as a final course for identification, but only a tool with which generally to locate a species, which may then have to be studied in more detail and compared with the descriptions, illustrations or accurately identified specimens. Of course, many of the more outstanding species can be placed by the use of the key alone. Both categories of each dichotomy should be read carefully before a decision is made as to what course to follow. It must be borne in mind that the genus is a large and taxonomically difficult one, and it must be treated accordingly.

Because a number of species are represented in the male sex only by dissected individuals, it has been difficult to assemble characters of the pygophore which are obvious without dissection and which may appear distinctive on the perfect individuals. It appears rather puzzling to me that so many of the species are known from only one or a few type specimens, whereas it is common knowledge among experienced collectors that many species are frequently abundant on their hostplants. Specialized collecting should change the picture, however.

In spite of the large number of species now known, many remain to be described. No one has described a new species of *Nesosydne* since Muir published his last descriptions in 1922. I have examined a number of new species, but lack of time prevents describing them. There may be more than 150 species living in Hawaii today, and it is probable that the number of species which have become extinct since the occupation of the islands by man is large.

Four species are not included in the following general key either because I have had no representatives of them, or because only females have been seen. However, the holotypes, which are in the British Museum, have been drawn, and these drawings included here will aid greatly in recognizing the species. I have been able to place some of the species in the geographical set of keys which follows the main key, however. I have not seen *nubigena* Kirkaldy. I have examined the female holotype of *hamadryas* Kirkaldy, one female of *procellaris* Kirkaldy, and two damaged females (?) of *haleakala* Kirkaldy.

Since the above notes and the main key were written, I have prepared a supplementary set of keys which contains a key to the species of each island. This second set of keys probably will prove to be more easily used than the long, complex main key. However, we do not have an accurate picture of the geographical distribution of all the species, and all of the keys must be used with care and caution.

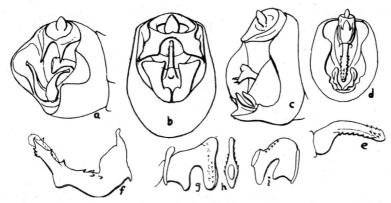

Figure 63—Details of *Nesosydne* genitalia: **a,** *N. koebelei* Muir, oblique view of pygophore; **b,** *N. nigriceps* Muir, pygophore from behind; **c,** *N. sola* Muir, oblique view of pygophore; **d,** *N. nephelias* Kirkaldy, rear view of pygophore; **e,** aedeagus of same; **f,** *N. asteliae* Muir, aedeagus; **g,** *N. nesogunnerae* Muir, lateral view of aedeagus; **h,** apical view of aedeagus of same; **i,** *N. gunnerae* Muir, aedeagus. (From Muir's original drawings.)

KEY SECTION I: PROVISIONAL GENERAL KEY TO THE HAWAIIAN NESOSYDNE

(Male specimens. See also the separate island keys on page 187.)

1.   First antennal segment not more than twice as long as broad, either less than twice as long as broad or approximately twice as long as broad. (Note: The measurements were made with an eyepiece micrometer, viewing the insect from the front and measuring the length along the *dorsal* margin of the antennal segment and the breadth at the apex from the same view. These measurements usually cannot be guessed at, because of optical illusion, and must be made carefully.) 2

First antennal segment more than twice as long as broad,
sometimes as much as three times as long as broad......58

2(1).   First antennal segment comparatively short or very short
for the genus, distinctly less than twice as long as
broad, in some only about as long as broad (measure
carefully) 3
First antennal segment approximately twice as long as
broad (use caution here; if the segment is two-thirds
as broad as long, it is *not* "approximately twice as long
as broad," although it may appear to be so without
measuring) 18

3(2).   Median carina of frons forking below middle of face and
thus double for most of its length.................... 4
Median carina of frons forking much nearer to vertex (or
rather obscure and ill-defined, or both)............... 5

4(3).   Vertex distinctly longer than broad, the median frontal
carinae where they come into view from above at apex
of vertex nearly fused and conspicuously protuberant;
length about 2.5 mm.; a moderately elongate species..
.... **kokolau** (Muir).
Vertex broader than long and appearing unusually broad,
median frontal carinae distinctly separated over fronto-
vertex angle; length about 1.6 mm.; a short, stocky
species...........................**ahinahina** (Muir).

5(3).   Face, including clypeus, entirely pale or nearly so, usually
pale yellowish, at least without dark marks or dark
vittae and not very brown.......................... 6
Frons and/or clypeus either largely dark, or with dark
vittae or maculae on frons or clypeus or both, but never
very pale overall, at least with darker coloration on
clypeus, if not on frons. (Caution: Confusion may be
caused at this point, for the character is not always
stable. You may have to try each section, especially
if you have a somewhat teneral individual.)...........41

6(5).   Frons as viewed from directly in front with its top produced into a median protuberance as in figure 71, c, and
elevated far above eyes; tegmina milky with conspicuous dark setigerous granules; on *Lipochaeta* on Oahu
(and Kauai ?).......................**leahi** (Kirkaldy).
Not such species; top of frons as viewed from in front
more as in figure 70, c............................. 7

7(6).   Head as viewed from side with distance between fore
edge of an eye and lateral facial carina nearly as great as,
as great as, or slightly greater than, distance from carina
to most remote point on profile of angle between frons
and vertex, never less than one-half as great, as in
figure 70, a..................................... 8
Head with distance between lateral facial carina and most
remote point on angle between vertex and frons, as seen
in profile as described above, obviously much greater
than distance between fore edge of an eye and lateral
carina, as in figure 74, c...........................16

8(7).   Spines of anal segment fang-like or short and stout,
          thorn-like or dentiform, never very long, slender or
          needle-like 9
          Anal spines very long, slender, needle-like.............11

9(8).   Tegmina conspicuously dotted with dark setigerous gran-
          ules; genital styles broad and flat, hooked on outer
          sides at apices; median carina of frons strongly formed
          and elevated......................**chambersi** Kirkaldy.
          Tegmina without dark setigerous granules; genital styles
          long and slender; median frontal carina low and rather
          obscure, apparently forking near lower ocular margins...10

10(9).   Kauai form.............................**viridis** (Muir).
          Hawaii form...............................**phyllostegiae** Muir.
          (Note: These forms are very closely allied and the differ-
          ences between them are difficult to define on the basis
          of the meager material available. See the drawings
          for differences found in the type series.)

11(8).   (Note: Here belongs a difficult assemblage of forms at-
          tached to *Acacia koa* and which may be termed the *koae*
          complex. All of them have macropterous forms, and
          brachypterous forms are known only for *koae*. These
          species are separated best by the characters of the male
          genitalia and by their food habits. Some are more
          readily distinguished in the living state, because they
          have then more distinctive facies.)
          Tegmina and wings milky hyaline (or yellowish?); teg-
          minal veins pale or white between granules, concolorous
          with membrane; granules dark and unusually conspic-
          uous, for the dark color extends entirely across veins
          and encroaches slightly on membrane, thus giving a
          characteristic dotted appearance to tegmina.........
          ....**koae-phyllodii** Muir.
          Tegmina not so dotted, granules usually hardly if any
          darker than veins, but if distinctly darker, then dark
          color is confined to veins which are darker than mem-
          brane and are often brown.........................12

12(11). Genital styles comparatively short and broad, broadly
          truncate at apex as in figure 77, c–e..................13
          Genital styles elongate, as in figures 70, b, and 78, p........14

13(12). (Note: Two species were originally placed here. After
          the removal of one of them, I have not renumbered the
          entire key because of the great risk of error involved
          in such a process. Therefore, only one name is included
          here.) ....**pseudorubescens** Muir.

14(12). When viewed from above, inner basal angles of genital
          styles only slightly protuberant caudad; pale forms
          (green when living)....................**koae** Kirkaldy.
          When viewed from above, inner basal angles of styles
          notably produced caudad to form distinct protuber-
          ances; comparatively dark forms...................15

15(14). "...average color is a light reddish brown with lighter
          carinae" (Muir, 1916:185); aedeagus with a row of
          strong spines running from apex to base............
          ....**rubescens** (Kirkaldy).

"The Kilauea, Hawaii, specimens are darker in color, especially the mesonotum of the males, which is sometimes nearly black, the anal spines are stouter and shorter, the dorsal row of spines on the aedeagus is represented by a few irregular spines...." (Muir, 1916:186).....................**rubescens pele** (Kirkaldy).

16(7).   (Note: Three closely allied forms belong here, and they are difficult to separate.)
Maui form; genital styles as in figure 73, a; aedeagus elongate, as in figure 73, b............**mauiensis** (Muir).
Hawaii forms; genital styles as in figures 74, a, and 77, f; aedeagus short and stout...........................17

17(16). Genital styles greatly prolonged at the "toe," as in figure 77, f..........................**raillardiae** Kirkaldy.
Genital styles not so acutely pointed at the "toe," but as in figure 74, a...................**neoraillardiae** (Muir).

18(2).   Pygophore with a conspicuous, tooth-like or stout, spine-like protuberance at middle of its lower caudal margin as in figure 65, d, h................................19
Pygophore without such a ventral process..............21

19(18). Vertex as seen from directly above with median line only slightly longer than its greatest basal breadth; anal segment transverse and with long converging anal spines; pygophore without hooks or lobes as in the two following species but with simple side margins...
....**amaumau** (Muir).
Vertex distinctly longer than broad; anal segment elongate, either without spines or with divergent spines.....20

20(19). Sides of pygophore, as seen from behind, with a conspicuous, recurved, somewhat hook-like tooth on inner margin above medio-ventral spine, the latter long and pointed; genital styles short; anal segment without large spines and unusually produced apically so that it is about a third longer than wide...........**sola** Muir.
Sides of pygophore broadly lobate as illustrated; ventro-median spine rather short and blunt; genital styles long and extending up to the prominent spines on anal segment which is also somewhat elongate, but not so much as in *sola*..............................**asteliae** Muir.

21(18). Apical margin of anal segment as viewed from directly above very deeply, broadly and unusually conspicuously emarginate, the emargination deeply V-shaped (fig. 66, i); armature on diaphragm of pygophore unusually large and protruding between and distinctly behind the styles which are formed as in figure 66, j....
..............................**coprosmicola** (Muir).
Apical margin of anal segment as seen from above (*not from below*) entire or only inconspicuously notched, never formed as in *coprosmicola* even if emarginate; other characters mentioned not as in *coprosmicola*.......22

22(21). Median frontal carina forking on face below vertex near lower level of eyes or farther distad, or, in *viridis* and

phyllostegiae, the carinae are vague and nearly obsolete
and apparently fork below vertex....................23
Median frontal carina forking at or on vertex...........30

23(22). Median frontal carina forking far down on face, near
apex, double for most of length....................24
Not such species, carina forking nearer lower level of eyes..26

24(23). Genital styles with their "toes" (or outer projection) bent
cephalad, instead of laterad as usual, so that when
viewed from side they appear bent forward at nearly
right angles beyond middle as in figure 77, i.........
....**rocki** Muir.
Genital styles obviously not so formed.................25

25(24). Pygophore very short, nearly vertical behind and mostly
concealed from above; both "heel" (or inner projection) and "toe" of genital styles produced into a sharp,
conspicuous projection (fig. 80, j).................
.... **wailupensis** (Muir).
Pygophore not so formed; genital styles with their apical
angles not projecting into slender points, but as in
figure 76, j..........................**painiu** (Muir).

26(23). Frontal carinae low and inconspicuous or in part difficult
to trace completely, or both; armature of diaphragm of
pygophore in form of a conspicuous, thin, vertical
plate; genital styles as in figures 78, f, and 80, i........27
Not such species....................................28

27(26). Kauai form.............................**viridis** (Muir).
Hawaii form........................**phyllostegiae** Muir.
(Note: These forms are closely allied and the differences
between them are difficult to define on the basis of the
meager material available. See the drawings for differences found in the type series.)

28(26). Pygophore shaped as in figure 82, f, in caudal view; genital styles long and slender; anal angles projecting
partly around anal segment; tegmina reaching about
to middle of abdomen....................**giffardi** Muir.
Pygophore more open, genital styles shorter, anal angles
not so produced and otherwise different from *giffardi;*
tegmina extending about to apex of abdomen..........29

29(28). Pygophore in rear view as in figure 82, c, genital styles
as in figure 78, d, aedeagus as in figure 82, h; anal
spines not very large; Maui..............**perkinsi** Muir.
Pygophore not exactly like *perkinsi,* styles as in figure
74, i; aedeagus as in figures 63, g, h, and 74, j; anal
spines large and blade-like; Lanai.................
.................................**nesogunnerae** Muir.
(Note: These forms are closely allied, and the dissected
holotypes at hand are inadequate material for proper
treatment of the species herein.)

30(22). "Toe" (or outer projection) of each genital style unusually
strongly produced laterally to form a long, heavy,
broad projection as in figure 67, g (do not confuse the
projecting "heel," or mesal part, with the ectal arm or
"toe")..............................**cyrtandricola** Muir.

Genital styles not so formed, the "toe" never so greatly
produced, although it is obviously produced in some
forms, but never as in *cyrtandricola*..................31

31(30). Anal segment as viewed from behind distinctly concave
and arch-like beneath, the concavity extending caudad
and dorsad so that top of arch is hind margin of anal
segment 32
Anal segment not so formed, entire beneath or nearly so,
or concavity is so far forward as to be obscure in normal rear view and not extended to margin of anal
segment 35

32(31). Genital styles with mesal-distal angles ("heels") strongly
prolonged inward to form a long narrow point, as in
figure 66, c........................**boehmeria** (Muir).
Genital styles with "heels" not so conspicuously more
produced than "toes"............................33

33(32). A line drawn between anal angles of pygophore passes
through hind margin of anal segment or only slightly
in front of it, and apical margin with or without a slight
median emargination when viewed from directly above...33a
Such a line passes through about middle of anal segment,
well in front of hind margin........................34

33a(33). Kauai species; inner edges of genital styles above basal
swelling for most part straight, the common space between them not O-shaped; anal segment without a
median emargination in hind edge; frons black only
between carinae; pronotum and mesonotum with limited dark coloring................**campylothecae** (Muir).
Lanai species; inner edges of genital styles above basal
swelling each concave so that the common space between them is sub-O-shaped; apical margin of anal segment with a small median notch, as seen from above;
face, pronotum and mesonotum almost all black; tegmina with an extensive dark cloud........**nigriceps** Muir.

34(33). Armature of diaphragm of pygophore comparatively
large and protruding outward to caudal level of genital
styles so that "heels" of styles appear to rest on its
apex............................**stenogynicola** (Muir).
Armature of diaphragm smaller, less conspicuous and not
protruding as mentioned above, but distant from genital styles........................**dubautiae** (Muir).

35(31). Genital styles comparatively long and slender (fig. 69, o),
comparatively narrowly exposed to caudal view; entire
pygophore in caudal view distinctive as in figure 82, b
...............................**ipomoeicola** Kirkaldy.
Genital styles comparatively broad and flat, broadly exposed in caudal view, or if slender, then pygophore is
conspicuously different in caudal view from that in
ipomoeicola.....................................36

36(35). Anal segment as viewed from above not extending caudad
of a line drawn between apices of anal angles of pygophore, but enclosed by such a line..................37

Anal segment with its posterior end extending distinctly
caudad of a line drawn between anal angles of pygophore 38

37(36). Inner apical angle of each genital style strongly produced
inward to form a long and conspicuous point, as in
figure 75, k; Oahu....................**oahuensis** Muir.
Inner apical angle of each style forming nearly a right
angle and not produced inward, as in figure 70, n;
Kauai ....**kuschei** (Muir).

38(36). Lanai species; aedeagus strongly barbed at apex to make
it appear arrowhead-like or harpoon-like, or from side as
in figure 69, e...........................**hamata** Muir.
(Note: I have seen only dissected specimens and entire
individuals should have additional characters to use
for separation from the following species.)
Aedeagus not so formed.............................39

39(38). Genital styles with inner edges of posterior faces on
approximately same vertical plane from extreme base
to apex, and when viewed from above there are seen to
be no caudal projections from these inner edges, neither
submedianly nor subbasally. (Note: If caution is not
used in measuring the first antennal segment accurately, *naenae* will run here.)...............**acuta** (Muir).
Genital styles with inner edges of their posterior faces
following an irregular vertical line, so that when they
are viewed from directly above they are seen to be protuberant submedianly and subbasally.................40

40(39). Vertex distinctly widening apically and at its widest
apical part (measured across carinae above, not down
on sides in front of eyes where measurement would be
obviously greater) slightly broader than at base.....
......................................**mamake** (Muir).
Vertex not widened distad, subequal or slightly narrower
between lateral carinae at apex than at base.........
....................................**nesopele** (Muir).

41(5). Pygophore in anal view as in figure 82, b, styles arranged
so as to suggest the shape of a lyre; aedeagus with a
characteristic strong hook or tooth, as in figure 69, q
.... **ipomoeicola** Kirkaldy.
Not so...42

42(41). Tegmina conspicuously spotted by comparatively large,
dark, setigerous granules.............................43
Tegminal granules not large and dark and not giving a
conspicuously spotted appearance to tegmina, or only
partly dark and at most feebly spotted...............45

43(42). Pygophore, as seen from behind, not obviously expanded
at sides, but distinctly higher than broad; tegmina in
some examples thick and entirely opaque...........
................................**tetramolopii** (Muir).
Pygophore broadened laterally and about as broad as
high; genital styles as in figures 66, a, h; 76, e.........44

44(43).   Hawaii species; genital styles with apical margin sloping slightly downward and outward as in figure 66, h; aedeagus long and slender, as in figure 66, g.........
. . . .**chambersi** Kirkaldy.
Maui species; genital styles with apical margin sloping slightly upward and outward as in figure 66, a. 44a

44a(44). Aedeagus with apex broadly expanded as in figure 76, g
. . . .**osborni** Muir.
Aedeagus slender, tapering to apex, not apically expanded. . . . . **bridwelli** (Muir).

45(42).   Tegmina either distinctly bicolored, broadly pale from humerus diagonally across to black mark at apex of clavus, and pale across most of apical cell area, or at least broadly pale basad, or with infuscation hardly perceptible and membrane hyaline; spaces between carinae on frons very dark and sharply and conspicuously contrasting with pale keels. .46
Without such a combination of characters; tegmina either largely opaque and with a rather granular texture, or more or less milky, or entirely dark or pale, or a combination of some of these characters. 51

46(45).   Underside of anal segment broadly and conspicuously concave and arch-like, anal spine conspicuous but not unusually large; genital styles each with a blunt, tooth-like boss at about middle of inner margin as in figure 78, i–k. . . . . , ...**pilo** (Muir).
Underside of anal segment either not so broadly concave or entire, but if concave, then without such knobs on genital styles. 47

47(46).   Underside of anal segment concave and with its sides strongly and heavily produced downward or spines unusually long and heavy; genital styles with "toes" obviously more strongly produced than "heels". 48
Without such a combination of characters; "heels" of genital styles as much produced as, or more so than, "toes" 49

48(47).   Lateral discal pronotal carinae curving slightly laterad at their apices and reaching or not reaching hind margin; pronotum and mesonotum almost entirely black; forks of median frontal carina low and almost obsolete on anterior part of vertex. . . . .**raillardiicola** (Muir).
Lateral discal pronotal carinae extending directly to hind margin; forks of median frontal carina strongly elevated, pale and conspicuous on entire vertex. . . . . . .
. . . .**bridwelli** (Muir).

49(47).   A line drawn between apices of anal angles of pygophore passes through hind margin of anal segment; anal spines (as seen in balsam mount) very long, slender and needle-like. . . . .**pipturi** Kirkaldy.
A line drawn between apices of anal angles of pygophore passes far anterior to apical margin of anal segment; anal spines not unusually long, slender or needle-like. . . .50

50(49).   Kauai species; aedeagus with a large, broad, flange-like
          subbasal tooth on lower right side as in figure 82, g...
          .... **naenae** (Muir).
          Maui species; aedeagus without such a flange, as in figure
          68, j.................................... **geranii** (Muir).

51(45).   Length of median keel of pronotum fully two-thirds as
          long as distance between hind ends of lateral pronotal
          discal keels.....................................52
          Length of median keel of pronotum only about equal to
          distance along hind margin between apex of median
          keel and apex of a lateral discal keel..................54

52(51).   Predominantly pale-yellowish species from Oahu; teg-
          mina nearly twice as long as thorax and head together,
          anal cells distinct (I have examined only the mutilated
          type, and there should be characters on the pygophore
          of perfect examples which would offer good characters
          to separate this species from the following two).....
          .... **incommoda** Muir.
          Predominantly brown or dark species from Maui; tegmina
          very short, little if any longer than distance between
          apex of vertex and hind margin of mesonotum; anal
          cells obsolete..53

53(52).   Very dark, nearly black-bodied species; in side view the
          genital styles are widely exposed and project strongly
          out of pygophore as in figure 65, g...............
          .... **argyroxiphii** Kirkaldy.
          Nota of thorax, top of head and legs pale; genital styles
          not so broadly exposed in side view, and pygophore
          almost entirely withdrawn beneath last complete ab-
          dominal tergite and nearly entirely concealed from
          above.................................. **eeke** (Muir).

54(51).   Tegmina almost or entirely dark, never milky-white;
          Maui forms...55
          Tegmina milky-white or yellowish-brown (on *Styphelia*)..56

55(54).   Anal segment as seen from behind with its underside
          arch-like, each side of arch produced into a large,
          fang-like tooth; lateral discal pronotal carinae thick-
          ened, curved laterad and not reaching hind pronotal
          margin; on *Coprosma*.............. **monticola** Kirkaldy.
          Anal segment entire beneath; lateral discal pronotal
          carinae evidently reaching hind margin and not apically
          curved outward toward sides; on *Styphelia* (*Cyathodes*)
          .... **nigrinervis** (Muir).

56(54).   Frons brownish-yellow or yellowish, but with apex in part
          or entirely and broadly dark and there concolorous
          with dark clypeus; Hawaii form...... **cyathodis** Kirkaldy.
          Frons vittate or nearly concolorous, but not apically fas-
          ciate..57

57(56).   Molokai species....................... **fullawayi** (Muir).
          Lanai species.......................... **lanaiensis** (Muir).

58(1).   Anterior profile of vertex as viewed from directly above
          with median carina conspicuously protuberant, as in
          figure 69, j...59

Anterior profile of vertex with median carina not so distinctly protuberant, more as in figure 69, k.............71

59(58). Profile of hind margin of pygophore, as seen from side, as in figure 76, l, with medio-ventral angle drawn out into a very prominent spine, and with a smaller spine at about midway up side (this may be partly concealed by long setae and may be difficult to see in certain lights); anal segment with apical part broad and each side expanded into a very large tooth which extends downward and obliquely outward to submedian lateral tooth on side of pygophore; apices of genital styles expanded and bifid, reaching anal segment; high mountains of Molokai.....................**palustris** Kirkaldy.

Not such species, even though medio-ventral angle of pygophore is protuberant and there is a tooth on side margin above it....................................60

60(59). Pygophore with ventro-median part produced into a very prominent spine and sides widely concave as viewed from side and enclosing anal segment in two prominent points which appear as in figure 76, a, when viewed from above.........................**olympica** (Muir).

Not so...61

61(60). Pygophore, as seen in profile from side, with hind margin as in figure 72, f, ventro-median angle produced to form a tooth-like process, and with a lateral, submedian tooth-like expansion (the former ventral process appearing pointed from the side, but when viewed from above it is blunt and rounded); anal segment with its ventro-lateral corners produced to form stout lobes as in figure 72, e.................**montis-tantalus** Muir.

Not so...62

62(61). Pygophore, as seen in profile from side, with a very large, broad, pointed tooth-like expansion as in figure 69, i; hind margin of anal segment turned caudad and downward at middle and there darker and more heavily sclerotized; genital styles narrow and horn-like, curving inwardly and tapering to points.......**gunnerae** Muir.

Pygophore not so formed.............................63

63(62). Pygophore as seen in profile from side with a large lobe-like expansion as in figure 69, a (genital styles partly twisted or otherwise placed so that their narrowest edges largely are presented to view from directly behind and their apices are subcontiguous or rather close together) 64

Pygophore not so formed, or if with a rather similar lobe-like expansion, then with apices of slender genital styles turned outward and assuming a sort of lyre-shape (as in fig. 63, a, of *koebelei*), or otherwise different......65

64(63). Tegmina leaving last two abdominal tergites plus pygophore exposed; length about 4.5 mm......**gigantea** (Muir).

Tegmina reaching nearly to apex of abdomen; length less than 4 mm......................**neowailupensis** (Muir).

(Note: These two forms appear to be close allies and
additional specimens should be studied to ascertain
their proper relationships.)

65(63). Pygophore as in figure 82, e (I am not sure that this
species belongs to this section, try also at 71.)........
....**cyrtandrae** Muir.
Not so...66

66(65). Pygophore crimped inward at edges toward apex of anal
segment (fig. 68, 1); anal segment unusually elongate,
with its hind margin heavily thickened, strongly produced, and not bearing teeth, and as in figure 68, k
..................................**gouldiae** Kirkaldy.
Pygophore not crimped in at hind edges of anal segment;
anal segment not thickened and produced posteriorly,
armed with a large, flange-like or fang-like tooth on
each side in all species except *timberlakei*..............67

67(66). Anal segment without spines; genital styles as seen in
broadest view as in figure 79, 1; aedeagus as in figure
79, k (I have seen only the dissected holotype); Oahu.
.... **timberlakei** Muir.
Anal segment with well-developed spines................68

68(67). Pygophore, in profile as viewed from side, with a prominent, lobe-like protuberance as in figure 77, m, of
sharpi, or if not the same, then as in figure 63, a, of
koebelei 69
Pygophore not so shaped...........................70

69(68). Genital styles slender, as in figure 77, 1, as seen from side
....**sharpi** Muir.
Genital styles broad and somewhat scythe-shaped as seen
from side, as in figure 70, j...............**koebelei** Muir.

70(68). Pale-yellow species from Maui with tegmina dark only
at apices of clavus and costal cell; aedeagus of unusual form, as in figure 79, d; genital styles apically
truncate with the angles slightly projecting. (Note:
I have not seen an entire example of this species.)....
....**sulcata** (Muir).
Yellowish-brown species from Oahu with tegmina extensively fuliginous; genital styles acuminate and with a
basal tooth-like process which is best seen from side
....**lobeliae** Muir.

71(58). Anal angles of pygophore conspicuously produced into
strong, pointed processes which largely surround anal
segment and project unusually far behind its caudal
margin (curved inward and downward as seen from
behind); armature of diaphragm very long, nearly as
long as inner side of a style beyond its basal angulation;
pygophore and appendages in anal and dorsal views
as illustrated. (Note: I have seen allied, similar-appearing new species from the type locality of this species
and taken with it.)..............**waikamoiensis** (Muir).
Not so...72

72(71). Pygophore as in figure 72, a, with anal angles produced
to form apically rounded processes which nearly meet
on median line and nearly enclose anal segment.....
....**longipes** (Muir).
Pygophore not so formed..............................73

73(72). Pygophore, in lateral profile, with a large, conspicuous,
submedian concavity in hind margin as in figure 72, j,
of *nephelias* or as in figure 64, a, of *aku*...............74
Pygophore not so shaped; if concave, then not as deeply
so and without such a contour......................76

74(73). Pygophore as in figure 82, e; genital styles with a tooth-
like lobe on inner side toward apex as in figures 67, c,
and 82, e.............................**cyrtandrae** Muir.
Pygophore obviously different; genital styles without
such a process so placed, if a lobe is present (*nephelias*),
it is placed distinctly lower down and apices of styles
are obviously differently shaped......................75

75(74). Pygophore, in full rear view, obviously distinctly broader
on a line drawn through bases of genital styles than
median height from same line to top of anal segment
....**aku** (Muir).
The pygophore very much narrower than high at above-
mentioned point.....................**nephelias** Kirkaldy.

76(73). A very large, robust species from highlands of Molokai,
about 4.5 mm. long.................**procellaris** Kirkaldy.
Not so...77

77(76). Underside of anal segment conspicuously concave, arch-
like; genital styles short; pygophore as in figure 62, c, d
.....................................**imbricola** Kirkaldy.
Underside of anal segment not arch-like...............78

78(77). Pygophore in lateral profile with submedian part of hind
(lateral) margin concave, as in figure 74, d, or rather
similar, more deeply concave in some species...........79
Pygophore with hind margin in profile not partly concave
as stated above.................................81

79(78). Large species, 4 mm. or longer; each genital style with a
small protuberance at its inner edge near base, which
when viewed from above is stoutly spine-shaped......
....**ulehihi** (Muir).
Smaller species, about 2 to 3 mm. long; genital styles
without such processes.............................80

80(79). Vertex about as broad as long; genital styles long, large
and heavy, extending up to level of anal segment.....
...............................**nephrolepidis** Kirkaldy.
Vertex nearly twice as long as broad; genital styles comparatively short and stocky, their apices remote from
anal segment............................**anceps** Muir.

81(78). Pygophore as viewed from directly behind as in figure
82, a; aedeagus shaped like an arrowhead and very
distinctive; ventral, caudal margin of pygophore with
a blunt, median protuberance.............**halia** Kirkaldy.
Without such characters..............................82

82(81). Anal segment transverse (fig. 80, f) ; a line drawn between
         apices of adjacent enclosing parts of pygophore (anal
         angles), as viewed from above, passes behind apex of
         anal segment; genital styles comparatively broad
         throughout......................**umbratica** Kirkaldy.
         Anal segment longer than broad; a line drawn between
         apices of adjacent enclosing parts of pygophore, as
         viewed from above, passing in front (cephalad) of
         hind margin of anal segment; genital styles broad or
         slender in caudal view.............................83

83(82). Pygophore in full rear view as in figure 82, d; genital
         styles broad; Oahu......................**swezeyi** Muir.
         Pygophore not so formed; genital styles slender in caudal
         view; Maui....................**neocyrtandrae** (Muir).

SECTION II: KEYS TO THE SPECIES OF EACH ISLAND

KEY TO THE KAUAI NESOSYDNE

(Males. Nine species.)

1.   Vertex of head strongly produced, distance between fore
         edge of an eye and apex is half or more than half as
         long as an eye when measured from side; tegmina
         milky with conspicuous dark granules on veins; male
         genital styles broad and flat; anal segment emarginate
         distad............................. **leahi** (Kirkaldy).
         Vertex not so produced, less than one-half as long as an
         eye as measured from side.......................... 2

2(1).   Median carinae of head conspicuously protuberant as
         viewed from directly above and obviously discontinu-
         ous with sides of apex of vertex, more as in figure
         69, j, than in 69, k.............................. 3
         Median carinae low and inconspicuous on vertex as seen
         from above, apex of vertex broadly rounded (do not
         be confused into believing median line is protuberant
         by differences in color of median line and adjacent
         areas of vertex, observe anterior silhouette only)...... 4

3(2).   Anal segment with prominent, divergent spines which
         have broad, semimembranous expansions and appear
         in rear view as in figure 66, f (spines extending down
         over tops of genital styles in holotype)..............
         ....**campylothecae** (Muir).
         Anal spines small, close together, obscure, not ordinarily
         visible from behind....................**kuschei** (Muir).

4(2).   Face vittate, black between pale median and lateral carinae. 5
         Face pale, not vittate................................. 6

5(4).   Pygophore and genitalia in rear view of a characteristic
         shape as in figure 82, b, as broad or broader than high;
         styles slender, widely separated, inner apical angles
         about twice as broadly separated as breadth of apex of
         a style..........................**ipomoeicola** Kirkaldy.

Pygophore of different shape, higher than broad; styles broad, their inner apical angles only as widely separated as breadth of apex of a style..............**naenae** (Muir).

6(4). Anal spines broad, stout, tooth-like; usually brachypterous..................................**viridis** (Muir).
 Anal spines long, slender, needle-like; usually macropterous 7

7(6). Tegmina with a characteristic, prominent dotting formed by unusually conspicuous dark granules on pale veins, dark color extending entirely across veins and slightly encroaching on membrane...........**koae-phyllodii** Muir.
 Tegmina not so spotted, granules hardly if any darker than veins, but if distinctly darker, then dark color is confined to veins which are darker than membrane and are often brown.................................. 8

8(7). Inner basal angles of genital styles, as seen from above, only slightly produced caudad; pale forms (green when living) ....**koae** Kirkaldy.
 Inner basal angles of genital styles distinctly produced into caudal knob-like protuberances (best seen obliquely from above); comparatively dark forms (reddish-brown or darker)............**rubescens** (Kirkaldy).

KEY TO THE OAHU NESOSYDNE

(Males. Twenty-nine species; *N. hamadryas* omitted.)

1. Ventral, caudal margin of pygophore with a conspicuous median protuberance (usually sub-spiniform).......... 2
 Pygophore without any median protuberance on lower hind edge...................................... 7

2(1). Anal segment with hind angles produced to form stout, round-ended processes............**montis-tantalus** Muir.
 Hind angles of anal segment not so produced............ 3

3(2). As viewed from above, with pygophore produced into long pointed processes which extend around and far beyond apex of anal segment (fig. 76, a)............
 .... **olympica** (Muir).
 Sides of pygophore not so formed.................... 4

4(3). Anal segment with hind margin turned caudad and downward at middle and there darker and more heavily sclerotized, shallowly concave and not elongated caudad
 .... **gunnerae** Muir.
 Anal segment not so formed, either produced caudad and more or less tongue-shaped, or normally rounded in shape 5

5(4). Anal segment normally rounded, not produced caudad, a line drawn between dorsal angles of pygophore passes at its hind edge (usual color pattern of males: generally pale species with contrasting dark pronotum and mesonotum and some dark maculae on tegmina usually most distinct at claval apices)................**halia** Kirkaldy.

Anal segment produced caudad and more or less tongue-
shaped 6

6(5).   Sides of pygophore, as seen from behind, with a conspicuous, recurved, somewhat hook-like tooth on inner margin above medio-ventral spine, the latter long and
pointed; genital styles short; anal segment without
large spines and unusually produced apically so that it
is about one-third longer than broad...........**sola** Muir.
Sides of pygophore broadly lobate as in figure 65, h,
ventro-median spine rather short and blunt; genital
styles long and extending up to the prominent anal
spines...................................**asteliae** Muir.

7(1).   Anterior edge of vertex, as viewed from directly above,
evenly or subcontinuously convex, median carinae not
or indistinctly protuberant and not obviously interrupting anterior outline............................ 8
Carinae, as they come into view over fore edge of vertex
as seen from above, distinctly protuberant and distinctly
interrupting anterior contour of vertex...............17

8(7).   First antennal segment, measured along dorsal edge from
front, longer than breadth of narrowest interocular
part of frons as seen from front..................... 9
First antennal segment shorter to much shorter than
breadth of narrowest interocular part of frons.........10

9(8).   Anal (dorsal) angles of pygophore produced into distinct
protuberances (as seen from above) which project distinctly behind caudal margin of anal segment, which is
strongly transverse and has its hind margin only
slightly arcuate, nearly subtruncate..................
................................**umbratica** Kirkaldy.
Anal angles of pygophore not produced; anal segment not
transverse, its hind margin projecting caudad of dorsal
angles of pygophore.....................**swezeyi** Muir.

10(8).   Anal angles of pygophore, as seen from above, appearing
to be produced into subtriangular protuberances which
partially envelop anal segment, a line drawn between
their hind edges passes through or slightly caudad of
hind margin of anal segment (intercarinal areas of
frons conspicuously dark; genital styles broad, and
heel and toe each produced so that from some angles
apex appears almost bifid; when viewed from side,
pygophore very nearly hides all enclosed structures
including styles)......................**oahuensis** Muir.
Anal angles of pygophore not so produced, or if slightly
produced, then anal segment projects behind anal angles..11

11(10). Face conspicuously vittate in all species except *nephrolepidis,* but even in that species intercarinal areas are
darker than carinae; genital styles either broadly expanded with inner apical angles well developed, or with
inner apical angles more strongly produced than outer
angles; never with combination of narrow genital styles
and concolorous face...............................12

Face nearly or quite concolorous and not vittate and not dark in all species except *ipomoeicola* which may have a distinctly vittate frons; genital styles in all species comparatively long and narrow and with inner apical angles at most moderately produced..................14

12(11). Pronotal keels dark; face at most vaguely vittate, never with carinae very pale with intercarinal areas black in sharp contrast; apices of genital styles broad and heavy, each with a small protuberance on inner margin below inner apical angle (best seen obliquely from above)........................**nephrolepidis** Kirkaldy.
Pronotal keels pale; face with keels pale and intercarinal spaces black, thus forming sharply contrasting vittae; genital styles not as described above..................13

13(12). Each genital style with inner apical angle strongly produced into a comparatively slender prolongation which is much longer than outer apical angle; on *Boehmeria* ....**boehmeria** (Muir).
Genital styles without such strongly prolonged inner apical angles, inner angles rather similar to outer apical angles; on *Pipturus*...................**pipturi** Kirkaldy.

14(11). First antennal segment about twice as long as broad; face usually vittate; pronotum and mesonotum usually dark; tegmina usually with a dark cloud...**ipomoeicola** Kirkaldy.
First antennal segment much shorter, either only about as long as broad or about two-fifths longer than broad, but never nearly twice as long as broad; face, pronotum and mesonotum usually pale, but if dark, then wings never with dark clouds.............................15

15(14). Face with round pale spots in derm; tegmina with a characteristic prominent dotting formed by unusually conspicuous dark granules on pale veins, dark color extending entirely across veins and slightly encroaching on membrane; first antennal segment about as broad as long.....................:**koae-phyllodii** Muir.
Face without such pale spots; tegmina not so spotted, granules hardly if any darker than veins, but if distinctly darker, then dark color is confined to veins which are darker than membrane and are often brown; first antennal segment one- or two-fifths longer along top edge than breadth.............................16

16(15). Inner basal angles of genital styles, as seen from above, only slightly produced; pale forms (green when living) ....**koae** Kirkaldy.
Inner basal angles of genital styles distinctly produced into caudal knob-like protuberances (best seen obliquely from above); more reddish-brown species...........
..............................**rubescens** (Kirkaldy).

17(7). Median frontal carina forking far down on front, near lower level of eyes or farther distad..................18
Median frontal carina forking near or on vertex..........20

18(17). Median frontal carina forking at or just above lower
level of eyes; anal segment produced caudad; pygophore in rear view as illustrated in figure 82, f;
aedeagus broadly expanded at apex........**giffardi** Muir.
Median frontal carina forking far down on face, between
lower edge of eyes and apex of frons.................19

19(18). Pygophore very short, nearly vertical behind and mostly
concealed from above; both inner and outer apical
angles of genital styles produced into sharp, conspicuous processes......................**wailupensis** (Muir).
Pygophore not so formed; genital styles with outer apical
angles bent cephalad instead of caudad as usual, so
that when viewed from side they appear bent forward
nearly at right angles beyond middle.........**rocki** Muir.

20(17). Vertex strongly produced and protuberant, as in figure
71, c; first antennal segment about as broad as long;
small, pale, lowland species with milky white tegmina
which are conspicuously spotted by coarse, dark granules on veins.......................**leahi** (Kirkaldy).
Vertex not so produced; first antennal segment obviously
longer than broad, usually conspicuously longer.......21

21(20). First antennal segment less than one-half as long as second (about one-third as long on holotype); (genital
styles broad and flat, inner apical angles broadly triangular and more produced than rounded outer apical
angles; aedeagus broad and thick at base, but rapidly narrowing to about middle, thence subequal in diameter,
strongly arched; only male seen is the dissected holotype
from which no characters of shape of pygophore can be
described)........................... **incommoda** Muir.
First antennal segment more than one-half as long as
second...22

22(21). Anal segment strongly produced caudad, its hind part
turned outward and downward and more or less shaped
like an extended tongue; pygophore, as seen from behind, pinched inward at hind edges of anal segment
..............................**gouldiae** Kirkaldy.
Anal segment not so formed.......................23

23(22). (Note: I have not examined an undissected specimen of
any of the following six species. Additional characters,
particularly of the pygophore, probably could be described if whole specimens were available for study.)
Pygophore, as seen in profile from side, with a large or
rather large lobe-like expansion as in figure 69, a;
(genital styles partly twisted or otherwise placed so
that their narrowest edges largely are presented to view
from directly behind and their apices are subcontiguous
or rather close together)..........................24
Pygophore not so formed, or if with a rather similar lateral lobe-like expansion, then with apices of slender
styles turned outward and assuming a sort of a lyre-
shape (as in figure of *koebelei*), or otherwise different...25

24(23). Tegmina leaving pygophore and last two abdominal ter-
           gites exposed; length about 4.5 mm.......**gigantea** (Muir).
         Tegmina reaching nearly to apex of abdomen; length less
           than 4 mm.....................**neowailupensis** (Muir).
25(23). Anal segment without spines; genital styles as seen in
           broadest view as in figure 79, 1; aedeagus as in figure
           79, k..............................**timberlakei** Muir.
         Anal segment with well-developed spines...............26
26(25). Aedeagus peculiarly shaped as in figure 77, j, greatly
           expanded dorsally and ventrally into a broad "head";
           anal spines long, slender, recurved, shaped like a
           snake's fangs (as seen from side), as in figure 77, k;
           genital styles shaped as in figure 77, l........**sharpi** Muir.
         Not such species, although anal spines may be fang-like...27
27(26). Genital styles curved outward (strongly divergent) be-
           yond middle (as seen from behind); styles, aedeagus
           and anal spines shaped as in figure 70, j–1............
           ....**koebelei** Muir.
         Genital styles slightly convergent (as seen from behind);
           styles, aedeagus and anal spines as in figure 71, h–j
           ....**lobeliae** Muir.

KEY TO THE MOLOKAI NESOSYDNE

(Males. Five species.)

1.   Median keels not strongly protuberant as they come into
           view over fore edge of vertex as seen from above,
           vertex rather evenly convex in front; lower hind mar-
           gin of pygophore without a median protuberance...... 2
         Median keels of vertex distinctly protuberant and discon-
           tinuous with remainder of profile of fore edge of ver-
           tex; caudal margin of pygophore produced into a con-
           spicuous protuberance at middle.................... 4
2(1).   A very large, bulky species about 4 mm. or more long;
           first antennal segment about three times as long as
           broad, about three-fourths as long as second segment
           and longer than breadth of narrowest interocular
           breadth of frons..................**procellaris** Kirkaldy.
         Much smaller species; first antennal segment either about
           as long as broad or about twice as long as broad,
           shorter than narrowest interocular breadth........... 3
3(2).   A tiny species about 1.5–2.0 mm. in length; first antennal
           segment only slightly longer than broad; genital styles
           broad, flat, expanded at apices on both inner and outer
           corners, so arranged that gap between them formed by
           their inner edges is O-shaped; tegmina not reaching
           end of abdomen.....................**fullawayi** (Muir).
         Usually over 2 mm. long; first antennal segment nearly
           twice as long as broad; genital styles long and slender,
           space between them U-shaped; tegmina surpassing
           apex of pygophore................**ipomoeicola** Kirkaldy.

4(1).   Pygophore shaped as in figure 76, 1, with a small spine-
line protuberance about half way up side, sides not
excavate (as seen from side).........**palustris** Kirkaldy.
Pygophore shaped as in figure 61, b, sides excavate at
about middle (as seen from side) and without a submedian spine on lateral margin, but with a spine on
lateral margin at about lower third.....**nubigena** Kirkaldy.

KEY TO THE LANAI NESOSYDNE

(Males. Seven species.)

1.   First antennal segment at most only slightly longer than
broad 2
First antennal segment much longer than broad........ 3

2(1).   Usually brachypterous; only about 1.5–2.0 mm. long;
genital styles comparatively broad and flat; on *Styphelia*
..................................**lanaiensis** (Muir).
Normally macropterous; over 2.0 mm. in body length
(4.5 mm. including tegmina); genital styles comparatively long and slender; on *Acacia*...................
..............................**rubescens** (Kirkaldy).

3(1).   Fore contour of vertex as viewed from above conspicuously interrupted by the strongly protuberant median
carinae; median frontal carina forking near (but obviously above) lower level of eyes.....**nesogunnerae** Muir.
Fore contour of vertex as seen from above subcontinuously convex and carinae not obviously protuberant..... 4

4(3).   Pygophore as viewed from side with two large, concave
excavations in caudal margin as in figure 61, e, f; dorsal anal angles of pygophore as seen from above, projecting, incurved and appearing to grasp anal segment;
genital styles shaped as in figure 72, k, l............
....................................**nephelias** Kirkaldy.
Not such species................................... 5

5(4).   Genital styles long, slender, erect, comparatively narrowly exposed in rear view, obviously distinct from
shape and proportions of following two species, space
between them broadly open and broadly U-shaped....
..............................**ipomoeicola** Kirkaldy.
Not so; styles broadly exposed in rear view, inner apical
angles, if brought together, with space between them
sub-O-shaped 6

6(5).   Face, genae, pronotum and scutellum mostly black;
aedeagus not shaped like an arrowhead............
....................................**nigriceps** Muir.
Face, genae, pronotum and scutellum marked with black
but mostly pale; aedeagus strongly barbed apically and
thus appearing arrowhead-like or harpoon-like in outline ....**hamata** Muir.

KEY TO THE MAUI NESOSYDNE

(Males. Thirty-four species; *N. haleakala* omitted.)

1.   First antennal segment rarely twice as long as broad, if
          about twice as long as broad, then never longer than
          narrowest interocular breadth of frons (measure length
          along top edge and breadth at apex)................. 2
        First antennal segment usually distinctly more than
          twice as long as broad, always fully as long as or dis-
          tinctly longer than narrowest interocular breadth........26

2(1).   Caudal margin of pygophore with a prominent, tooth-like
          or blunt, spine-like, median protuberance on lower
          margin............................**amaumau** (Muir).
        Pygophore without a median protuberance on lower hind
          margin 3

3(2).   Median frontal carina forking far down on face, at or
          below lower level of eyes, thus double for most of its
          length 4
        Median carina forking much higher on face, nearer fore
          angle of vertex..................................... 7

4(3).   Vertex, when viewed from directly above, unusually
          short and broad, median line shorter than breadth of
          base; a tiny species, tegmina less than 1.0 mm. long on
          male holotype; first antennal segment about 0.7 as
          long as broad......................**ahinahina** (Muir).
        Vertex conspicuously longer than broad and/or tegmina
          over 1.5 mm. long................................... 5

5(4).   Median frontal carina forking at about lower level of
          eyes; vertex little longer along median line than
          breadth of base..........................**perkinsi** Muir.
        Median frontal carina forking below lower level of eyes,
          nearer apex; vertex conspicuously longer than broad.... 6

6(5).   Protuberance formed on vertex by median frontal carinae
          narrow and comparatively sharply and narrowly pro-
          tuberant; genae and areas between carinae on frons and
          clypeus yellowish-brown, not black; first antennal seg-
          ment about one-third longer than broad...**kokolau** (Muir).
        Protuberance formed on vertex by median carinae of face
          broad and low; genae and intercarinal areas on clypeus
          and frons black; first antennal segment about twice as
          long as broad..........................**painiu** (Muir).

7(3).   First antennal segment less than twice as long as broad,
          usually distinctly shorter (measure carefully, for op-
          tical illusions may confuse you)..................... 8
        First antennal segment approximately twice as long as
          broad...21

8(7).   Tegmina usually subopaque and whitish, but always con-
          spicuously spotted by comparatively large, coarse, dark
          granules on veins................................... 9
        Tegmina not conspicuously spotted, even if whitish or
          subopaque, granules not prominent...................11

9(8). Outer apical angles of genital styles not strongly produced as in *osborni* (fig. 76, e) and *bridwelli* (fig. 66, a),
but inner apical angle appearing more produced; lateral
outlines of caudal margin of pygophore as seen directly
from rear arcuate but not very lobate (as in fig.
81, d) thus appearing comparatively narrow and higher
than broad........................**tetramolopii** (Muir).

Outer apical angles of genital styles strongly produced
as in figures 66, a, and 76, e; lateral outlines of caudal
margin of pygophore as seen from directly behind
rather strongly, broadly lobate (as in fig. 81, c)........10

10(9). Aedeagus expanded at apex as in figure 76, g...........
....**osborni** Muir.

Aedeagus slender, acuminate, as in figure 66, b........
..................................**bridwelli** (Muir).

11(8). Distance between fore edge of an eye and lateral facial
carina only about one-half as great as distance from
lateral facial carina to apex of angle between frons and
vertex (as seen in profile from side); an entirely pale
species; as seen from directly above, top of pygophore
broadly concave behind as in figure 73, c, not notched in a
sub-V-shape, anal segment conspicuously exposed from
above...............................**mauiensis** (Muir).

Distance from fore edge of an eye to lateral facial carina
greater than, as great as, or nearly as great as distance
from lateral facial carina to apex of frons as seen from
side; either pale or dark species, but if pale, pygophore
not shaped as above................................12

12(11). Tegmina very short, not reaching pygophore............13
Tegmina reaching or surpassing pygophore.............15

13(12). Pronotum short, median keel only about as long as distance between its apex and apex of a lateral keel, or
shorter..........................**nigrinervis** (Muir).

Median keel of pronotum fully two-thirds or three-
fourths as long as distance between hind ends of lateral
pronotal keels 14

14(13). Very dark species, most of body black; pygophore exposed from above and with styles fully and broadly
exposed from side (as in fig. 65, g)...............
..............................**argyroxiphii** Kirkaldy.

Paler, brownish species with nota of thorax, top of head
and legs pale; pygophore almost entirely withdrawn
beneath last complete abdominal tergite and almost
entirely concealed from above and from side.........
....**eeke** (Muir).

15(12). Face pale between carinae; tegmina without dark maculae; macropterous forms....................16

Face black between carinae; tegmina with dark maculae;
brachypterous forms 17

16(15). Genital styles short and broad........**pseudorubescens** Muir.
Genital styles long and slender........**rubescens** (Kirkaldy).

17(15). An almost entirely black species, keels of face and thoracic nota all black; pygophore shaped as in figure
72, i; genital styles short, not or barely extending up
beyond dorsal edge of diaphragm, their ectal angles
more strongly produced than inner apical angles and
near where their tips reach sides of pygophore there is
a rather obscure (usually) inwardly projecting boss-
like protuberance of inner wall of edge of pygophore
..................................**monticola** Kirkaldy.
Not such species....................................18

18(17). Genital styles each with a prominent boss or protuberance
on posterior face at about middle of inner edge, appearing conspicuously protuberant when viewed from directly above 19
Without such protuberances on genital styles............20

19(18). Protuberance on inner edge of genital styles round and
boss-like as in figure 78, i–k; aedeagus angulate at apex
....**pilo** (Muir).
Protuberance on inner edge of genital styles elongate,
not round, as in figure 69, l, m; aedeagus roundly subtruncate at apex...................**imbricola** Kirkaldy.

20(18). Outer apical angles of genital styles more strongly produced than inner angles, space between inner edges
of styles more nearly inverted keyhole-shaped than
O-shaped; underside of anal segment conspicuously
concave ....**raillardiicola** (Muir).
Inner apical angles of styles more strongly produced than
outer angles, space between inner edges O-shaped;
underside of anal segment not concave.....**geranii** (Muir).

21(7). Genital styles long and slender, reaching anal segment,
space between them wide-open and U-shaped........
..............................**ipomoeicola** Kirkaldy.
Genital styles not so formed, broad and flat as seen from
behind 22

22(21). Genital styles short, not extending above top edge of
diaphragm, distant from lower edge of anal segment,
which is grooved or arch-like beneath................23
Genital styles longer, extending above diaphragm to near
lower edge of anal segment which is not grooved or
arch-like beneath except in *dubautiae*..................24

25(22). Anal segment broadly concave and arch-like beneath,
anal spines far distant from aedeagus; genital styles,
as seen from directly above, each with a prominent protuberance projecting caudad at about middle of inner
side.............................**imbricola** Kirkaldy.
Anal segment comparatively narrowly grooved beneath,
anal spines close to aedeagus; genital styles plain, without any protuberance from inner edges.............
..............................**stenogynicola** (Muir).

24(22). Genital styles peculiarly formed as in figure 74, f, outer
apical angle broadly and strongly produced, inner edge
strongly irregular in posterior outline as seen from

side, with a conspicuous protuberance below inner apical angle..................**nephrolepidis** Kirkaldy.
Genital styles not so formed.........................25

25(24). Inner basal angles of styles not strongly produced, space between inner margins of styles thus collectively elongate-lenticular in outline from base to apex; underside of anal segment not obviously arch-like...........
....**mamake** (Muir).
Inner basal angles of styles strongly protuberant, space between their inner margins roughly inverted subcordate in shape from just below middle to apex; underside of anal segment arch-like with anal spines widely separated and divergent..............**dubautiae** (Muir).

26(1). Dorsal apical (anal) angles of pygophore produced so that a line drawn between their apices encloses anal segment 27
Anal angles of pygophore not produced, a line drawn between their apices passes in front of caudal margin of anal segment 29

27(26). Anal angles of pygophore not so strongly produced nor curved inward as described below; diaphragm normally concealed by styles, much narrower at sides of armature than distance between lower end of armature and lowest part of caudal margin of pygophore; armature broad and heavy........................**umbratica** Kirkaldy.
Anal angles of pygophore unusually strongly prolonged, curved strongly inward and downward toward aedeagus when viewed from behind, projecting far beyond anal segment when viewed from directly above and curved inward toward each other so that their apices are closer together than breadth of anal segment; diaphragm unusually wide, longer at side of armature than distance from lower end of armature to lowest part of caudal margin of pygophore, broadly exposed; armature long and narrow 28

28(27). Pygophore, when viewed directly from side, with projecting anal angles distinctly visible as in figure 81, a, and appearing somewhat as hook-like protuberances; inner margin of genital style with an irregularity or projection slightly basad of middle................
.............................**waikamoiensis** (Muir).
Pygophore, when viewed directly from side, with projecting anal angles not visible, as in figure 72, a; inner margin of genital style with a tooth-like protuberance just distad of middle...................**longipes** (Muir).

29(26). Genital styles broad and flat, expanded to very broad apices, without protuberances on inner margin above middle...30
Genital styles comparatively long and slender and/or narrowing distad and/or with a protuberance on inner margin above middle...........................31

30(29). When viewed from directly above, inner hind margins of genital styles are seen to be on an even plane from base

to apex and not made irregular by protuberances or
irregularities of contour..................**acuta** (Muir).
Genital styles, as seen from directly above, with inner
margins obviously discontinuous, projecting somewhat
caudad at about middle and with basal angles protuberant.............................**nesopele** (Muir).

31(29). (Note: I have examined only the holotypes of the following three species. The pygophores had been removed
and the parts mounted in balsam on slides.)
Anal spines very large, curved caudad or outward; aedeagus unusually broad, apex blunt, with transverse rows
of teeth and a deep dorsal groove (fig. 79, d); genital
styles as in figure 79, e..................**sulcata** (Muir).
Anal spines curved cephalad; aedeagus slender, acuminate, teeth arranged in longitudinal rows; genital styles
each with a well-developed, tooth-like, subapical protuberance as in figures 67, c, and 73, e.................32

32(31). Genital styles, anal spines and aedeagus as in figure
67, c–e ....**cyrtandrae** Muir.
Genital styles, anal spines and aedeagus as in figure
73, e, g, h.......................**neocyrtandrae** (Muir).

KEY TO THE HAWAII NESOSYDNE

(Males. Seventeen forms.)

1.   First antennal segment distinctly less than twice as long
as broad 2
First antennal segment about twice as long as broad or
distinctly longer 11

2(1).   Tegmina conspicuously dotted by prominent setigerous
granules; median carinae of frons and vertex prom-
inently raised; genital styles broad and flat, outer
apical angles sub-hook-shaped; anal segment broadly
arch-like beneath, anal spines broadly separated......
................................**chambersi** Kirkaldy.
Without such a combination of characters.............. 3

3(2).   Tiny species from *Styphelia,* usually distinctly less than 2
mm. long; tegmina less than 1 mm. long, subopaque,
milky-white; vertex and most of frons yellow, most
of genae, clypeus and a broad band across apex of frons
dark; length of median pronotal carina shorter than
distance between its caudal end and apex of a lateral
carina...........................**cyathodis** Kirkaldy.
Not such species................................... 4

4(3).   Anal segment (as viewed from directly above) with hind
margin deeply, broadly, conspicuously emarginate as
in figure 66, i...................**coprosmicola** (Muir).
Anal segment without such a deep, broad emargination,
at most only slightly emarginate (compare *neoraillardiae*). 5

5(4).   Genital styles (as seen from directly behind) broad and
flatly exposed or short and broad..................... 6

Genital styles (as seen from directly behind) elongate, comparatively long and slender and/or comparatively narrow as seen from behind...... 8

6(5). Genital styles short, not strongly expanded at outer apical angles; anal segment not broadly arch-like beneath...
............**pseudorubescens** Muir.
Genital styles broadly expanded outward at outer apices as in figures 74, a, and 77, f; anal segment broadly concave beneath 7

7(6). Genital styles each expanded at outer apical angles to form long expansions as in figure 77, f (on *Raillardia*)
............**raillardiae** Kirkaldy.
Genital styles with outer apical angles less strongly produced as in figure 74, a (on *Lipochaeta*)............
.... **neoraillardiae** (Muir).

8(5). Diaphragm of pygophore appearing more nearly horizontal than vertical; armature thin, lamella-like, long from back to front, its dorsal edge armed with a pair of divergent spines............**phyllostegiae** Muir.
Diaphragm placed more nearly vertical; armature thick, stout 9

9(8). When viewed from directly above, inner basal angles of genital styles only slightly protuberant caudad; pale forms (green when living)............**koae** Kirkaldy.
When viewed from above, inner basal angles of styles comparatively strongly protuberant; comparatively dark forms 10

10(9). Mesonotum yellowish-brown......**rubescens** (Kirkaldy).
Mesonotum dark brown or mostly black............
............**rubescens pele** (Kirkaldy).

11(1). Anal angles of pygophore(as seen from directly above) produced into distinct protuberances which project distinctly caudad of hind margin of anal segment......12
Anal angles of pygophore not produced and not protuberant 13

12(11). Pygophore, as seen directly from side, with hind edge only slightly concave below protuberant anal angle and without an angle on margin at about middle, not as in figure 64, a......**umbratica** Kirkaldy.
Pygophore with caudal margin deeply excavated below protuberant anal angle and with an angle at about middle, as in figure 64, a......**aku** (Muir).

13(11). First antennal segment fully three times as long as broad, one-third longer than narrowest interocular breadth..
.... **ulehihi** (Muir).
First antennal segment only about twice as long as broad and at most barely longer than narrowest interocular breadth 14

14(15). Genital styles long and rather slender, comparatively narrowly exposed from rear view, apices widely separated, space between them widely open and U-shaped......
.... **ipomoeicola** Kirkaldy.
Styles broadly and flatly exposed to rear view......15

15(14). Outer apical angle of each genital style strongly produced to
form a long, acute triangle, its dorsal margin nearly
straight as in figure 67, g; inner margins without any
protuberances above base............**cyrtandricola** Muir..
Genital styles not so formed, inner margins expanded or
protuberant above middle........................16

16(15). Median length of vertex only slightly longer than breadth
at base; genital styles extending up to level of anal
segment, shaped as in figure 74, f......................
....................................**nephrolepidis** Kirkaldy.
Median length of vertex about twice as long as breadth
across base; genital styles rather short, not extending
much above dorsal level of diaphragm.......**anceps** Muir.

All the species in the following list are brachypterous in both sexes. as far as
is known, unless otherwise mentioned.

The types of Muir's species are in the collection of the Hawaiian Sugar Planters'
Association Experiment Station in Honolulu, and those of Kirkaldy's are in
the British Museum with the exception of those mentioned below as being now
in the Bishop Museum.

Nesosydne acuta (Muir), new combination (fig. 64, g–j).
Ilburnia acuta Muir, 1919:96, pl. 4, figs. 9, 11.

Endemic. Maui (type locality: "Ridge South of Iao Valley").
Hostplant: *Cyrtandra mauiensis.*

Nesosydne ahinahina (Muir), new combination (fig. 64, f).
Ilburnia pulla Muir, 1919:98, pl. 3, fig. 6; pl. 4, fig. 17. Not Muir, 1916:186.
Ilburnia ahinahina Muir, 1922:102.

Endemic. Maui (type locality: Mount Eke (Eeke), 5,000 feet).
Hostplant: *Argyroxiphium* ("ahinahina"; the native word means silvery gray
and refers to the color of *Argyroxiphium,* the silversword plant).

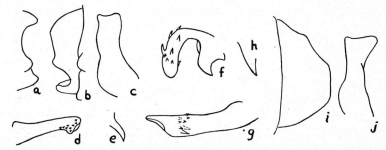

Figure 64—Details of *Nesosydne* genitalia. **a–e,** *N. aku* (Muir): **(a)** outline of caudal margin of pygophore of holotype from left side, at a more dorsally oblique angle than **b**; **(b)**
same as **a**, but directly from right side of paratype; **(c)** right style in balsam; **(d)** aedeagus
in balsam; **(e)** anal spine in balsam. **f,** *N. ahinahina* (Muir), aedeagus in balsam. **g–j,** *N.*
acuta (Muir): **(g)** aedeagus in balsam; **(h)** anal spine in balsam; **(i)** outline of caudal
margin of pygophore as seen from right side; **(j)** right style in balsam.

Nesosydne aku (Muir), new combination (fig. 64, a–e).
Ilburnia aku Muir, 1921:513, pl. 8, figs. 14, 14a.

Endemic. Hawaii (type locality: Olaa, 23 miles, 2,300 feet).
Hostplant: *Cyanea tritomantha* ("aku").

Nesosydne amaumau (Muir), new combination and emendation (fig. 65, a–d).
Ilburnia amamau Muir, 1921:512, pl. 8, figs. 19, 19a.

Endemic. Maui (type locality: Mount Haleakala, 6,100 feet).
Hostplant: *Sadleria* fern ("amaumau").
"The nymphs are uniformly light brown. There is the usual tendency for some specimens to be lighter than others and for the females to be lighter than the males. This species comes next to *I. painiu* Muir, to which it is closely related." (Muir, 1921:513.)

Because of a misspelling in Hillebrand's *Flora of the Hawaiian Islands,* Muir called this species *"amamau"* instead of *"amaumau."* He obviously named the insect after its hostplant, and we should correct the spelling.

Nesosydne anceps Muir (fig. 65, e, f).
Nesosydne anceps Muir, 1916:187, pl. 2, fig. 34.
Ilburnia anceps (Muir), of authors.

Endemic. Hawaii (type locality: Glenwood).
Hostplant: *Freycinetia* (Giffard, 1918:411, notes).

Nesosydne argyroxiphii Kirkaldy (fig. 65, g).
Nesosydne argyroxiphii Kirkaldy, 1908:203, fig. 1; pl. 4, fig. 6. 1910:590.
Ilburnia argyroxiphii (Kirkaldy) Muir, 1919:89, female.

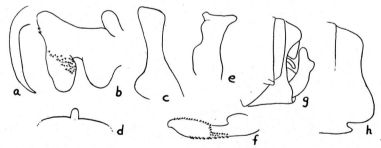

Figure 65—Details of *Nesosydne* genitalia. **a–d,** *N. amaumau* (Muir): **(a)** anal spine; **(b)** aedeagus; **(c)** right style (**a–c,** in balsam); **(d)** ventral part of hind margin of pygophore as seen from directly above to show median protuberance. **e, f,** *N. anceps* Muir: **(e)** right style in balsam; **(f)** aedeagus in balsam (anal spines long and slender, but not drawn because of their poor position on the slide). **g,** *N. argyroxiphii* Kirkaldy, outline of pygophore as seen from left side. **h,** *N. asteliae* Muir, cotype, outline of caudal margin of pygophore from left side.

Endemic. Maui (type locality: Haleakala Crater, about 10,000 feet).

Hostplant: *Argyroxiphium sandwicense.*

Kirkaldy (1910:590) described the last instar nymphs as follows: "brownish testaceous, largely suffused with dark fuscous." The insect feeds upon young silversword plants.

The eggs are evidently parasitized by a *Polynema* mymarid wasp.

The holotype is in the British Museum. Perkins says in his letter that "I found this species in great abundance, together with the larvae of a remarkable (undescribed) Phycitid moth, but I suppose the leaf-hoppers were lost." The moth referred to was later described by Hampson as *Rhynchephestia rhabdotis.*

Nesosydne asteliae Muir (figs. 63, f; 65, h).

Nesosydne asteliae Muir, 1917:307, pl. 5, fig. 13.

Ilburnia asteliae (Muir), of authors.

Endemic. Oahu (type locality: Mount Kaala, 4,000 feet).

Hostplant: *Astelia veratroides.*

This appears to be an ally of *halia.*

Nesosydne boehmeria (Muir), new combination (fig. 66, c).

Ilburnia boehmeria Muir, 1921:514, pl. 8, figs. 12, 12a.

Endemic. Oahu (type locality: Makaleha Valley).

Hostplant: *Boehmeria.*

This form is much like *pipturi.*

Nesosydne bridwelli (Muir), new combination (figs. 66, a, b; 81, c).

Ilburnia bridwelli Muir, 1919:90, pl. 3, fig. 3; pl. 4, fig. 20.

Endemic. Maui (type locality: Mount Haleakala, about 7,000 feet, near Puu Nianiau).

Hostplants: *Argyroxiphium virescens, Argyroxiphium sandwicense, Dubautia.*

"The nymph is dark brown, lighter on carinae, at base of abdomen and mottled over tegminal pads." (Muir, 1919:91.)

This form is so much like *osborni* that I feel further study is required to clarify its position.

Nesosydne campylothecae (Muir), new combination (fig. 66, d–f).

Ilburnia campylothecae Muir, 1922:97, pl. 3, fig. 11.

Endemic. Kauai (type locality: Kumuwela).

Hostplant: *Campylotheca.*

Nesosydne chambersi Kirkaldy (fig. 66, g, h).

Nesosydne chambersi Kirkaldy, 1908:202, pl. 4, figs. 10–12; 1910:590. Muir, 1916:142, pl. 3, fig. 44.

Ilburnia chambersi (Kirkaldy), of authors.

Endemic. Hawaii (type locality: Kilauea, 4,000 feet).

Hostplant: *Raillardia ciliolata.*

The type mount consisting of two pairs is now in the Bishop Museum. Perkins remarks in his letter that "I could not find specimens of this with name attached, but one card of mine had a red label and are clearly this species. They are not the earliest I took, however. It is curious that K. should have omitted reference to my specimens of this species because he must have known it was in connection with these small species on *Raillardia* that I made special observations on *Pipunculus.* He apparently did not describe at all the extremely abundant species on *Pipturus,* on which I particularly noticed *Stylops, Gonatopus,* and *Pipunculus* and also the ineffective attacks of *Nesomimesa* at Kilauea."

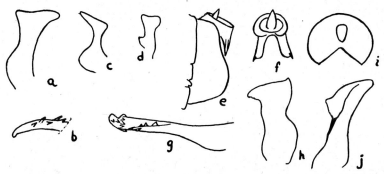

Figure 66—*Nesosydne* genitalia details. **a, b,** *N. bridwelli* (Muir): **(a)** right style; **(b)** apical part of aedeagus as seen protruding from holotype, dry. **c,** *N. boehmeria* (Muir): right style (dry) of holotype. **d–f,** *N. campylothecae* (Muir): **(d)** right style, in balsam; **(e)** pygophore as seen from left side; **(f)** anal segment from behind. **g, h,** *N. chambersi* Kirkaldy: **(g)** aedeagus, in balsam; **(h)** left style. **i, j,** *N. coprosmicola* (Muir): **(i)** anal segment as seen from above; **(j)** right style of paratype.

Nesosydne coprosmicola (Muir), new combination (fig. 66, i, j).

Ilburnia coprosmicola Muir, 1919:103, pl. 4, fig. 18.

Endemic. Hawaii (type locality: Olaa, 27 miles).

Hostplant: *Coprosma ernodioides.*

The nymphs are dark brown with paler markings.

Nesosydne cyathodis Kirkaldy (fig. 67, a, b).

Nesosydne cyathodis Kirkaldy, 1910:589. Muir, 1916:192, pl. 3, fig. 48.

Ilburnia cyathodis (Kirkaldy), of authors.

Endemic. Hawaii (type locality: Kilauea, 4,000 feet).

Hostplant: *Styphelia (Cyathodes) tameiameiae.*

Kirkaldy (1910:589) described the last instar nymphs.

There is a group of closely allied forms centering around this species. Muir (1919:91) decided that they were equivalent to subspecies and varieties and he listed varieties *fullawayi, lanaiensis,* and *nigrinervis* and subspecies *eeke* hereunder. He said that these forms "are of great interest as among them we have considerable chroötic but practically no phallic differences." However, I believe that there are quite distinct phallic differences. The two forms with most closely similar aedeagi and genital styles are *fullawayi* and *lanaiensis,* but, as my sketches illustrate, the other forms have greater differences. The differences evident in the drawings together with external differences which are striking in some of the species lead me to consider that these forms are entitled to specific rank.

Perkins, in a letter, states that he took this species and *raillardiae* in 1903 when he was collecting a *Pipunculus* which flew around the plants infested by the species, but Kirkaldy did not credit him with taking either of the species.

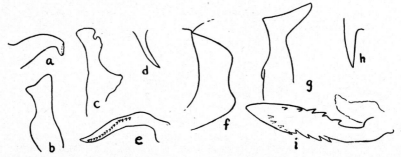

Figure 67—*Nesosydne* genitalia. **a, b,** *N. cyathodis* Kirkaldy: **(a)** aedeagus, in balsam; **(b)** right style, in balsam. **c–e,** *N. cyrtandrae* Muir, holotype, parts in balsam: **(c)** right style; **(d)** anal spine; **(e)** aedeagus. **f–i,** *N. cyrtandricola* Muir: **(f)** outline of pygophore as seen from left side; **(g)** right style of cotype; **(h)** anal spine in balsam; **(i)** aedeagus in balsam.

Nesosydne cyrtandrae Muir (figs. 67, c–e; 82, e).

Nesosydne cyrtandrae Muir, 1916:189, pl. 3, fig. 38; pl. 4, figs. 67, 69.

Ilburnia cyrtandrae (Muir), of authors.

Endemic. Maui (type locality: Nahiku).

Hostplant: *Cyrtandra.*

The male holotype is a dissected, teneral individual with the right side of the interocular part of the frons collapsed to such an extent that I cannot be certain of the degree of protuberance of the median carina on the fronto-vertex angle. The original description is inadequate.

Nesosydne cyrtandricola Muir (fig. 67, f–i).

Nesosydne cyrtandricola Muir, 1918:407, figs. 1, 2.

Ilburnia cyrtandricola (Muir), of authors.

Endemic. Hawaii (type locality: Glenwood, Olaa, 2,300 feet).

Hostplants: *Cyrtandra, Charpentiera obovata.*

"The young nymphs are light green, later acquiring dark marks similar to the adults. The species comes near to *N. anceps* but is quite distinct." (Muir, 1918:407.)

Nesosydne dubautiae (Muir), new combination (fig. 68, a, b).

Ilburnia dubautiae Muir, 1921:510, pl. 8, fig. 10.

Endemic. Maui (type locality: ridge south of Iao Valley, 2,000 feet).

Hostplant: *Dubautia plantaginea.*

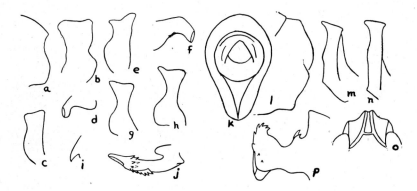

Figure 68—Genitalia of *Nesosydne*. **a, b,** *N. dubautiae* (Muir): **(a)** hind margin of pygophore as seen from left; **(b)** left style. **c, d,** *N. eeke* (Muir): **(c)** right style in balsam; **(d)** aedeagus in balsam. **e, f,** *N. fullawayi* (Muir), holotype: **(e)** right style; **(f)** aedeagus, dry dissection. **g–j,** *N. geranii* (Muir): **(g)** right style, paratype, in balsam; **(h)** right style of another example from a slightly different angle, in balsam; **(i)** anal spine in balsam; **(j)** aedeagus, in balsam. **k–o,** *N. gouldiae* Kirkaldy: **(k)** anal segment; **(l)** hind edge of pygophore as seen from left side; **(m)** right style, oblique caudad view; **(n)** right style directly from rear; **(o)** vertex as seen from above. **p,** *N. giffardi* Muir, aedeagus, dry dissection.

Nesosydne eeke (Muir), new combination (fig. 68, c, d).

Ilburnia cyathodis subspecies *eeke* Muir, 1919:92.

Endemic. Maui (type locality: Mount Eke (Eeke), 5,000 feet).

Hostplant: *Argyroxiphium.*

I have raised this form to full specific rank, for I believe that its characters indicate that it is not just a subspecies of *cyathodis*. Its facies is really quite distinct from that of *cyathodis*.

Nesosydne fullawayi (Muir), new combination (fig. 68, e, f).

Ilburnia fullawayi Muir, 1916:192.

Ilburnia cyathodis variety *fullawayi* (Muir) Muir, 1919:91.

Endemic. Molokai (type locality: Kamoku).

Hostplant: *Styphelia (Cyathodes)*.

Muir (1916:193) recorded this species from Maui, but I doubt that it occurs on that island. I consider this form specifically distinct from *N. cyathodis* (see the discussion under that species).

Nesosydne gcranii (Muir), new combination (fig. 68, g–j).

Ilburnia geranii Muir, 1921:515, pl. 8, figs. 13, 13a.

Endemic. Maui (type locality: Mount Haleakala, 6,000 feet).

Hostplant: *Geranium arboreum*.

According to Muir, the nymphs are pale brown with dark brown at the bases of the tegminal pads and on the sides of the abdominal tergites.

This species was originally called *geraniorum* by Muir and his type series was so labeled; then the labels were written over to *geranii* (the published name), but the correction is not always very distinct on the specimen labels.

Nesosydne giffardi Muir (figs. 68, p; 82, f).

Nesosydne giffardi Muir, 1916:194, pl. 3, fig. 54; pl. 4, fig. 74.

Ilburnia giffardi (Muir), of authors.

Endemic. Oahu (type locality: Mount Tantalus).

Hostplants: *Cyrtandra grandiflora, Rollandia crispa*.

Nesosydne gigantea (Muir), new combination (fig. 69, a, b).

Ilburnia gigantea Muir, 1921:517, pl. 8, fig. 15.

Endemic. Oahu (type locality: Castle Trail, about 2,000 feet).

Hostplant: *Pritchardia* palm.

This species shares with *I. procellaris* the distinction of being the largest in the genus (4.5 mm.). It is closely similar to *I. neowailupensis* in structure of the pygophore and its appendages.

Nesosydne gouldiae Kirkaldy (fig. 68, k–o).

Nesosydne gouldiae Kirkaldy, 1910:586. Muir, 1916:189, pl. 3, fig. 39.

Ilburnia gouldiae (Kirkaldy), of authors.

Endemic. Oahu (type locality: Mount Tantalus).

Hostplants: *Cyrtandra grandiflora, Cyrtandra* sp. (The species was originally recorded from *Gouldia,* and so specifically named, but the host record was erroneous.)

The nymphs have been described by Kirkaldy (1910:586). The type is supposedly in the British Museum.

Nesosydne gunnerae Muir (figs. 63, i ; 69, h–j).
  Nesosydne gunnerae Muir, 1917:305, pl. 5, fig. 15.
  Ilburnia gunnerae (Muir), of authors.

Endemic. Oahu (type locality: Mount Kaala, about 4,000 feet).
  Hostplants: *Gunnera petaloidea* (adults and nymphs mostly along the under-sides of the midribs of old leaves); accidental (?) captures on *Pelea, Coprosma longifolia* and *Myrsine* (*Suttonia*).

Nesosydne haleakala Kirkaldy (fig. 62, e).
  Nesosydne haleakala Kirkaldy, 1910:587. Muir, 1916:197.
  Ilburnia haleakala (Kirkaldy), of authors.

Endemic. Maui (type locality: Mount Haleakala, 5,000 feet).
  I have seen only two damaged specimens, both (?) females, which are in the Bishop Museum and which are apparently the specimens originally examined by Kirkaldy. It will take considerable comparative study to place this species properly,

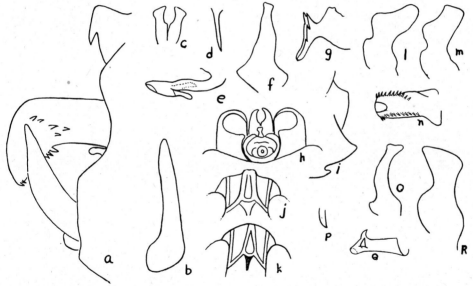

Figure 69—*Nesosydne* genitalia. **a, b,** *N. gigantea* (Muir): **(a)** pygophore as seen from right side (aedeagus may have more teeth, but this sketch was made from a dry specimen); **(b)** right style from directly behind. **c–e,** *N. hamata* Muir: **(c)** styles from behind, in balsam; **(d)** anal spine, holotype, in balsam; **(e)** aedeagus, holotype, in balsam. **f, g,** *N. halia* Kirkaldy: **(f)** left style in balsam; **(g)** aedeagus in balsam. **h–j,** *N. gunnerae* Muir: **(h)** pygophore viewed from above; **(i)** caudal margin of pygophore seen from left side; **(j)** front part of vertex as seen from above to show protuberant median keels. **k–n,** *N. imbricola* Kirkaldy: **(k)** front part of vertex seen from above to show non-protuberant median keels; **(l)** broad view of style; **(m)** style from slightly different angle (**l,** and **m,** in fluid); **(n)** aedeagus, in balsam (from paratype of *"coprosmae"*). **o–q,** *N. ipomoeicola* Kirkaldy: **(o)** right style in balsam; **(p)** anal spine in balsam; **(q)** aedeagus in balsam. **r,** *N. incommoda* Muir, holotype, right style.

because no males have as yet been associated with it. When additional material is assembled, it should be compared with *amaumau* (Muir). The holotype, also a female, is in the British Museum, and it is figured here. The one example at the Bishop Museum, which has its anal segment intact, does not have it concave behind as the artist has indicated on the holotype. This is a large species similar to *amaumau* (judging from the female), if it is not the same.

Nesosydne halia Kirkaldy (figs. 69, f, g; 82, a).

> *Nesosydne halia* Kirkaldy, 1908:202, pl. 4, fig. 8; 1910:584. Muir, 1916:194, pl. 3, fig. 52.
> *Ilburnia halia* (Kirkaldy), of authors.
> *Nesosydne halia* "var." Kirkaldy, 1910:585.
> *Ilburnia halia* variety *fuscovittata* Metcalf, 1943:308. New synonym.

Endemic. Oahu (type locality: Mount Tantalus, 1,300 feet).
Hostplants: *Dubautia plantaginea, Freycinetia.*
Parasite: *Polynema ciliata* Perkins (Hymenoptera: Mymaridae), in the eggs.
The type should be in the British Museum.
There is no reason to maintain Metcalf's name, which he erected without knowing what Kirkaldy labeled as a variety. The coloration on the tegmina varies individually. This species is rather similar to *asteliae.*

Nesosydne hamadryas Kirkaldy.

> *Nesosydne hamadryas* Kirkaldy, 1910:587.
> *Ilburnia hamadryas* (Kirkaldy), of authors.

Endemic. Oahu (type locality: Mount Tantalus).
Only the long-winged female holotype is known. Muir did not know the species. The holotype is now in the Bishop Museum, and I have been unable to associate it with any other species, but I have not compared it with all of the known long-winged females. The first antennal segment is slightly more than twice as long as broad, about three-fourths the length of the second and as long as the narrowest interocular breadth of the frons. The outline of the front part of the vertex as viewed from above is convex without a protuberant median line. It looks superficially like *N. rubescens pele,* or one of the other associates of *koae,* but the elongate first antennal segment is distinctive.

Nesosydne hamata Muir (fig. 69, c–e).

> *Nesosydne hamata* Muir, 1917:309, pl. 5, figs. 17, 17a.
> *Ilburnia hamata* (Muir), of authors.

Endemic. Lanai (type locality: 3,000 feet).

Nesosydne imbricola Kirkaldy (figs. 62, b–d; 69, k–n).

Nesosydne imbricola Kirkaldy, 1910:590.

Ilburnia imbricola (Kirkaldy), of authors.

Ilburnia coprosmae Muir, 1919:93, pl. 3, fig. 2; pl. 4, fig. 21 (type from Olinda). New synonym.

Endemic. Maui (type locality: Mount Haleakala, 5,000 feet).

Hostplant: *Coprosma montana.*

The male holotype is in the British Museum, and a drawing of it is presented here. An examination of Muir's type material of his *coprosmae,* plus some fresh specimens collected by me in 1945, with the aid of the drawing of Kirkaldy's holotype of *imbricola* have enabled me to establish the above synonymy.

Nesosydne incommoda Muir (fig. 69, r).

Nesosydne incommoda Muir, 1916:193, pl. 3, fig. 47.

Ilburnia incommoda (Muir), of authors.

Endemic. Oahu (type locality: Kaumuohona).

Nesosydne ipomoeicola Kirkaldy (figs. 69, o–q; 82, b).

Delphax pulchra Stål, Öfv. Svenska Vet. Akad. Förh. 11:246, 1854 (I have not seen this reference); 1859:275, redescription (name preoccupied in *Delphax*).

Nesosydne ipomoeicola Kirkaldy, 1907:120; 1908:202, pl. 4, fig. 4; 1910:586. Muir, 1916:194, pl. 3, figs. 51, a–c.

Ilburnia ipomoeicola (Kirkaldy) Muir, 1921:517.

Endemic. Kauai, Oahu (type locality: Honolulu), Molokai, Maui, Hawaii.

Hostplants: *Antidesma,* Bermuda grass, *Cibotium, Cyrtandra, Dolichos lablab, Gouldia elongata, Ipomoea bona-nox, Jussiaea villosa,* leafy cabbage, *Lythrum maritimum, Mucuna gigantea, Pipturus, Polygonum,* potato, *Rumex, Sadleria, Strongylodon lucidum,* sweet potato.

Some of these hostplants probably have been recorded on the basis of accidental captures and they do not serve as breeding plants. I have seen long-winged individuals resting on bush beans and lima beans and have seen examples which had been confused with the taro leafhopper because they were caught resting on taro. Swezey found it to be particularly attached to *Sadleria* ferns, in the young, tender frond stalks of which it lays numerous eggs. William Look reported finding eggs abundant in stray Irish potato plants on Hawaii in March, 1945. The species breeds on *Ipomoea.*

This was the first Hawaiian delphacid to be described. It has been collected mostly from 1,500 feet down to sea level. Kirkaldy considered it to be the commonest of the native delphacids. It is a variable species, and Muir thought that it consisted of a number of varieties or subspecies. Both sexes have short- and long-winged individuals. Some examples examined have the thoracic nota and tegmina largely pale, whereas others have these parts extensively dark and in others they are predominantly or almost entirely black.

Perkins (1913:clxxxiii) said that at least two *Pipunculus* flies are parasitic on this species, but he did not cite their names.

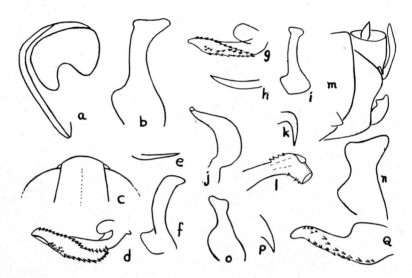

Figure 70— Details of *Nesosydne* genitalia. **a–f,** *N. koae* Kirkaldy: **(a)** head from side; **(b)** right style; **(c)** head from front (beneath) to show convexity of front of vertex; **(d)** aedeagus; **(e)** anal spine; **(f)** right style **(d–f,** from balsam slide of same example from Mount Tantalus, Oahu). **g–i,** *N. koae-phyllodii* Muir: **(g)** aedeagus; **(h)** anal spine; **(i)** right style **(g–i,** balsam mount of same example). **j–l,** *N. koebelei* Muir, holotype (parts in balsam): **(j)** left style, full lateral view; **(k)** anal spine; **(l)** aedeagus. **m, n,** *N. kuschei* (Muir), holotype: **(m)** view of pygophore from left side, anal segment turned up and out showing aedeagus (small teeth on aedeagus not shown here); **(n)** right style. **o–q,** *N. kokolau* (Muir), holotype, parts in balsam: **(o)** right style; **(p)** anal spine; **(q)** aedeagus.

Nesosydne koae Kirkaldy (figs. 47, d; 70, a–f).

   Nesosydne koae Kirkaldy, 1907:161; 1908:202, pl. 4, fig. 2; 1910:583. Muir, 1916:185, pl. 2, fig. 32 (this figure is misleading); 1917:299. Genotype of *Nesosydne*.

   Ilburnia koae (Kirkaldy), of authors.

Endemic. Kauai (?), Oahu (type locality: Mount Tantalus), Hawaii (variety ?). Hostplant: *Acacia koa*—breeds on the young leaves.

Muir (1917:299) stated that the female "only oviposits in the young shoots bearing leaves..."; he described the ovipositor and compared it with that of *rubescens*. Both nymphs and adults, when living, are the same bright green as the young leaves of koa. Macropterous and brachypterous forms occur in both sexes of this species.

Perkins notes in his letter that Kirkaldy "... named specimens from Hawaii also as *koae* and a similar sp. was in the S.I.C. [Sandwich Islands Committee] coll. from Molokai (taken on *Acacia koaia*) but I do not know what became of the latter." The type is evidently in the British Museum.

Nesosydne koae-phyllodii Muir (fig. 70, g–i).
Nesosydne koae-phyllodii Muir, 1916:186, pl. 2, fig. 31.
Ilburnia koae-phyllodii (Muir), of authors.

Endemic. Kauai (type locality: Waimea), Oahu (variety ?).
Hostplant: *Acacia koa*.
The eggs are deposited in the edges of the koa phyllodes, not in the leaves. Only macropterous forms have been found.

Nesosydne koebelei Muir (figs. 63, a; 70, j–l).
Nesosydne koebelei Muir, 1917:308, pl. 5, figs. 10, 10a.
Ilburnia koebelei (Muir), of authors.

Endemic. Oahu (type locality: Punaluu).

Nesosydne kokolau (Muir), new combination (fig. 70, o–q).
Ilburnia kokolau Muir, 1919:95, pl. 4, figs. 4a, b.

Endemic. Maui (type locality: ridge south of Iao Valley).
Hostplant: *Campylotheca* ("kokolau").

Nesosydne kuschei (Muir), new combination (fig. 70, m, n).
Ilburnia kuschei Muir, 1922:96, pl. 3, fig. 10.

Endemic. Kauai (type locality: near Waialae Falls, 4,000 feet).
Hostplant: *Cyrtandra*.

Nesosydne lanaiensis (Muir), new combination (fig. 71, a, b).
Ilburnia fullawayi subspecies *lanaiensis* Muir, 1917:309.
Ilburnia cyathodis variety *lanaiensis* (Muir) Muir, 1919:92.

Endemic. Lanai (holotype from Waiopaa; allotype from Kaiholena).
Hostplant: *Styphelia* (*Cyathodes*).
This species has been listed as occurring on Maui (Muir, 1919:92), but I am not convinced that it occurs there. I believe that it is specifically distinct from *cyathodis*. It is closely similar to *fullawayi*.

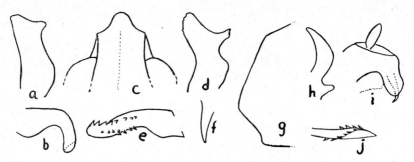

Figure 71—Details of *Nesosydne*. **a, b,** *N. lanaiensis* (Muir), holotype (parts in balsam):
(a) left style; **(b)** aedeagus. **c–f,** *N. leahi* (Kirkaldy): **(c)** front of head (from beneath) to
show protuberant nature of frons and vertex; **(d)** left style in balsam; **(e)** aedeagus in
balsam; **(f)** anal spine in balsam. **g–j,** *N. lobeliae* Muir: **(g)** outline of hind margin of pygophore as seen from right; **(h)** left style, full side view; **(i)** anal segment, from side; **(j)**
aedeagus.

Nesosydne leahi (Kirkaldy) (fig. 71, c–f).

Megamelus leahi Kirkaldy, 1904:176.

Nesosydne leahi (Kirkaldy) Kirkaldy, 1908:202.

Ilburnia leahi (Kirkaldy), of authors.

Endemic. Oahu (type locality: Diamond Head ["Leahi"]), Kauai (?).

Hostplant: *Lipochaeta calycosa.*

Parasite: *Anagrus frequens* Perkins (Hymenoptera: Mymaridae), in the eggs.

Muir (1916:193, pl. 3, fig. 49) described and figured the male terminalia of a
specimen from *Lipochaeta* which may be this or another species. Kirkaldy omitted
the species from his 1910 *Fauna Hawaiiensis* report.

Both sexes are represented in collections by macropterous and brachypterous
specimens.

Perkins states in his letter: "I believe I still have one or two of the original
specimens, captured on the side of Diamond Head on some isolated specimens of
its food plant. Kirkaldy could not find these original plants from my direction,
but obtained the insect in the crater itself. The specimens he had of mine and of
his own were I think nearly all destroyed during the time he was in hospital." The
type is presumably in the British Museum.

This species displays a slight indication in the produced vertex of its head that
is suggestive of a tendency toward the development of a cephalic horn such as
that of *Dictyophorodelphax.*

Nesosydne lobeliae Muir (fig. 71, g–j).

Nesosydne lobeliae Muir, 1916:212; 1917:306, pl. 5, figs. 7, 7a.

Ilburnia lobeliae (Muir) Muir, 1919:108; 1921:520, pl. 8, figs. 3, 3a.

Endemic. Oahu (type locality: Kaumuohona Ridge).

Hostplant: *Lobelia hypoleuca.*

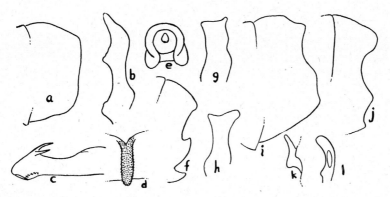

Figure 72—*Nesosydne* genitalia details. **a–d**, *N. longipes* (Muir): **(a)** outline of hind margin of pygophore; **(b)** right style, dry on paratype, oblique rear view to side; **(c)** aedeagus in balsam; **(d)** armature of diaphragm in balsam. **e, f**, *N. montis-tantalus* Muir: **(e)** anal segment; **(f)** rear margin of pygophore as seen from left side. **g**, *N. mamake* (Muir), right style in balsam. **h**, *N. naenae* (Muir), right style of paratype. **i**, *N. monticola* Kirkaldy, outline of hind margin of pygophore from left side (example compared with type by Perkins). **j–l**, *N. nephelias* Kirkaldy: **(j)** outline of hind margin of pygophore from left side (from a cotype of "*disjuncta*"); **(k)** lateral view of right style; **(l)** full rear view of right style.

Nesosydne longipes (Muir), new combination (fig. 72, a–d).

Ilburnia longipes Muir, 1919:93, pl. 3, fig. 4; pl. 4, fig. 15.

Endemic. Maui (type locality: Olinda, 4,200 feet).
Hostplant: *Cyrtandra mauiensis.*

Nesosydne mamake (Muir), new combination (fig. 72, g).

Ilburnia mamake Muir, 1919:101, pl. 4, fig. 8.

Endemic. Maui (type locality: Waikamoi Gulch, 4,000 feet).
Hostplant: *Pipturus* ("mamake").
Muir described the nymphs.

Nesosydne mauiensis (Muir), new combination (fig. 73, a–d).

Ilburnia mauiensis Muir, 1919:99, pl. 3, fig. 10; pl. 4, fig. 5.

Endemic. Maui (type locality: Wailuku Common).
Hostplants: *Campylotheca mauiensis, Lipochaeta integrifolia, Raillardia menziesii, Tetramolopium artemisia.*

Nesosydne monticola Kirkaldy (fig. 72, i).

Nesosydne monticola Kirkaldy, 1910:591. Muir, 1916:197.
Ilburnia monticola (Kirkaldy) Muir, 1919:90, pl. 4, fig. 10.

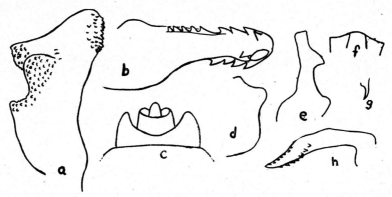

Figure 73—*Nesosydne* genitalia details. **a–d,** *N. mauiensis* (Muir): **(a)** right style, in balsam; **(b)** aedeagus, in balsam; **(c)** pygophore as seen from above; **(d)** outline of hind margin of pygophore as seen from side. **e–h,** *N. neocyrtandrae* (Muir): **(e)** left style in balsam; **(f)** fore margin of vertex as seen from above; **(g)** anal spine, in balsam; **(h)** aedeagus, in balsam.

Endemic. Maui (type locality: Mount Haleakala, 8,000 feet).

Hostplant: *Coprosma montana.*

This is much like *imbricola,* but it is darker, has a shorter first antennal segment and somewhat different terminalia.

The type is supposedly in the British Museum.

Nesosydne montis-tantalus Muir (fig. 72, e, f).

Nesosydne montis-tantalus Muir, 1916:195, pl. 5, fig. 55.

Ilburnia montis-tantalus (Muir), of authors.

Endemic. Oahu (type locality: Mount Tantalus).

Hostplants: *Lobelia hypoleuca, Broussaisia arguta* (reported to be common on small plants and seedlings close to the ground).

Nesosydne naenae (Muir), new combination (figs. 72, h; 82, g).

Ilburnia naenae Muir, 1922:98, pl. 3, fig. 12.

Endemic. Kauai (type locality: Alakai Swamp).

Hostplants: *Dubautia* ("naenae"), *Raillardia.*

Nesosydne neocyrtandrae (Muir), new combination (fig. 73, e–h).

Ilburnia neocyrtandrae Muir, 1919:100, pl. 3, fig. 9; pl. 4, fig. 7.

Endemic. Maui (type locality: Waikamoi Trail, 4,000 feet).

Hostplant: *Gunnera mauiensis.*

"The nymphs have the two median frontal carinae and the first joint of antennae very short, as is usual in the genus; the head, tegminal pads and apical portion of the abdomen are dark, the rest light." (Muir, 1919:100.)

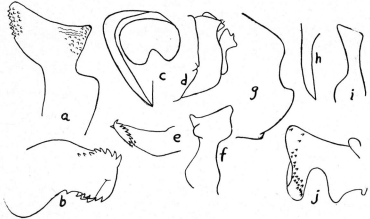

Figure 74—*Nesosydne* details. **a–c,** *N. neoraillardiae* (Muir) : **(a)** left style, in balsam as seen with the compound microscope; **(b)** aedeagus, in balsam, under the compound microscope; **(c)** outline of head from side. **d–f,** *N. nephrolepidis* Kirkaldy : **(d)** view of pygophore from left side (outline of style varies with extent it is rotated outward and will not appear the same unless seen from exactly the same angle) ; **(e)** aedeagus in balsam; **(f)** right style in balsam. **g,** *N. neowailupensis* (Muir), outline of hind margin of pygophore from left side ; **h–j,** *N. nesogunnerae* Muir, holotype : **(h)** anal spine in balsam; **(i)** right style in balsam; **(j)** aedeagus in balsam.

Nesosydne neoraillardiae (Muir), new combination (fig. 74, a–c).
   Ilburnia neoraillardiae Muir, 1921 :517, pl. 8, fig. 17.

Endemic. Hawaii (type locality : Kahuku, Kau, 1,800 feet).
Hostplant : *Lipochaeta subcordata.*
   This species is so close to *raillardiae* that more study is required before an opinion is formed as to the distinctive features between the two. However, the genital styles are less expanded outward on this form.

Nesosydne neowailupensis (Muir), new combination (fig. 74, g).
   Nesosydne wailupensis 1916 :191, pl. 3, fig. 43 ; pl. 4, fig. 66 (name preoccupied).
   Ilburnia neowailupensis Muir, 1919 :108.

Endemic. Oahu (type locality : Wailupe).
Hostplant : *Coprosma longifolia.*
   This species has much in common with *gigantea.*

Nesosydne nephelias Kirkaldy (figs. 61, d–f ; 63, d, e ; 72, j–l).
   Nesosydne nephelias Kirkaldy, 1910 :588. Muir, 1916 :197 ; 1917 :308, pl. 5, fig. 8 (this species ?).
   Ilburnia nephelias (Kirkaldy), of authors.
   Nesosydne disjuncta Muir, 1917 :306, pl. 5, figs. 12, 12a. Synonymy by Muir, 1919 :6.

Endemic. Lanai (type locality, 2,000 feet or above).

Kirkaldy's type is in the British Museum. Muir's type of *disjuncta* came from 3,000 feet on Lanai. Kirkaldy's series contained more than one species. A specimen in the Bishop Museum from the original lot is quite different from the holotype, and this may have confused Muir.

Nesosydne nephrolepidis Kirkaldy (fig. 74, d–f).
> *Nesosydne nephrolepidis* Kirkaldy, 1908:203, pl. 4, fig. 1. Muir, 1916:189, pl. 3, fig. 40; pl. 4, fig. 79.
> *Ilburnia nephrolepidis* (Kirkaldy), of authors.

Endemic. Oahu (type locality: Mount Tantalus), Maui, Hawaii.
Hostplant: *Nephrolepis exaltata*.

Nesosydne nesogunnerae Muir (figs. 63, g, h; 74, h–j).
> *Nesosydne nesogunnerae* Muir, 1917:305, pl. 5, figs. 16, 16a.
> *Ilburnia nesogunnerae* (Muir), of authors.

Endemic. Lanai (type locality: Lanaihale, 3,000 feet).

Nesosydne nesopele (Muir), new combination (fig. 75, a–d).
> *Ilburnia nesopele* Muir, 1921:511, pl. 8, figs. 6, 6a.

Endemic. Maui (type locality: Ukulele Pipe Line, Haleakala, 5,000 feet).
Hostplant: *Astelia veratroides*.
Muir described the nymphs as being "yellow, brown on face, clypeus, wing pads, hind femora and apical tarsi."

Nesosydne nigriceps Muir (figs. 63, b; 75, e–g).
> *Nesosydne nigriceps* Muir, 1917:308, pl. 6, figs. 33, 33a.
> *Ilburnia nigriceps* (Muir) Muir, 1921:511, pl. 8, fig. 7, aedeagus ("*nigroceps*").

Endemic. Lanai (type locality: 2,300 feet).

Nesosydne nigrinervis (Muir), new combination (fig. 75, h, i).
> *Ilburnia cyathodis* variety *nigrinervis* Muir, 1919:92.

Endemic. Maui (type locality: Mount Haleakala).
Hostplant: *Styphelia (Cyathodes)*.
This is a very dark or black form, and I consider it to be fully specifically distinct from *cyathodis*. The males are only about 1.5 mm. long although they appear larger. It has been taken in series at the summit of Haleakala (10,000 feet).

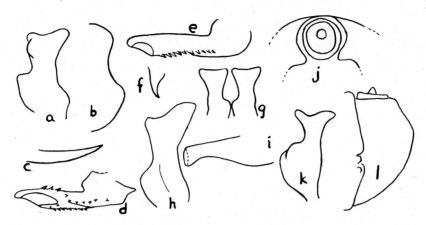

Figure 75—Details of *Nesosydne* genitalia. **a–d,** *N. nesopele* (Muir) : **(a)** right style in balsam; **(b)** outline of hind margin of pygophore of holotype; **(c)** anal spine in balsam; **(d)**
aedeagus in balsam. **e–g,** *N. nigriceps* Muir : **(e)** aedeagus of holotype in balsam; **(f)** anal
style of holotype in balsam; **(g)** genital styles in balsam. **h, i,** *N. nigrinervis* (Muir) : **(h)**
right style in balsam; **(i)** aedeagus in balsam. **j–l,** *N. oahuensis* Muir : **(j)** anal segment and
surrounding anal angles of pygophore; **(k)** right style in balsam; **(l)** lateral view of pygophore.

Nesosydne nubigena Kirkaldy (fig. 61, a–c).

Nesosydne nubigena Kirkaldy, 1910:589.
Ilburnia nubigena (Kirkaldy), of authors.

Endemic. Molokai (type locality: "forest above Pelekunu").

The type is in the British Museum. I have not seen this species, but the illustrations show that it is a distinctive form. The tooth-like process on the sides
of the male pygophore above the medio-ventral process recalls the similar processes
on *Nesosydne sola*. The ventro-median process on this species is broad and blunt
(as seen from above), but on *sola* it is pointed in both dorsal and lateral views.

Nesosydne oahuensis Muir (fig. 75, j–l).

Nesosydne oahuensis Muir, 1916:188, pl. 2, fig. 37.
Ilburnia oahuensis (Muir), of authors.

Endemic. Oahu (type locality: Mount Tantalus).
Hostplant: *Charpentiera obovata*.

Nesosydne olympica (Muir), new combination (fig. 76, a–d).

Ilburnia olympica Muir, 1921:520, pl. 8, figs. 16, a, b.

Endemic. Oahu (type locality: Castle Trail, about 2,000 feet).
Hostplant: *Lobelia*.
This distinctive species evidently lacks anal spines.

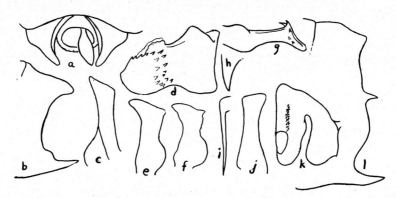

Figure 76—*Nesosydne* genitalia. **a–d,** *N. olympica* (Muir): **(a)** pygophore as seen from above, holotype; **(b)** outline of hind margin of pygophore as seen from left side, holotype; **(c)** right style obliquely from side, holotype; **(d)** aedeagus in balsam. **e–h,** *N. osborni* Muir: **(e)** left style of holotype, dry; **(f)** left style as seen in balsam preparation; **(g)** aedeagus in balsam; **(h)** anal spine in balsam. **i–k,** *N. painiu* (Muir), holotype, parts in balsam: **(i)** anal spine; **(j)** right style; **(k)** aedeagus. **l,** *N. palustris* Kirkaldy, hind margin of pygophore as seen from side.

Nesosydne osborni Muir (fig. 76, e–h).

Nesosydne osborni Muir, 1916:192, pl. 3, fig. 46 (this figure erroneous).
Ilburnia osborni (Muir) Muir, 1919:99, pl. 4, fig. 6.

Endemic. Maui (type locality: Haleakala Crater).
Hostplant: *Raillardia.*

Nesosydne bridwelli is identical in external appearance with this species, but the aedeagus is broadly expanded at the apex in the holotype of *N. osborni,* whereas it is narrowed to a slender apex on the holotype of *bridwelli.* These differences are also evident on other examples studied, but the shape of the aedeagus is some-what variable. It is obvious that the two forms are closely allied, and more infor-mation regarding them is desirable. I have taken typical *bridwelli* breeding com-monly on *Dubautia* or *Raillardia.*

Nesosydne painiu (Muir), new combination (fig. 76, i–k).

Ilburnia painiu Muir, 1919:102, pl. 4, fig. 16, *a–c.*

Endemic. Maui (type locality: ridge south of Iao Valley).
Hostplant: *Astelia veratroides* ("painiu").

Nesosydne palustris Kirkaldy (fig. 76, 1).

Nesosydne palustris Kirkaldy, 1908:202, pl. 4, fig. 7; 1910:589.
Ilburnia palustris (Kirkaldy), of authors.

Endemic. Molokai (type locality: 4,500–4,950 feet; high, wet bog).

Nesosydne perkinsi Muir (figs. 78, d ; 82, c, h).
  Nesosydne perkinsi Muir, 1916:190, pl. 3 (not pl. 2 as stated in original de-
    scription), fig. 42; pl. 4, fig. 73.
  Ilburnia perkinsi (Muir), of authors.

Endemic. Maui (type locality: Mount Haleakala, 5,000 feet).

Nesosydne phyllostegiae Muir (fig. 78, e–h).
  Nesosydne phyllostegiae Muir, 1918:405, figs. 3, 4.
  Ilburnia phyllostegiae (Muir), of authors.

Endemic. Hawaii (type locality: Puuwaawaa, North Kona, 3,700 feet).
Hostplant: *Phyllostegia racemosa.*
Macropterous females and brachypterous males and females are known.

Nesosydne pilo (Muir), new combination (fig. 78, i–k).
  Ilburnia pilo Muir, 1922:99, pl. 3, figs. 14, 14a.

Endemic. Maui (type locality: Haleakala, 5,800 feet).
Hostplant: *Coprosma ernodioides* ("pilo").
Brachypterous males and females and macropterous females have been reported.
This species is very close to *imbricola,* but the styles have a rounded boss on their
inner sides which is distinct from that of *imbricola.*

Nesosydne pipturi Kirkaldy (fig. 78, l–n).
  Nesosydne pipturi Kirkaldy, 1908:202, pl. 4, fig. 3; 1910:584. Muir, 1916:191,
    pl. 3, fig. 45.
  Ilburnia pipturi (Kirkaldy) Muir, 1921:515, pl. 8, figs. 11, 11a.

Endemic. Oahu (type locality: the mountains behind Waialua, according to
Perkins' letter).
Hostplant: *Pipturus.*
Parasite: *Pipunculus swezeyi* Perkins (Diptera: Pipunculidae).
The type should be in the British Museum.
The nymphs are pale green. This species and *boehmeria* are very similar.

Nesosydne procellaris Kirkaldy (fig. 62, a).
  Nesosydne procellaris Kirkaldy, 1910:588. Muir, 1916:197.
  Ilburnia procellaris (Kirkaldy), of authors.

Endemic. Molokai (type locality: above Pelekunu, 3,000 feet).
This is a large species (4.5 mm. in length), and it does not seem to have been
collected since the type pair was taken by Perkins. What I have taken to be

the female specimen from the original material has been found in the Bishop Museum. I have labeled it "Allotype ?" and placed it in the type collection. The number beneath the card on which the specimen is mounted refers to Perkins' collecting area at 3,000 feet, above Pelekunu, Molokai. The holotype is in the British Museum, and, as the drawing included here shows, it is a broken specimen. Kirkaldy stated that it was the bulkiest of the Hawaiian delphacids known to him. I do not know why he should have stated that "This species is very probably now extinct." The type material came from a locality which has been poorly collected. From the included drawing, it may appear that the type is macropterous, but it is a brachypterous form, the tegmina of which do not reach to the apex of the abdomen in the male but surpass it in the female.

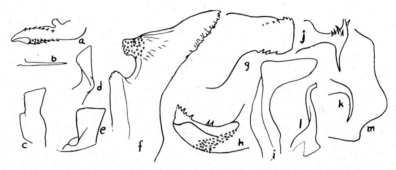

Figure 77—Details of *Nesosydne* genitalia. **a-e,** *N. pseudorubescens* Muir: (**a**) aedeagus in balsam; (**b**) anal spine in balsam; (**c**) right style in balsam; (**d**) right style on holotype viewed obliquely from the inside (left side), dry; (**e**) the same, in direct rear view. **f, g,** *N. raillardiae* Kirkaldy, parts in balsam under the compound microscope: (**f**) right style; (**g**) aedeagus. **h, i,** *N. rocki* Muir, holotype: (**h**) aedeagus, dry dissection; (**i**) right style from right side. **j–m,** *N. sharpi* Muir, holotype, dry dissection: (**j**) aedeagus; (**k**) anal spine; (**l**) full left view of left style; (**m**) outline of hind margin of pygophore as seen from side.

Nesosydne pseudorubescens Muir (fig. 77, a–e).

  Nesosydne pseudorubescens Muir, 1916:186, pl. 2, fig. 34.
  Ilburnia pseudorubescens (Muir) Muir, 1919:88.
  Nesosydne pele, misidentification by Muir, 1916:188, pl. 2, fig. 36; pl. 4, fig. 78.
  Ilburnia pele, misidentification by Muir, 1921:512, pl. 8, figs. 9, 9a.

  Endemic. Maui, Hawaii (type locality: Olaa, 29 miles).

  Hostplants: *Acacia koa* (on the phyllodes); *Lobelia* and *Clermontia parviflora,* accidental (?) captures.

  Muir did not see Kirkaldy's type of *pele,* and he confused with it the broad-styled species he called *pseudorubescens.* The styles bend cephalad at about the middle, and this angulation confused Muir into considering that each had a pyramidal projection on the posterior face as he illustrated for *"pele"* (1916:221, pl. 4, fig. 78). I have examined the original material which Muir called *"pele,"* including the slide of the genitalia which served as a basis for his illustration, and find it to be the same as the type of *pseudorubescens.*

"In coloration this species is very similar to *rubescens,* but the fuscous hind margin from clavus to apex is very distinctive...." (Muir, 1916:186.) I believe that this dark coloration is individually variable. Only macropterous males and females have been reported.

Nesosydne raillardiae Kirkaldy (fig. 77, f, g).

Nesosydne raillardiae Kirkaldy, 1908:203, pl. 4, fig. 5; 1910:590. Muir, 1916: 194, pl. 3, fig. 50.
Ilburnia raillardiae (Kirkaldy) Muir, 1921:516, pl. 8, fig. 18.

Endemic. Hawaii (type locality: Kilauea, 4,000 feet).
Hostplants: *Raillardia scabra, Raillardia ciliolata, Rollandia.*
Macropterous females have been found in addition to the short-winged males and females. The type should be in the British Museum. This is close to *neoraillardiae.*

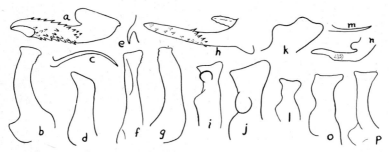

Figure 78—Details of *Nesosydne* genitalia. **a–c,** *N. rubescens pele* (Kirkaldy), parts in balsam: **(a)** aedeagus (the number and arrangement of the teeth is subject to individual variation); **(b)** right style; **(c)** anal spine. **d,** *N. perkinsi* Muir, right style of holotype. **e–h,** *N. phyllostegiae* Muir: **(e)** anal spine of holotype in balsam; **(f)** right style of paratype, from rear, dry; **(g)** left style of holotype, flat in balsam; **(h)** aedeagus in balsam. **i–k,** *N. pilo* (Muir): **(i)** right style of paratype as seen in balsam; **(j)** right style as seen from behind; **(k)** right style as seen obliquely from side. **l–n,** *N. pipturi* Kirkaldy, parts in balsam: **(l)** right style; **(m)** anal spine; **(n)** aedeagus. **o,** *N. raillardiicola* (Muir), right style. **p,** *N. rubescens* (Kirkaldy), right style oblique from side.

Nesosydne raillardiicola (Muir), new combination (fig. 78, o).

Ilburnia raillardiicola Muir, 1919:102, pl. 4, fig. 14; 1921:512, pl. 8, fig. 5.

Endemic. Maui (type locality: Mount Haleakala, 7,000–8,000 feet).
Hostplants: *Raillardia menziesii, Raillardia platyphyllum.*
Muir (1919:102) described the nymphs as being "ochraceous orange, brownish over the head and thorax."

Nesosydne rocki Muir (fig. 77, h, i).

Nesosydne rocki Muir, 1916:196, pl. 3, fig. 56; pl. 4, fig. 71, a, b.
Ilburnia rocki (Muir), of authors.

Endemic. Oahu (type locality: Konahuanui).

Nesosydne rubescens (Kirkaldy) (fig. 78, p).

Nesosydne koae variety *rubescens* Kirkaldy, 1907:161; 1910:584.
Nesosydne rubescens (Kirkaldy) Muir, 1916:185, pl. 2, fig. 30.
Ilburnia rubescens (Kirkaldy), of authors.

Endemic. Kauai, Oahu (type locality: Mount Tantalus), Maui, Hawaii.
Hostplant: *Acacia koa* (eggs deposited in edges of leaves and phyllodes).
Kirkaldy (1910:584) says that the nymphs are green tinged with roseate. Only macropterous males and females are known.
If a holotype were ever designated, it should be in the British Museum.

Nesosydne rubescens variety **pele** (Kirkaldy), new combination (fig. 78, a–c).

Nesosydne pele Kirkaldy, 1910:585.
Nesosydne rubescens variety *pulla* Muir, 1916:186.
Ilburnia rubescens variety *pulla* (Muir), of authors.
Muir's *Nesosydne pele,* 1916:188, pl. 2, fig. 36; pl. 4, fig. 78, and his *Ilburnia pele,* 1921:512, pl. 8, figs. 9, 9a, apply to *pseudorubescens.*

Endemic. Hawaii (type locality: Kilauea).
Hostplant: *Acacia koa* (also recorded, probably from accidental captures or misidentifications, from *Broussaisia pellucida, Cyrtandra* and *Platydesma campanulata*).
This is a darker form; the males have dark, nearly black, mesonota. Only macropterous males and females have been reported. Further study is needed to elucidate the status of the forms of this species. It might be questioned whether the supposed varietal differences are stable or whether they represent individual or colonial variation.
The type mount, which consists of two male examples on the same card, is now in the Bishop Museum. Muir was misled (perhaps by a specimen which was considered a cotype of this species but actually was *pseudorubescens*) and redescribed this species under the name *pulla.* He did not see the type, and he could not obtain adequate information from Kirkaldy's description.
This variety is named for Pele, the Hawaiian goddess of the volcano.

Nesosydne sharpi Muir (fig. 77, j–m).

Nesosydne sharpi Muir, 1916:195, pl. 3, fig. 53, a, b; pl. 4, fig. 65.
Ilburnia sharpi (Muir), of authors.

Endemic. Oahu (type locality: Punaluu).
Hostplants: *Broussaisia, Boehmeria stipularis.*

Nesosydne sola Muir (figs. 63, c; 79, a).

Nesosydne sola Muir, 1917:307, pl. 5, figs. 11, 11a.
Ilburnia sola (Muir), of authors.

Endemic. Oahu (type locality: Punaluu).

See the comparative notes under *nubigena*. This is a peculiar species with an unusual aedeagus and an elongate anal segment.

Nesosydne stenogynicola (Muir), new combination (fig. 79, b, c).
Ilburnia stenogynicola Muir, 1919:94, pl. 3, fig. 5; pl. 4, fig. 22.

Endemic. Maui (type locality: Olinda, 4,200 feet).
Hostplant: *Stenogyne kamehameha*.

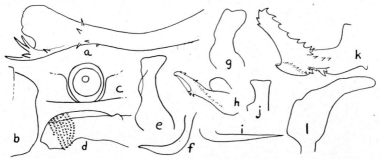

Figure 79—*Nesosydne* genitalia details. **a,** *N. sola* Muir, aedeagus, holotype, dry dissection; **b, c,** *N. stenogynicola* (Muir), paratype: **(b)** outline of hind edge of pygophore from side; **(c)** anal segment as seen from above. **d–f,** *N. sulcata* (Muir), holotype, parts in balsam: **(d)** aedeagus; **(e)** right style; **(f)** right anal spine. **g–i,** *N. swezeyi* Muir, holotype, dry dissection: **(g)** right style; **(h)** aedeagus; **(i)** anal spine. **j,** *N. tetramolopii* (Muir), holotype, upper part of right style. **k, l,** *N. timberlakei* Muir, holotype, parts in balsam: **(k)** aedeagus; **(l)** right style.

Nesosydne sulcata (Muir), new combination (fig. 79, d–f).
Ilburnia sulcata Muir, 1921:516, pl. 8, fig. 4.

Endemic. Maui (type locality: ditch trail east of Keanae, about 1,500 feet).
Hostplant: *Cyrtandra*.

Nesosydne swezeyi Muir (figs. 79, g–i; 82, d).
Nesosydne swezeyi Muir, 1916:187, pl. 2, fig. 33; pl. 4, fig. 68.
Ilburnia swezeyi (Muir), of authors.

Endemic. Oahu (type locality: Mount Olympus).

Nesosydne tetramolopii (Muir), new combination and emendation (figs. 79, j; 81, d).
Ilburnia tetramalopii Muir, 1919:88, pl. 3, fig. 7; pl. 4, fig. 19.

Endemic. Maui (type locality: Mount Haleakala, 7,000 feet).
Hostplant: *Tetramolopium humile*.
The nymphs are described by Muir.

A typographical error in the original description makes the change in spelling of the specific name necessary.

Nesosydne timberlakei Muir (fig. 79, k, l).

Nesosydne timberlakei Muir, 1917:304, pl. 5, fig. 14; 1918:398.
Ilburnia timberlakei (Muir), of authors.

Endemic. Oahu (type locality: Waiahole).
Hostplants: *Cyrtandra garnotiana, Cyanea truncata.*

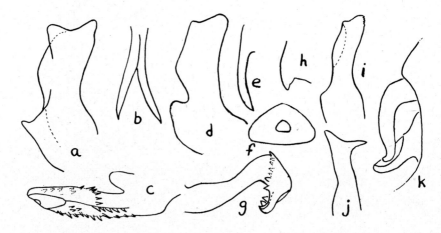

Figure 80—Details of *Nesosydne* genitalia. **a–c,** *N. ulehihi* (Muir), parts in balsam: **(a)** right style; **(b)** anal spines; **(c)** aedeagus. **d–g,** *N. umbratica* Kirkaldy: **(d)** right style, drawn flat in fluid; **(e)** anal spine in balsam; **(f)** anal segment; **(g)** aedeagus in balsam. **h, i,** *N. viridis* (Muir), paratype, parts in balsam: **(h)** anal spine; **(i)** right style, viewed from flat side (it appears longer and narrower when seen from behind). **j, k,** *N. wailupensis* (Muir): **(j)** right style; **(k)** side view of part of pygophore to show aedeagus and armature of diaphragm.

Nesosydne ulehihi (Muir), new combination (fig. 80, a–c).

Ilburnia ulehihi Muir, 1919:104, pl. 4, fig. 12.

Endemic. Hawaii (type locality: Olaa, 27 miles).
Hostplant: *Smilax sandwicensis* ("ulehihi").

Nesosydne umbratica Kirkaldy (fig. 80, d–g).

Nesosydne umbratica Kirkaldy, 1910:585.
Ilburnia umbratica (Kirkaldy), of authors.
Nesosydne blackburni Muir, 1916:189, pl. 3, fig. 41; pl. 4, fig. 70, a, b. New synonym.
Ilburnia curvata Muir, 1919:96, pl. 4, figs. 1, 3. New synonym.

Endemic. Oahu, Maui, Hawaii (type locality: Kilauea).
Hostplants: *Charpentiera obovata, Clermontia* (several species), *Cyrtandra, Pipturus, Stenogyne, Urera sandwicensis.*

This species has not been recognized under Kirkaldy's name since it was described. The types, however, are in the Bishop Museum, and I have found the above synonymy necessary. When Muir described his *blackburni* (1916:190) he said, "It is possible that this is *umbratica* Kirkaldy, but the description is useless for identification." The holotype mount of *blackburni* consists of two female examples, and there are two additional female specimens in Perkins' collection at the Bishop Museum. I have compared female paratypes of *blackburni* with these female examples and have found them to be conspecific. Kirkaldy did not mention the sex of his specimens, the locality or the hostplant in his brief and unsatisfactory original description. The types were collected from *Clermontia* by Perkins at Kilauea in July, 1906.

Muir's type of *blackburni* came from Kilauea, Hawaii. Muir's *curvata* (described from a unique male from Lupe Ditch Trail, 1,200 feet, Kailua District, Maui) was separated from *blackburni* because of differences in the shape of the apex of the aedeagus. However, the holotype is somewhat teneral, the genitalia evidently have been boiled too long in caustic potash and they are distorted. The anal spines are badly deformed, and, in my opinion, the apex of the aedeagus is also damaged. I have examined several slides of cleared genitalia of "*blackburni*" and have found no two individuals exactly alike. I can find no characters on the holotype of *curvata* to warrant its separation from the series of examples of *umbratica* which have been assembled.

This is a variable species, and the wings may be almost entirely clear or they may be nearly entirely fuscous. Macropterous and brachypterous forms have been reported for both sexes.

Nesosydne viridis (Muir), new combination (fig. 80, h, i).
Ilburnia viridis Muir, 1922:99, pl. 3, figs. 13, 13a.

Endemic. Kauai (type locality: Nualolo).
Hostplant: *Phyllostegia*.

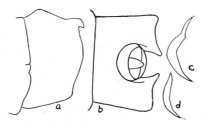

Figure 81—Details of *Nesosydne* genitalia. **a, b**, *N. waikamoiensis* (Muir): **(a)** outline of pygophore as seen from right side; **(b)** outline of pygophore as seen from directly above. **c**, outline of left side of pygophore of *N. bridwelli* (Muir), as seen from behind. **d**, the same of *N. tetramolopii* (Muir).

Nesosydne waikamoiensis (Muir), new combination (fig. 81, a, b).

Ilburnia waikamoiensis Muir, 1919:97, pl. 3, figs. 1, 8; 1921:514, pl. 8, fig. 2 (correction of former figure).

Endemic. Maui (type locality: Waikamoi Gulch, 4,000 feet).

Hostplants: *Cyanea aculeatiflora, Pipturus.*

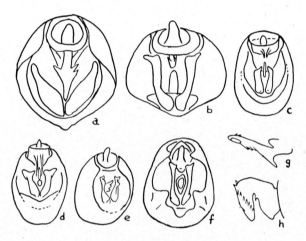

Figure 82—Rough sketches of male genitalia of some *Nesosydne* species. **a**, *N. halia* Kirkaldy, rear view of pygophore; **b**, the same of *N. ipomoeicola* Kirkaldy; **c**, the same of *N. perkinsi* Muir; **d**, the same of *N. swezeyi* Muir; **e**, three-quarters view of pygophore of *N. cyrtandrae* Muir (the aedeagus is incorrectly shown, see fig. 67, e); **f**, rear view of pygophore of *N. giffardi* Muir; **g**, aedeagus of *N. naenae* (Muir); **h**, aedeagus of *N. perkinsi* Muir. (**a, b**, original; **c–f, h**, after Muir, 1916; **g**, after Muir, 1922.)

Nesosydne wailupensis (Muir), new combination (fig. 80, j, k).

Aloha wailupensis Muir, 1916:181, pl. 2, fig. 22.

Ilburnia wailupensis (Muir) Muir, 1919:108.

Endemic. Oahu (type locality: Wailupe).

Hostplant: *Rollandia crispa.*

The aedeagus turns downward at nearly a right angle so that its apex lies against the peculiarly elongated armature of the diaphragm which is hollowed out on its dorsum and projects back between the bases of the styles—an unusual combination of characters.

Tribe DELPHACINI Lambertie, 1910

Araeopini Metcalf, 1938:299.

With the exception of the native species of *Kelisia,* the members of this tribe found in Hawaii are immigrants. The group may be distinguished from the Alohini by the structure and form of the metatibial calcar. In the Delphacini, the calcar, instead of being solid and transversely convex, is either more or less foliaceous or thin, or partly so, or it is distinctly concave on one side. The teeth are reduced to minute dentes and form a minutely denticulate margin on the calcar as figure 46, a, b, indicates.

With the exception of the species of *Megamelus,* which feeds on water lilies, and *Tarophagus,* which feeds on taro, all our Delphacini are attached to grasses—in sharp contrast to the Alohini, none of which feeds on grasses.

Key to the Genera of Delphacini Found in Hawaii

1.   First and second antennal segments flattened, the first sub-
         triangular in outline..............**Perkinsiella** Kirkaldy.
      First and second antennal segments subcylindrical, not
         compressed 2
2(1). Median carina of frons forking at a point near lower
         edges of eyes......................**Peregrinus** Kirkaldy.
      Median frontal carina forking on, or close to, the vertex.... 3
3(2). Taro- and water-lily-infesting species; prothorax nearly
         twice as broad as head across eyes and/or predom-
         inantly dark-colored species; first antennal segment ob-
         viously longer than broad, two-thirds as long as second
         or longer 4
      Pallid (except in some examples of *Liburnia*), grass-feed-
         ing species; pronotum less than one-fourth broader than
         head across eyes; first antennal segment only slightly
         longer than broad, always much shorter than second..... 5
4(3). Taro-frequenting species; median carinae of head very
         slightly protuberant at apex of vertex, and head not
         strongly prolonged beyond eyes, as in figure 90 (our
         species with pro- and mesonotum pale yellow between
         carinae so as to form a common, broad, pale vitta con-
         spicuous to the unaided eyes and with a similar vitta on
         last two or three abdominal tergites; tegmina shiny;
         pronotum only about one-seventh broader than head
         across eyes; spur of hind tibia V-shaped in cross sec-
         tion; first antennal segment comparatively slender—7:4,
         male, 10:4, female)..............**Tarophagus,** new genus.
      Water-lily species; median carinae of head strongly pro-
         tuberant at fore edge of vertex and head prolonged in
         front of eyes, as in figure 90 (our species with head,
         across eyes, only about five-eighths as broad as pro-

notum ; pro-' and mesonotum not conspicuously bicolored
as in *Tarophagus;* first antennal segment stout (7 :5) ;
tegmina appearing minutely granular ; hind tibial spur
very large and broad, broadly C-shaped in cross section,
leaf-like)........................**Megamelus** Fieber.

5(3). Antennae without dark vittae, at most first segment with
a dark apical ring ; anal segment of male entire, not concave beneath, with anal spines arising from a common
median point and close together ; anal angles of pygophore projecting behind anal segment; genital styles
expanded distad........................**Liburnia** Stål.

Antennae, as seen from front, with dark vittae ; anal segment of male conspicuously concave beneath, with long,
strong anal spines widely separated at their origins ;
anal angles of pygophore not projecting behind anal
segment; genital styles attenuated and apically pointed
....**Kelisia** Fieber.

Genus **PERKINSIELLA** Kirkaldy, 1903:179

This genus was originally erected to receive the infamous sugarcane leafhopper.
It now contains 23 described species, and it is believed that a number of new
species await discovery. The center of development of the genus lies in the Malay
Archipelago, and species occur naturally as far west as India and as far east as
Fiji. Some species have been spread by man accidentally as far as Africa and east-
ward to Hawaii. Kirkaldy considered the genus a derivative of the world-wide
Dicranotropis Fieber. It bears a remarkable superficial resemblance to the American genus *Stobaera* Stål, and this led Kirkaldy (1907 :135, footnote) to say that
the two genera were closely allied. This statement may cause some confusion,
however, for the two genera are now considered as belonging to different tribes.
The species are almost exclusively attached to sugarcane and only occasionally do
they take to other grasses. A list of the species together with bibliographic references to scores of published writings on the group is included in Metcalf's catalogue
(1943) of the family.

This genus is easily recognized in the Hawaiian insect fauna because of its expanded and flattened antennal segments, the first of which is subtriangular in
outline. There are other characters which widely separate the genus from other
local Delphacini, but they need not all be detailed here. The male terminalia are
distinctive. The median part of the ventral caudal margin of the pygophore is
produced into a process which in turn bears a pair of spiniform processes. Brachypterous and macropterous forms occur in both sexes in some species. In *Perkinsiella saccharicida* no true brachypterous males have yet been discovered—Giffard's
record (1922 :109) to the contrary is evidently in error.

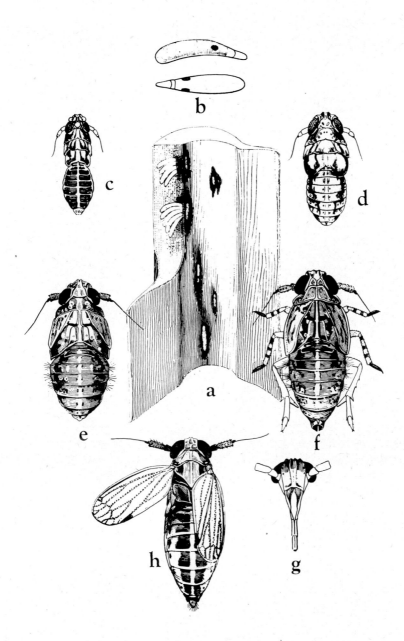

Figure 83—*Perkinsiella saccharicida* Kirkaldy, the sugarcane leafhopper. **a**, section of sugar-cane midrib showing eggs in place; **b**, eggs; **c**, first instar nymph; **d**, second instar; **e**, third instar; **f**, fourth instar; **g**, face of fourth instar nymph; **h**, brachypterous adult female. (After Kirkaldy, 1906.)

Perkinsiella saccharicida Kirkaldy (figs. 46, b; 83, a–h; 84, a–f; 85).

Perkinsiella saccharicida Kirkaldy, 1903:179. Genotype.

Kirkaldy, 1906:406, pl. 26, pl. 27, figs. 1–5; 277–286, notes. 1907:137, pl. 11, figs. 5–8; pl. 13, figs. 11–13.

For detailed bibliography, see Metcalf, 1943:137–141.

The sugarcane leafhopper (Hawaiian name: "umu-ko").

Kauai, Oahu (type locality: Honolulu), Molokai, Lanai, Maui, Hawaii.

Immigrant. First found in the Territory by Perkins, who collected it at a light at Waialua, Oahu, in 1900. Perkins (1903:6) considered that it had gained a foothold in the islands in 1897 or 1898. It is a widespread species now recorded from Queensland, New South Wales, Java, Formosa, Malaya, South China, Mauritius and South Africa. It is considered to be a Queensland insect. (Metcalf, 1943:137–141, has erroneously recorded the species from Amboina and the Philippines. The record for Fiji is based upon a single example, probably mislabeled. Considerable collecting in Fiji has failed to reveal the species there.)

Hostplants: sugarcane (Pemberton, 1919:194, reported finding the leafhopper breeding in seven grasses and three sedges on the island of Hawaii, but the identities of the plants, other than "Hilo grass" and *Paspalum conjugatum,* are not available now).

Parasites: *Paranagrus optabilis* Perkins, *Paranagrus perforator* Perkins, *Anagrus frequens* Perkins (Hymenoptera: Mymaridae); *Ootetrastichus beatus* Perkins, *Ootetrastichus formosanus* Timberlake (Hymenoptera: Eulophidae), all in the eggs. *Haplogonatopus vitiensis* Perkins (attacks the nymphs, seldom the adults), *Pseudogonatopus hospes* Perkins (attacks the adults, only rarely the nymphs), *Echthrodelphax fairchildii* Perkins (Hymenoptera: Dryinidae) (attacks the nymphs). *Pipunculus hawaiiensis* Perkins, *Pipunculus juvator* Perkins, and *Pipunculus terryi* Perkins (Diptera: Pipunculidae) parasitize the young leafhoppers.

Predators: *Cyrtorhinus mundulus* (Breddin) (Heteroptera: Miridae) sucks the eggs (see vol. 3, page 206, for discussion). *Conocephalus saltator* (Saussure) (Orthoptera: Tettigoniidae) feeds on nymphs and adults. *Chelisoches morio* (Fabricius) and *Euborellia annulipes* (Lucas) (Dermaptera) feed upon the nymphs and adults. *Zelus renardii* Kolenati (Heteroptera: Reduviidae) attacks nymphs and adults; *Nabis capsiformis* Germar and *Nabis blackburni* White (Heteroptera: Nabidae) feed upon the nymphs and adults, particularly on the nymphs; *Orius persequens* (White) and *Physopleurella mundula* (White) (Heteroptera: Anthocoridae) prey upon the nymphs; *Oechalia kaonohi* Kirkaldy (confused in literature under the name of *Oechalia grisea*) (Heteroptra: Pentatomidae). *Chrysopa microphya* McLachlan, *Anomalochrysa deceptor* Perkins, *Anomalochrysa gayi* Perkins, *Anomalochrysa proteus* Perkins and *Anomalochrysa raphidioides* Perkins (Neuroptera: Chrysopidae) feed upon the nymphs, particularly. *Nesomimesa hawaiiensis* Perkins (Hymenoptera: Mimesidae) stores its burrow nests with adult leafhoppers which it stings and paralyzes.

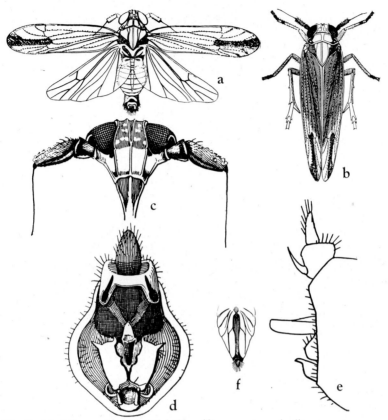

Figure 84—*Perkinsiella saccharicida* Kirkaldy. The sugarcane leafhopper. **a,** macropterous male; **b,** macropterous female; **c,** face; **d,** rear view of male pygophore; **e,** outline of male pygophore from side; **f,** ventral view of apical part of abdomen of female. (Rearranged from Kirkaldy, 1906 and 1907.)

A number of spiders have been recorded as feeding upon the leafhopper. Among these are *Pagiopalus atomarius* Simon, *Tetragnatha mandibulata* Walckenaer, *Heteropoda regia* (Fabricius), *Adrastidea nebulosa* Simon, *Plexippus paykulli* (Audouin), *Hasarius adansoni* (Audouin), *Mollica microphthalmus* (Koch) and *Bavia aericeps* Simon.

Entomophthora, Cordyceps and *Sporotrichium* fungi have been identified as attacking the leafhopper, especially in the regions of heavier rainfall.

Detailed notes on most of the above-listed parasites and predators have been assembled by Swezey in his paper on the "Biological Control of the Sugarcane Leafhopper in Hawaii" (1936), and the reader is referred to that paper for a detailed discussion. His records of parasites and predators refer to the time of great abundance of the leafhopper.

Life history: A clutch of one to as many as 12 slender, curved, whitish eggs is deposited in a slit cut by the ovipositor into the midrib of a leaf (the favorite place for oviposition), in the internode of a stalk, in a leaf sheath, in a leaf blade or in a shoot. One female may lay as many as 300 eggs in the month or two of her adult life. Although eggs may be deposited in both sides of a leaf, the preferred place of oviposition is low down on the inner (stalk) side of the leaf. The eggs usually tend to be deposited at an angle in the plant tissue, and the outer ends of the eggs, which project slightly above the plant epidermis, are covered over by a deposit of white wax. The incubation period varies with the temperature: in warm weather it may be as short as two weeks, but may extend over a period up to five or six weeks in the cooler seasons or at higher elevations. The incubation period may also be prolonged by dryness, and eggs in cane cuttings may not hatch for several weeks because of dryness.

The incisions made for the reception of the eggs make way for the entrance of a "red rot" fungus, *Physalospora tucumanensis* Spegazzini (*Colletotrichum falcatum* Went). This, and fermentation of the injured tissues, cause a reddish discoloration at the oviposition site, and the infested parts of the cane may become conspicuously reddish or closely red-spotted. These "claret-colored egg spots" are characteristic of leafhopper infestation, and have served to diagnose infestations even in the absence of nymphs and adults.

The first nymphal instar is conspicuous on account of the produced head. The vertex is a trifle longer than wide, extending well in front of the eyes and wider between them than an eye. I cannot trace any transverse or discal keels. On the frons there are *two keels* (which do not meet on the vertex or elsewhere), which are rounded convexly. These do not unite at the apical margin of the frons, nor do they meet the lateral keels there. The frons exterior to these submedian keels is wide and covered with sensory organs. The second segment of the antennae is large and stout but short. I cannot trace any sensory organs. The tarsi are bisegmentate, the posterior pair being provided each with a small mobile spur.

The second and third instars are not remarkable, except that the spur lengthens, the head shortens and the usual changes take place in the thorax. The fourth instar is very close to the adult, except that the body is still covered with sensory organs and the submedian keels are still separate, not uniting at the apical margin of the frons. In this instar, the sensory organs on the antennae are very conspicuous. (Kirkaldy, 1906:278–279.)

The length of each of the five instars was found by Van Dine (1904) to range from 4 to 9 days, with an average of about 7 days each, with the entire life cycle requiring 56 days at an average temperature of about 72 degrees, or 48 days at an average temperature of 77 degrees.

Kershaw (1913:185–186) notes that the food reservoir of the alimentary canal "... enters the head. The malpighian tubes are forked distally for a considerable length, the forked and about half the single portion being lobulate, the rest smooth. The color varies from pale pink to dark purple-red."

The nymphs and adults congregate in large numbers toward the bases of the leaves. They are more active at night than during the day, and the macropterous forms are attracted readily to lights. Copulation, oviposition and dispersal or migration usually take place at night. "... when disturbed in the daytime [it] flies but a short distance, or is even unwilling to fly at all, trusting to its leaping

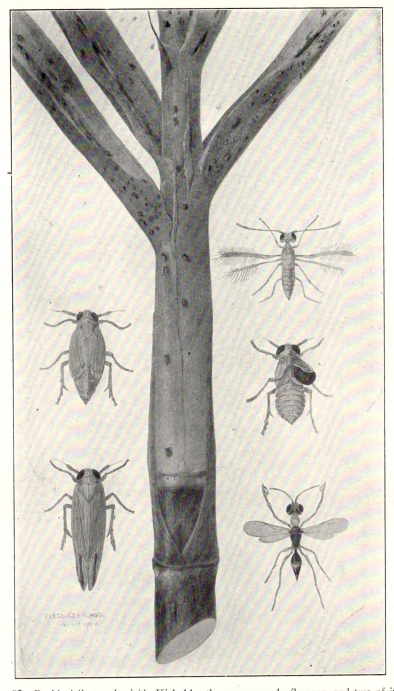

Figure 85—*Perkinsiella saccharicida* Kirkaldy, the sugarcane leafhopper, and two of its para-sites. The plate shows an infested stalk of sugarcane as it appeared when the leafhopper was abundant. Short- and long-winged females on the left, the egg parasite *Paranagrus optabilis* Perkins (top right), a nymph (middle right) showing the protruding black larval sac of the dryinid parasite *Echthrodelphax fairchildii* Perkins (bottom right). (From a painting in the Experiment Station, H.S.P.A., by W. R. Potter; after Swezey, 1915.)

powers to escape, or is content to sidle round the leaf or stem out of sight, or to run backwards when threatened from the front." (Perkins, 1903:9.) "On certain occasions, however, they have been seen flying in one direction in the day time in such numbers as to form a migratory swarm, quite like that which occurs in the case of certain locusts, dragon-flies, butterflies and other insects." (Perkins, 1903:11.)

Williams (1931:122–123) describes the stridulation of the leafhopper as follows: it is an intermittent noise, "...a sort of chirping, commencing with a staccato note, followed after a short pause, by a diminuendo of short rasping strokes, the whole lasting about two seconds. In addition, the insect may produce a sort of brisk tattoo suggestive of flapping the wings against a surface. These noises were audible from a distance of about eight feet, and were heard in my room [where a number of leafhoppers were enclosed in a large jar] in the afternoon and night and also once or twice in the field at 10:40 A.M. during bright warm weather. No movement could be detected in the stridulating insects." On still evenings the stridulation of thousands of leafhoppers in canefields sounded like the approach of a rain squall.

During the cooler seasons of the year, brachypterous females are developed in numbers, whereas they are only rarely found in the warmer seasons. The brachypterous females appear to be more prolific than the macropterous forms, and, consequently, the leafhopper populations increase more rapidly in the cooler seasons and the damage is then most severe.

Because of the copious amounts of honeydew produced, molds find unusually favorable conditions for growth upon the plants, and "...in bad attacks whole fields of cane may be black with the usual black fungus, or in striking contrast, white with another species, or the black smut may be followed and overgrown with the white fungus." (Perkins, 1903:11.)

The result of leaf-hopper attack when very severe is seen in the drying up of the leaves (from the constant sucking of their juices) before their full functions are performed. In consequence of this the joints of the stem, even at the time when they should be thickening, become on the contrary tapering and contracted, so much so sometimes that the crown topples over and is even entirely destroyed, further growth, of course, being at an end. Young cane is sometimes entirely killed out before any considerable length of stem has been produced. (Perkins, 1903:12.)

The astounding abundance of the leafhopper at the height of its development in Hawaii can be appreciated only by those men who actually had experience in the fields at that time. A sour odor hung over the fields during periods of severe epidemic. Most of the present plantation men really have no idea of, nor can they truly appreciate, the overwhelming numbers of leafhoppers which swarmed over the cane during the "leafhopper years" and the great damage caused. If undisturbed, the offspring of a single pair of leafhoppers might exceed a half billion individuals within a year.

The story of discovery, study, exploration and biological control of the leafhopper and of the development and advancement of Hawaiian entomology following its establishment in Hawaii is an epic. To tell it fully and adequately would require a separate volume. The whole future of the economic stability of the Territory appeared at one time to hinge upon the success or failure in the control of the leafhopper. The economic foundation of Hawaii is rooted in sugar, and that foundation was rapidly dissolving in 1903 and 1904 at the height of the leafhopper attacks—only two years after the insect was first discovered damaging the cane. At a time when the tonnage of sugar produced should have been increasing, it dropped from 437,991 to 367,475 tons, or a loss of 70,516 tons in a year, because of the ravages of the leafhopper. This reduction in yield represented a loss of more than five million dollars in a single year. Some plantations were almost wiped out. "The most severely injured plantation on the Island [Hawaii] was the Hawaiian Agricultural Company·at Pahala, where the Yellow Bamboo cane was the variety chiefly grown, and it proved to be more susceptible to leafhopper attack than any other variety. The damage was so extensive here that whole fields of great area were practically killed outright, and the plantation, which had a crop of 18,888 tons in 1903, was reduced to crops of 1,620 tons in 1905 and 826 tons in 1906." (Swezey, 1936:61.) With successful control, by 1940 the yield of 96° sugar for the Territory was 976,677 tons, representing a value of nearly 54 million dollars.

Inasmuch as the leafhopper has been intercepted at quarantine in Honolulu in sugarcane cuttings from Australia (eggs inserted in the stalks), it is presumed that it was by this means that the insect first gained entrance to Hawaii.

Although it was first collected in 1900, it was not until the next year that the leafhopper was reported by entomologists as attacking cane (Koebele's report in the *Hawaiian Planters' Monthly,* 21:20-26, 1902). Soon thereafter the reports of damage on various plantations throughout the islands came in rapid succession, and it was evident that the worst pest in the history of the industry had secured a firm foothold.

At that date there were no entomologists on the staff of the Hawaiian Sugar Planters' Association Experiment Station. Albert Koebele had been employed by the Hawaiian Board of Agriculture and Forestry in 1893 after his remarkable success in the biological control of the cottony cushion scale in California. He spent much of his time away from Hawaii in search of beneficial insects for introduction. At the time of the leafhopper outbreak, Dr. Perkins was employed as Koebele's assistant. The Hawaii Agricultural Experiment Station (a Federal station) had then been organized for only a couple of years but had begun entomological research with D. L. Van Dine as entomologist. The University of Hawaii had not yet been founded, and Bishop Museum did not have a department of entomology. Thus the number of entomologists working in Hawaii was small, and there were no routine entomological inspections made on the sugar plantations. With Koebele in Mexico searching for insects to control the *Lantana* weed pest, Perkins and Van Dine carried on independent research on the leafhopper after it was discovered to be a cane pest. Inasmuch as the Hawaiian Sugar Planters' Association had been subsidizing the work of Koebele and Perkins, in 1902 they asked for the recall of Koebele to Hawaii for the purpose of concentrating his efforts on the leafhopper. Koebele returned to Honolulu early in 1904, after having convalesced at Alameda, California, from illness contracted in the tropics (malaria ?), and later (1903) having studied, at the recommendation of L. O. Howard, with O. H. Swezey, who at that time was in Ohio and had worked there on leafhoppers and their parasites under Herbert Osborn. In 1904 Koebele and Perkins went to Australia in search of parasites.

During Koebele's absence in America, Perkins had ascertained that the leafhopper (which had been determined as a genus and species new to science) was an Australian insect. In 1903 G. W. Kirkaldy and F. W. Terry were added as entomological assistants in the Territorial Board of Agriculture and Forestry.

By 1904 the losses to the sugar plantations were so great that it became essential that an adequately staffed division of entomology be established in the Hawaiian Sugar Planters' Association Experiment Station. Thus, Perkins was appointed director of the new division, with Koebele as consulting entomologist, Kirkaldy and Terry as assistant entomologists, and Swezey was brought from Ohio especially for breeding parasites and inspection work and later had charge of the distribution of parasites to plantations and the progress of their establishment and spread in the fields. Hence, while Perkins and Koebele were searching for parasites in Australia, the new Division of Entomology of the Sugar Planters' Experiment Station had an active staff in Honolulu.

Koebele and Perkins arrived in Queensland in June, 1904, and immediately discovered that the leafhopper was kept under control by a number of parasites. Cultures of some of these parasites were shipped back to Honolulu. Perkins returned to Honolulu at the end of 1904, and Koebele followed in 1905, stopping in Fiji to obtain parasites on the way, but left Hawaii to retire that summer. In the fall of 1905 Frederick Muir was employed to fill Koebele's place in foreign exploration for parasites.

The parasites which became established in Hawaii as a result of the Koebele and Perkins expedition were the following small Hymenoptera: *Paranagrus optabilis* Perkins (sent from Queensland), *Paranagrus perforator* Perkins (from Fiji), *Anagrus frequens* Perkins (from Queensland), and *Ootetrastichus beatus* Perkins (introduced from Fiji, but also found in Australia). Of these, *Paranagrus optabilis* Perkins was the most successful.

As the result of the attacks of parasites and predators, by 1907 a fairly effective leafhopper control had been established. However, damage was still caused, local outbreaks continued to occur, and although the Hawaiian sugar industry had been saved from utter disaster, further attempts were made to procure additional parasites.

Muir continued the exploration and introduction work begun by Koebele and Perkins, and the parasites sent to Hawaii by him included *Haplogonatopus vitiensis* Perkins, introduced from Fiji in 1906; *Pseudogonatopus hospes* Perkins, introduced from China in 1906; *Ootetrastichus formosanus* Timberlake, introduced from Formosa in 1916; and *Cyrtorhinus mundulus* (Breddin), introduced from Queensland in 1920. Of all the enemies introduced, the *Cyrtorhinus* bug proved to be the most efficacious.

In 1919 C. E. Pemberton was added to the staff as assistant entomologist and as a field assistant for Muir. When Muir was in Queensland he discovered that the *Cyrtorhinus* sucked the eggs of the sugarcane leafhopper. This bug belongs to the family Miridae, which is normally a plant-sucking group and contains many well-known and important crop pests. Pemberton studied a small lot of the bugs brought by Muir to Honolulu on June 21, 1920. He found that the bugs confined their attacks entirely to leafhopper eggs and would starve if eggs were not available. With the beneficial habits of the bugs fully ascertained, Muir and Pemberton released a few individuals in the fields of the Ewa Plantation on July 19, 1920. In 1920 Pemberton went to Fiji, where Muir had previously found the bug without having discovered its egg-sucking habits, and made several shipments of bugs to Honolulu in the fall of that year.

Cyrtorhinus quickly became established and widespread, and it reached Molokai and Maui without having been purposely introduced to those islands. By 1923, the bug was generally distributed over all sugarcane areas in the islands and the leafhopper was everywhere under control and even difficult to find. The leafhopper has remained under control ever since, and whenever there is a local upbuilding of leafhopper populations, the subsequent increase of *Cyrtorhinus* reduces the numbers of leafhoppers. It is now frequently difficult to obtain leafhoppers for exhibition or classroom work without considerable search.

So successful has been the control of the leafhopper by *Cyrtorhinus* that it is considered that had entomologists of the Hawaiian Sugar Planters' Association Experiment Station found the bug early in their search for parasites it alone could have accomplished complete control, and none of the other introductions would have been necessary. Large sums of money could have been saved by such a fortunate discovery, not only from the expenses of extensive field work, but also in the earlier control of the leafhopper. Had there been an adequate museum collection of Pacific insects in Honolulu in those early days, the task of finding parasites and predators would have been aided considerably. As it was, the field searchers went abroad with meager information, but luck was with them and they accomplished what they set out to do with marked success. Confusion had arisen soon after the appearance of the leafhopper in Hawaii because it had been misidentified as a Javanese species by a worker at the National Museum. Had the error not been quickly corrected by Kirkaldy, who had access to the extensive collections at the British Museum, much delay and additional expense probably would have resulted.

This leafhopper is capable of transmitting the dreaded Fiji disease of sugarcane. A disaster might fall at any time in Hawaii should that terrible disease become established here.

The story of the biological control of the sugarcane leafhopper in Hawaii belongs high in the annals of entomological history.

For bibliographies pertaining to the sugarcane leafhopper, see Swezey, 1936: 98–100, and Metcalf, 1943:137–141.

Genus **PEREGRINUS** Kirkaldy, 1904:175

This is a monotypic genus. In our fauna it most closely resembles *Perkinsiella,* but the genotype is a more slender insect which does not have the expanded antennal segments that make *Perkinsiella* so distinctive. Brachypterous and macropterous forms occur in both sexes. For a detailed list of references to the genus, see Metcalf's world catalogue (1943).

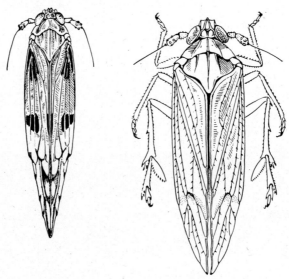

Figure 86—*Peregrinus maidis* (Ashmead), the corn leafhopper, left; *Liburnia paludum* (Kirkaldy), right, drawn to one-third larger scale than *Peregrinus* (this is a macropterous female, but most Hawaiian specimens are brachypterous). (Abernathy drawings.)

Peregrinus maidis (Ashmead) (figs. 86, 87, 88).

    Delphax maidis Ashmead, 1890:323, figs. *a–g.*

    Peregrinus maidis (Ashmead) Kirkaldy, 1904:176. Genotype.

    For detailed synonymy and a bibliography of about 140 titles, see Metcalf's catalogue (1943:252–256).

The corn leafhopper.

Kauai, Oahu, Molokai, Lanai, Maui, Hawaii.

Immigrant. Tropicopolitan, but extending into the temperate zones in North America, Australia and Africa; described from Florida. It may be a native of Malaysia, but I do not believe that its place of origin is known within narrower limits. Specimens were collected in the Territory by Perkins in 1892, but there is reason to believe that the species was established in the islands about 1880.

Hostplant: corn. Although the leafhoppers may occasionally be found on sorghum, sugarcane, Job's tears and perhaps on other grasses, such occurrences are apparently accidental, for in Hawaii they appear to be able to breed successfully only on corn. Muir (1917:147) noted that he found this species breeding on native grasses in the Malay Archipelago and in the Philippines.

Parasites and predators: *Paranagrus optabilis* Perkins, *Paranagrus osborni* Fullaway (this is either the same species as *P. optabilis* or is a difficult-to-separate ally of that species), *Anagrus frequens* Perkins (Hymenoptera: Mymaridae) and *Ootetrastichus beatus* Perkins (Hymenoptera: Eulophidae) parasitize the eggs. *Haplogonatopus vitiensis* Perkins (Hymenoptera: Dryinidae) parasitizes the nymphs and adults. The known predators in Hawaii include spiders, the voracious ant *Pheidole megacephala* (Fabricius) which eats both eggs and nymphs, coccinellid beetles including *Coelophora inaequalis* (Fabricius), the bug *Zelus renardii* Kolenati, the mirid bug *Cyrtorhinus mundulus* (Breddin), the earwig *Chelisoches morio* (Fabricius), and chrysopid lacewings.

In addition to these, the predaceous mirid bug, *Cyrtorhinus lividipennis* Reuter (a near relative of the sugarcane egg-sucking bug), was imported to feed on the eggs, but it failed to become established. This insect should be reimported with every effort made to obtain its successful establishment here.

Figure 87—*Peregrinus maidis* (Ashmead), the corn leafhopper.

Peregrinus maidis is a serious pest of corn, and the damage resulting from infestation may cause crop failure. Populations of the leafhoppers may increase rapidly to great numbers, and the sucking of the plant juices causes a wilting of the plants which resembles drought wilt. Also, the lesions caused by feeding and oviposition make way for fungus infection. Moreover, the leafhopper is the vector for the serious corn mosaic ("yellow stripe") disease.

Corn mosaic, a virus disease, is the most destructive of the enemies of corn in Hawaii. Kunkel (1921:45–46) states that

Under conditions such as exist in Hawaii it is one of the most destructive corn diseases known to pathologists.... Mottling or striping of the leaves and dwarfing of the plant are the most striking symptoms of corn mosaic. The leaves, leaf sheaths and rind of the stalk are mottled or striped with areas of lighter green color. In certain instances the color in the dark green areas is more intense than is common for normal healthy tissues of healthy plants. This heightens the contrast between the light and dark green areas. The shade of green in the lighter areas varies considerably in different plants and during different stages of the disease.

Kunkel also notes that the dwarfing symptom is even more striking than the striping and mottling and that all infected plants are more or less dwarfed, and he says (p. 47),

Plants that become diseased while young are severely dwarfed, even in the more resistant varieties. Plants attacked before they reach the tasselling stage never produce good ears of corn. If the plant is several feet high before contracting the disease the dwarfing will be less marked. Even in cases of extreme dwarfing the disease does not seem either to hasten or delay the time at which plants mature. Diseased plants show their silk and tassel at the same time as healthy ones. They frequently produce one or more small nubbins. The disease does not have much effect on the yield of plants that are attacked only shortly before they reach maturity. Mosaic has not been observed to kill young plants outright. Mature diseased plants die and dry up earlier than do normal ones.

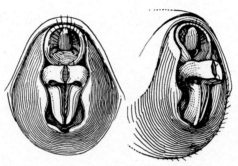

Figure 88—*Peregrinus maidis* (Ashmead). Two views of the male pygophore. (After Kirkaldy, 1907.)

The control of mosaic has centered around the introduction and breeding of resistant varieties of corn. Control of the leafhopper by biological or chemical means does not appear to result in successful control of the disease, for a small population of infected leafhoppers can infect a field of corn even though a large leafhopper population is prevented from developing. However, this should not discourage future introduction of promising leafhopper parasites and predators.

The corn leafhopper is a lowland insect, and corn grown at elevations above 2,000 feet is rarely attacked by the hoppers. Corn grown at high elevations is free from mosaic.

Fullaway (1918) has published descriptions of the early stages of the insect, and the following paragraph of data has been abstracted from his paper.

The 0.8 mm. long, cylindrical, curved, somewhat pyriform, pearly white eggs are deposited principally in the midrib of the upper sides of the leaves, but sometimes in the stalk, in cavities made by the saw-toothed ovipositor. From one to four eggs are placed (head, or narrow end, outward) in each cavity which is marked externally by a scar and a little whitish wax. They are often laid in regular rows, sometimes double rows, a slight distance apart. The eggs hatch in nine days in summer, and the hatching time is retarded in cooler weather and by dryness. Up to 300 or more eggs may be laid by one female at rates as high as more than 50 per day. About 200 eggs per female is considered an average number. The durations of the nymphal instars are as follows: I, 3 to 4 days; II, 2 to 4 days; III, 3 to 4 days; IV, 3 to 4 days; V, 4 to 5 days. Wing pads appear in the third instar.

The adults of both sexes may be brachypterous or macropterous, but the long-winged forms have been found to be about twice as abundant as the short-winged forms. Also, females are more abundant than males. The adults will live for at least a month under favorable conditions. The life cycle in the lowlands in the summer is about a month. Thus, several generations of leafhoppers may develop on a corn crop before it is harvested, for it requires about 100 to 120 days for corn to mature here. The hoppers usually attack the corn several days after it appears above the ground, and new immigrants arrive continually. The accumulation of leafhoppers on the corn plant is rapid. As many as 50 adult hoppers have been counted on a single plant in a new field adjacent to older plantings. As many as 1,000 eggs per leaf on a 12-leafed, two-month-old plant have been observed. The abundance of the hoppers can most easily be demonstrated by bending the leaves away from the stalk and observing the masses of individuals that congregate on the inner sides near the leaf bases where they are protected by the proximity of the leaf base to the stalk.

The abundance of honeydew produced affords a favorable pabulum for extensive growth of molds and attracts numbers of insects seeking sweets.

Genus **LIBURNIA** Stål, 1866

Sogata Distant, 1906.

This genus, which contains about 60 forms, is the second largest of the family, being outnumbered by *Nesosydne* only. It is a difficult assemblage of small leafhoppers. It is nearly cosmopolitan in distribution, but the largest number of species has been recorded from the Indo-Pacific regions. A detailed bibliography of the genus and its species is supplied by Metcalf's 1943 world catalogue, which should be consulted for details.

A single immigrant species occurs in our fauna, and for many years it was placed with the similar-appearing species assigned to the genus *Kelisia*. This one species is not very different from our *Kelisia* species, and it cannot be separated on the basis of characters used in keys in certain published reports consulted. Muir and Giffard (1924:12) noted that "This genus is a convenient home for a certain number of species with weak and uncertain generic character, which, if placed in other genera, break down their characters." I have found the non-vittate antennae in combination with the structures of the male terminalia to be the most reliable characters for the separation of *Liburnia paludum* from our *Kelisia* species.

Liburnia paludum (Kirkaldy) (figs. 86; 89, a).

  Kelisia paludum Kirkaldy, 1910:579. Muir, 1917:310, 330, pl. 5, figs. 18, 18a.
  Sogata paludum (Kirkaldy) Muir and Giffard, 1924:13, pl. 6, figs. 134, 135.
  Liburnia paludum (Kirkaldy) Metcalf, 1943:366.

  Kauai (?), Oahu (type locality: Waikiki, Honolulu), Molokai, Lanai (?), Maui (?), Hawaii (?), Laysan, Pearl and Hermes Reef, Midway, Kure (Ocean Island).

  Immigrant. A widespread Pacific species recorded from Samoa, Fiji, Australia, Java, the Philippines, Ceylon and Jamaica and presumably of Indo-Malayan origin although originally described from Hawaii.

  Hostplants: *Herpestis monnieria, Juncus,* "sedge."

  Parasites: *Aphelinoidea xenos* Timberlake (Hymenoptera: Trichogrammatidae) and *Anagrus frequens* Perkins (Hymenoptera: Mymaridae) on the eggs; *Haplogonatopus vitiensis* Perkins and *Echthrodelphax fairchildii* Perkins (?) (Hymenoptera: Dryinidae) on the nymphs and adults.

  This is essentially a lowland form which apparently usually frequents swampy or damp areas. Only a few macropterous Hawaiian individuals have been seen, but large numbers of brachypterous examples have been collected here.

  Muir (1917:330) has called attention to the confusing differences in the color of this species in different localities. All, or nearly all, of a large series from many localities in Hawaii are pale. A large series from Samoa is very dark, with the metanotum black on some. Also, the Samoan specimens are generally smaller. Since this text was written, a few long-winged males have been taken at a light trap at Pearl Harbor (November, 1947). These were considered at first to represent a new immigrant, for they are the dark form such as is found in Samoa. The genitalia appear similar in the two forms, however. Further work on this complex is required. The dark form may be a wet-season color variant.

Genus **KELISIA** Fieber, 1866

  This is one of the larger genera of Delphacidae. It is cosmopolitan in distribution and contains fifty-odd forms. A large mass of literature has been assembled on the genus, and Metcalf's world catalogue should be consulted for detailed references.

  In the Hawaiian fauna, this group can be separated easily from all the genera of the Delphacini excepting the single immigrant species of *Liburnia* which was assigned originally to *Kelisia*. The color pattern of the antennae and the structure of the male terminalia will serve to separate the species of the two genera now known in our fauna, but the generic differences need amplification and strengthening.

  Muir (1917:310) said that the Hawaiian members of this genus "have the face slightly broader and the sides more arcuate than in the type species."

  The five forms known from Hawaii have been considered possible immigrants by some authors, but there appears to me to be reason for considering them endemic.

I believe that the group has gained entrance to the Hawaiian Islands relatively recently, geologically speaking, as compared with our other native delphacids. I do not doubt that further collection and study will result in the discovery of additional new species. The known forms are closely allied, and some difficulty may be encountered when naming specimens, but, as the drawings show, the male genitalia are distinctive.

These insects differ from our other native Delphacidae in habit because they are attached to grasses. None of the other Hawaiian delphacids are grass-feeders.

Long-winged females of *Kelisia eragrosticola, sporobolicola* and *swezeyi* have been seen.

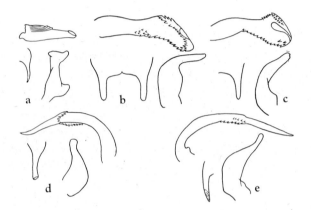

Figure 89—Details of the male genitalia of some delphacids. Each group of figures shows the aedeagus (top), anal spine (left), and a genital style (right). Figure **b** includes a rear view of both anal spines and shows the concave hind edge of the anal segment. All drawings made from balsam mounts; setae omitted. **a,** *Liburnia paludum* (Kirkaldy); **b,** *Kelisia eragrosticola* Muir; **c,** *Kelisia emoloa* Muir; **d,** *Kelisia sporobolicola* Kirkaldy; **e,** *Kelisia swezeyi* Kirkaldy.

KEY TO THE HAWAIIAN SPECIES OF KELISIA

1.   Granules of tegminal veins darker than veins and conspic-
        uous or comparatively conspicuous..................... 2
        Granules of tegminal veins not distinctly darker than veins,
        usually inconspicuous or obsolete...................... 3

2(1).   Tegmina so abbreviated that three or four abdominal ter-
        gites (exclusive of pygophore) are left exposed; lateral
        carinae of pro- and mesonotum conspicuously oblique
        and not nearly in line longitudinally; pygophore of
        female entirely pale...............**sporobolicola** Kirkaldy.
        Tegmina more elongate so that only two or two and a part
        of a third abdominal tergites are exposed; lateral carinae
        on pro- and mesonotum not very oblique and nearly in
        line longitudinally; anal angles of pygophore of female
        conspicuously dark adjacent to anal segment.........
        ....**swezeyi** Kirkaldy.

3(1). Anterior contour of vertex, as seen from directly above,
        broadly and rather flatly arcuate, distance across lateral
        carinae there subequal to distance across basal angles,
        and latter distance subequal to median length; genital
        styles of male not strongly bent, only slightly sinuate
        on their outer edges........**sporobolicola immaculata** Muir.
        Vertex comparatively pointed or roundly pointed, distance
        across carinae there less than basal breadth across basal
        angles, and latter distance less than or subequal to
        median length; genital styles of male strongly and con-
        spicuously bent laterad or dorso-cephalad or both....... 4
4(3). Frons with areas between carinae darker than carinae,
        sometimes rather strikingly contrasted, especially at
        front of vertex......................**eragrosticola** Muir.
        Frons entirely pale.........................**emoloa** Muir.

Kelisia emoloa Muir (fig. 89, c).
  Kelisia emoloa Muir, 1917:311, pl. 5, figs. 19, 19a.

Endemic. Oahu (type locality: Palolo Valley).
Hostplant: *Eragrostis variabilis* ("emoloa"). .

Kelisia eragrosticola Muir (figs. 55; 89, b).
  Kelisia eragrosticola Muir, 1919:85, pl. 4, fig. 2.

Endemic. Oahu, Maui (type locality: Iao Valley).
Hostplant: *Eragrostis variabilis*.

Kelisia sporobolicola Kirkaldy (fig. 89, d).
  Kelisia sporobolicola Kirkaldy, 1910:578. Muir, 1917:310, pl. 5, figs. 21, 21a;
    1919:86, pl. 4, fig. 13; 1921:509.

Endemic. Kauai, Oahu (type locality: Honolulu), Maui, Hawaii.
Hostplants: *Eragrostis atropioides, Sporobolus virginicus, Vincentia angustifolia*.
Predator: *Cyrtorhinus mundulus* (Breddin) (Hemiptera: Miridae) has been
recorded feeding upon the eggs.
What is apparently the type mount (a card containing three specimens) is now
in Perkins' collection at the Bishop Museum. It bears the locality label "Honolulu
XI.1903 R.C.L.P.," Kirkaldy's manuscript name "maritima" written on a slip
of paper (torn, not cut, out of a larger sheet), and "? are these the types of K.
sporobolicola K. R.C.L.P." I have placed this material in the type collection at
the Bishop Museum.

Kelisia sporobolicola immaculata Muir.
  Kelisia sporobolicola variety *immaculata* Muir, 1921:509.

Endemic. Hawaii (type locality: Kilauea).

Hostplants: *Deschampsia australis, Vincentia angustifolia.*

Parasite: *Anagrus frequens* Perkins (Hymenoptera: Mymaridae) in the eggs.

Kelisia swezeyi Kirkaldy (fig. 89, e).

Kelisia swezeyi Kirkaldy, 1910:578.

Endemic. Kauai, Oahu (type locality: Kalihi, Honolulu).

Hostplants: *Eragrostis variabilis, Gahnia* ("coarse sedge"?).

Genus **TAROPHAGUS**, new genus

Metcalf (1943) lists about 35 species under *Megamelus,* but it is obvious that the species of this assemblage belong to more than one genus. Our taro leafhopper is not congeneric with the genotype, *Megamelus notula,* and it must be removed from that genus. There appears to be no genus in which to place it, and a new one must be erected to receive it.

Megamelus is well developed in Europe and North America, and it has extended its range to South America. It does not appear to have invaded Africa or the Orient. The eight Pacific species now assigned to it must be removed. I would assign the well-known taro leafhopper and *M. proserpinoides* Muir, 1917 (Philippines), and *M. persephone* Kirkaldy, 1907 (Queensland), to the new genus and suggest that the following species may belong here; further study and additional

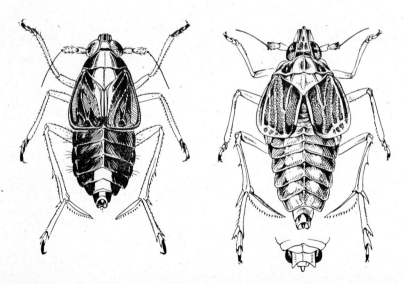

Figure 90—*Tarophagus proserpina* (Kirkaldy), the taro leafhopper, brachypterous female, left; *Megamelus angulatus* Osborn, the water lily leafhopper, brachypterous female, right, with sketch of male pygophore from above to show inflated sides. (Abernathy drawings.)

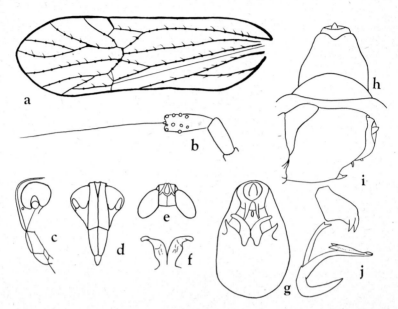

Figure 91—Diagrams of features of *Tarophagus proserpina* (Kirkaldy): **a**, fore wing of a macropterous male paratype (the venation is subject to variation); **b**, antenna; **c**, outline of front of head from side, male paratype; **d**, the same, full front view; **e**, the same, dorsal view; **g**, ventral view of pygophore; **h**, the same, dorsal view; **i**, the same, lateral view; **j**, lateral view of anal segment and aedeagus.

material of these five species are needed before conclusions can be reached regarding them: *M. geranor* (Kirkaldy) Muir, 1917 (Queensland); *M. kaha* (Kirkaldy) Muir, 1917 (Queensland); *M. leimonias* (Kirkaldy) Muir, 1917 (Queensland); *M. muiri* Metcalf, 1943 (*albicollis* Muir, 1917) (Philippines); and *M. sponsa* Kirkaldy, 1907 (Queensland). I have seen also new species which belong to *Tarophagus*.

The most striking differences between *Megamelus* and *Tarophagus* are displayed in the male terminalia. *Megamelus* has the sides of the pygophore characteristically inflated (as shown in my illustration) and the structure of the appendages and their arrangement are quite distinct. Muir (1926) has illustrated the genitalia of some *Megamelus* species, and his drawings may be consulted for a clear picture of the *Megamelus* type of terminalia. My sketches of *proserpina* illustrate the terminalia of the genotype of *Tarophagus*. The carinae are not strongly protuberant on the apex of the vertex of the head on *Tarophagus,* but they are strongly protuberant on *Megamelus,* and the vertex is longer on *Megamelus* as the drawings show. The appendages of *Tarophagus* are proportionately longer and more slender than those of *Megamelus*. For example, on *Tarophagus* the hind tibiae have the inner or shortest tibial length (excluding the terminal expansion and spines) as long as the entire tarsus. On our *Megamelus,* however, the corresponding tibial length is not as long as the two basal tarsal segments. The head of *Tarophagus* is loosely compacted to the pronotum as compared with *Megamelus* on which the hind edges of the eyes seem almost to be shallowly inserted into the pronotum, as compared with *Tarophagus*. The wing venation of the genotype of *Tarophagus* is as illustrated. When series of species of each genus are available, other characters of generic importance may be drawn up, but the differences pointed out here are sufficient for our present purpose.

Genotype: *Megamelus proserpina* Kirkaldy.

I am indebted to Mr. R. G. Fennah for concurrence of opinion regarding the establishment of the new genus.

Tarophagus proserpina (Kirkaldy), new combination (figs. 46, a; 90; 91, a–j).
Megamelus proserpina Kirkaldy, 1907:147, pl. 10, figs. 5–7; pl. 12, figs. 19–21.

The taro leafhopper.

Kauai, Oahu, Hawaii.

Immigrant. A widespread species found in Java, the Philippines, Guam, Amboina, Australia, New Hebrides, Fiji (type locality: Suva), Tonga, Niue, Samoa, the Society Islands and elsewhere in the Pacific. This species was first found in the Territory in 1930 by Swezey and Fullaway, who reported it as being abundant at Waianae, Oahu.

Hostplant: *Colocasia esculenta* (taro).

Parasites: *Haplogonatopus vitiensis* Perkins (Hymenoptera: Dryinidae) attacks nymphs and adults; *Ootetrastichus megameli* Fullaway (Hymenoptera: Eulophidae) attacks the eggs.

Predators: *Cyrtorhinus fulvus* Knight, and *Cyrtorhinus mundulus* (Breddin) (Heteroptera: Miridae) suck the eggs; the former is the more important predator on this leafhopper.

A considerable effort was made by the Board of Agriculture and Forestry in attempting to eradicate this species when it was first discovered. The torch was applied to rather large areas of taro, but in spite of the control efforts, the species spread about the island.

Mr. Fullaway made a trip to the Philippines to obtain parasites and predators and recorded some life history notes in his 1937 report (pp. 405–406) on the species. The following résumé is from his report:

The eggs, which are less than 1 mm. in length, are pearly white, spindle-shaped with pointed ends and are deposited, usually in pairs, in cavities hollowed out in the taro tissue. They hatch in 8 to 9 days. The adult stage is reached in 13 days, after four molts at 3- to 4-day intervals. The eggs are fully developed in 3-day-old adults. Most individuals are brachypterous, but long-winged forms are said to be found occasionally in winter.

Large colonies of leafhoppers may build up on irrigated taro.

Genus **MEGAMELUS** Fieber, 1866

See the commentary under *Tarophagus* for notes on this genus.

Megamelus angulatus Osborn (fig. 90).

Megamelus angulatus Osborn, 1905:374.

The water-lily leafhopper.

Oahu.

Immigrant. An eastern United States species, described from Delaware. First reported in the Territory by Fullaway from examples collected at Aiea, Oahu, in 1941.

Hostplant: *Nymphaea* water lilies.

Parasite: *Polynema ciliata* (Say) (Hymenoptera: Mymaridae) attacks the eggs. This parasite was brought to Honolulu from Michigan in 1941 by Fullaway and it quickly established itself on local leafhopper colonies.

This leafhopper may at times cause concern to growers of water lilies, but complaints have not heretofore been common. It has been wrongly called *Megamelus davisi* Van Duzee in some Hawaiian literature.

Family **FLATIDAE** Spinola, 1839

A single immigrant species represents this family in Hawaii. The group is most conspicuously developed in the continental tropics and adjacent islands, and many of the species are large and showy. They are considered the most highly evolved of the Fulgoroidea.

The one species now in our fauna can be confused with no other local group. Its vertically held, broad, subtriangular tegmina which have granulate clavi, together with the characters outlined in the family key, readily will distinguish the family.

Subfamily FLATINAE

Genus **SIPHANTA** Stål, 1860

This genus has its headquarters in Australia.

Siphanta acuta (Walker) (fig. 92).

Poeciloptera acuta Walker, 1851:448.

Phalainesthes schauinslandi Kirkaldy, 1899:359. (Genotype of *Phalainesthes*). Synonymy by Kirkaldy, 1902:117.

Kirkaldy, 1907:100, pl. 3, figs. 2, 4; pl. 6, figs. 13–14, 17–20.

The torpedo bug.

Kauai, Oahu, Molokai, Lanai, Maui, Hawaii.

Immigrant. An Australian species which has been artificially spread elsewhere, including Tasmania and New Zealand. It was established in Hawaii prior to 1898, or thereabout. "By 1900 it had become so extremely numerous, that in some of the forests on Oahu it was actually destroying large numbers of certain native trees, besides being injurious to coffee and other cultivated plants. A Proctotrupoid egg-parasite (*Aphanomerus pusillus*), introduced by Koebele in 1904, has done excellent service in many localities in diminishing the numbers of this pest. In wet districts it frequently is destroyed by a parasitic fungus." (Perkins, 1913:cciv.)

Hostplants: *Acacia, Cheirodendron, Citrus,* coffee (at one time considered a pest on this plant), *Coprosma, Eucalyptus,* guava, *Metrosideros, Moraea iridioides, Rubus, Styphelia (Cyathodes),* sumac, *Myrsine (Suttonia), Tetraplasandra* and many other kinds of plants.

Parasites and predators: *Chrysopa microphya* McLachlan (Neuroptera) preys upon the nymphs; *Aphanomerus pusillus* Perkins (Hymenoptera: Scelionidae) attacks the eggs; an undetermined fungus; *Nesomimesa antennata* (Smith) (Hymenoptera: Mimesidae) stores its nests with paralyzed individuals; certain coccinellid beetles prey upon the eggs.

This common, widespread hopper, called "torpedo bug" because of its great leaping powers, is one of the most characteristic members of our introduced fauna. The hind edges of the green, truncated tegmina are edged with pink. The life history in New Zealand has been reported upon by Myers (1922:256).

The eggs are deposited in sub-circular masses about 5 mm. in diameter on the leaves of plants. The egg-mass is slightly convex because the eggs in the middle of the mass are placed more nearly upright than those along the margins. The entire clutch of up to more than 100 eggs is glued together and partially covered by a cement.

Figure 92—*Siphanta acuta* (Walker), the torpedo bug.

The green and red nymphs of the five instars have been adequately described and discussed by Myers. The young nymphs prefer to feed upon leaves, but older ones feed upon stems.

They are very inactive, sitting for hours with their beaks applied to the stem. Occasionally an abdomen commences to vibrate—the vibrations pass gradually to an up-and-down thrashing—and at the moment of greatest amplitude of the movement, on the summit of an up-stroke, a perfectly spherical bead of honeydew, almost as big as the width of the abdomen at its tip, is exuded, and rapidly jerked away between the tufts of filaments which lie on each side of the anal extremity, and which are parted for the purpose. The younger instars are less forcible in this process, and frequently show a bead of honeydew held by the caudal filaments long after it has left the body.... All of the nymphs have a peculiar habit of swaying rhythmically from side to side—either when stationary or during the act of walking slowly. ... The fifth instar nymphs can jump as far as 2 ft. The adult plant-hopper, if it jumps at all, almost always spreads its wings while in the air.... The older nymphs are often surrounded by a mealy halo of white pruinose material from the filaments, which are easily detachable. The formation of such circles, between which and the body itself of the insect is always a clear space, would be best explained by the supposition that the nymphs move round frequently without changing to a like extent the position of the rostrum. (Myers, 1922:262–263.)

At Kula, Maui, in 1944, I saw 15 adult specimens on 10 inches of stem of *Moraea iridioides*. Their peculiar motion reminds one of a dance—a bug "hula."

Kershaw (1913:175) published a detailed, illustrated study of the alimentary canal of this species. He reported that the adults live about two months in Hawaii, and that the eggs hatch in between 10 and 20 days.

LITERATURE CONSULTED

ALFKEN, J. D.
1904. BEITRAG ZUR INSECTENFAUNA DER HAWAIISCHEN UND NEUSEELANDISCHEN INSELN (ERGEBNISSE EINER REISE NACH DEM PACIFIC. SHAUINSLAND 1896–97). Zoologische Jahrbücher, Systematik 19:561–628, colored pl. 32.

AMYOT, C. J. B.
1847. ENTOMOLOGIE FRANCAIS, RHYNCHOTES. Ann. Soc. Ent. France (II) 5:143–238. [This reference is sometimes given as: Methode Mononymique, 1848, pp. 339–434, but this is evidently a reprint.]

ASHMEAD, W. H.
1890. THE CORN DELPHACID, DELPHAX MAIDIS. Psyche 5 (166) :321–324, figs. *a–g.*

BALL, E. D.
1927. THE GENUS DRAECULACEPHALA AND ITS ALLIES IN NORTH AMERICA. Florida Entomologist 11 (3) :33–40.

BEAMER, R. H., and P. B. LAWSON.
1945. A REVISION OF THE GENUS STRAGANIA (BYTHOSCOPUS OF AUTHORS) IN AMERICA NORTH OF MEXICO. Kansas Ent. Soc. 18 (2) :49–66, pls. 1–3.

BRIDWELL, J. C.
1917. NOTES ON DICTYOPHORODELPHAX MIRABILIS. Proc. Hawaiian Ent. Soc. 3 (4) :279–280.

————
1918. NOTES ON THE ENTOMOLOGY OF HAWAIIAN EUPHORBIA WITH THE DESCRIPTION OF A NEW DICTYOPHORODELPHAX. Proc. Hawaiian Ent. Soc. 3 (5) :385–387.

————
1919. DICTYOPHORODELPHAX PRAEDICTA SP. NOV. Proc. Hawaiian Ent. Soc. 4 (1) :72–73.

BRITTON, W. E., et al.
1923. THE HEMIPTERA OR SUCKING INSECTS OF CONNECTICUT. In: Guide to the Insects of Connecticut. Part IV. Connecticut Geological and Nat. Hist. Survey Bull. 34:1–807, figs. 1–169, pls. 1–20.

BRYAN, E. H., JR., and O. H. SWEZEY.
1926. HEMIPTERA. In: Insects of Hawaii, Johnston Island, and Wake Island. Bernice P. Bishop Mus. Bull. 31:80–81.

CARTER, WALTER.
1941. PEREGRINUS MAIDIS (ASHM.) AND THE TRANSMISSION OF CORN MOSAIC. Ann. Ent. Soc. America 34 (3) :551–556.

CECIL, RODNEY.
1930. THE ALIMENTARY CANAL OF PHILAENUS LEUCOPHTHALMUS L. Ohio Jour. Science 30 (2) :120–127.

CHINA, W. E., and R. G. FENNAH.
1945. ON THE GENERA TETIGONIA GEOFF., TETTIGONIA F., TETTIGONIELLA JAC., AND IASSUS FAB. Ann. Mag. Nat. Hist (XI) 12:707–712.

COMSTOCK, J. H.
1933. AN INTRODUCTION TO ENTOMOLOGY. i-xix, 1–1044, figs. 1–1228. Comstock Publishing Co., Ithaca, New York.

CRAWFORD, D. L.
1914. A CONTRIBUTION TOWARD A MONOGRAPH OF THE HOMOPTEROUS INSECTS OF THE FAMILY DELPHACIDAE OF NORTH AND SOUTH AMERICA. Proc. U. S. National Mus. 46:557–640, pls. 44–49.

DAVIS, C. J., and A. L. MITCHELL.
1946. HOST RECORDS OF PHILAENUS SPUMARIUS (LINN.) AT KILAUEA, HAWAII NATIONAL PARK. Proc. Hawaiian Ent. Soc. 12 (3) :515–516.

DEGEER, CARL.
1773. MEMOIRES POUR SERVIR A L'HISTOIRE DES INSECTES. 3:i–viii, 1–696. Stockholm.

DELONG, D. M.
1923. See BRITTON, W. E., et al., 1923.

1931. A REVISION OF THE AMERICAN SPECIES OF EMPOASCA KNOWN TO OCCUR NORTH OF MEXICO. U. S. Dept. Agr. Tech. Bull. 231:1–60, figs. 1–11.

ESCHSCHOLTZ, J. F.
1822. ENTOMOGRAPHIEN. 1:1–128, 2 pls. Reimer, Berlin.

Evans, J. W.
    1938. A CONTRIBUTION TO THE STUDY OF THE JASSOIDEA. Papers and Proc. Royal Soc. Tasmania
        for 1938. 19–55, pls. 4–11.

    1946–1947. A NATURAL CLASSIFICATION OF LEAFHOPPERS. PART 1. Trans. Royal Ent. Soc. London.
        96 (3) :47–60, figs. 1–25 (1946). PART 2. 97 (2) :39–54, 3 figs. (1946). PART 3. 98 (6) :105–271,
        36 figs. (1947).

Fabricius, J. C.
    1775. SYSTEMA ENTOMOLOGIAE. 1–832. Korte, Flensburg.

    1794. ENTOMOLOGICA SYSTEMATICA. 4:1–472. Proft, Hafniae.

    1803. SYSTEMA RHYNGOTORUM. 1–314. Reichard, Brunsvigae.

Fennah, R. G.
    1944. NOMENCLATORIAL NOTES ON LATERNARIA L., FULGORA L., AND DELPHAX FABR. Proc. Biological
        Soc. Washington 57:43–44.

Fullaway, D. T.
    1937. NOTES ON THE TARO LEAFHOPPER (MEGAMELUS PROSERPINA KIRK.). Proc. Hawaiian Ent. Soc.
        9 (3) :405–406.

    1940. AN ACCOUNT OF THE REDUCTION OF THE IMMIGRANT TARO LEAF-HOPPER (MEGAMELUS PROSER-
        PINA) POPULATION TO INSIGNIFICANT NUMBERS BY THE INTRODUCTION AND ESTABLISHMENT OF
        THE EGG-SUCKING BUG CYRTORHINUS FULVUS. Proc. Sixth Pacific Science Congress 4:345–346.

Funkhouser, W. D.
    1927. CATALOGUE OF THE MEMBRACIDAE. In: General Catalogue of the Hemiptera. 1–581. Smith
        College, Massachusetts.

Giffard, W. M.
    1917. REFERENCE TABLES OF THE HAWAIIAN DELPHACIDS AND THEIR FOOD-PLANTS. Proc. Hawaiian
        Ent. Soc. 3 (4) :339–348.

    1918. NOTES ON DELPHACIDS COLLECTED ON A SHORT VISIT TO PORTIONS OF THE INTERMEDIATE FORESTS
        IN OLAA AND IN NORTH AND SOUTH KONA, ISLAND OF HAWAII. Proc. Hawaiian Ent. Soc.
        3 (5) :407–412.

    1921. THE SYSTEMATIC VALUE OF THE MALE GENITALIA OF DELPHACIDAE. Ann. Ent. Soc. America
        14 (2) :135–140, figs. 1–4.

    1922. THE DISTRIBUTION AND ISLAND ENDEMISM OF HAWAIIAN DELPHACIDAE WITH ADDITIONAL LISTS
        OF THEIR FOOD PLANTS. Proc. Hawaiian Ent. Soc. 5 (1) :103–118.

    1925. A REVIEW OF THE HAWAIIAN CIXIIDAE, WITH DESCRIPTIONS OF SPECIES. Proc. Hawaiian Ent.
        Soc. 6 (1) :51–171, figs. 1–142.

Goding, F. W.
    1895. SYNOPSIS OF THE SUBFAMILIES AND GENERA OF NORTH AMERICAN CERCOPIDAE, WITH A BIBLIO-
        GRAPHICAL AND SYNONYMICAL CATALOGUE OF THE DESCRIBED SPECIES OF NORTH AMERICA.
        Bull. Illinois State Laboratory Nat. Hist. 3:483–501.

Hacker, Henry.
    1925. THE LIFE HISTORY OF OLIARUS FELIS KIRK. Mem. Queensland Mus. 8 (2) :113–114.

Hadden, F. C.
    1928. SUGAR CANE MOSAIC AND INSECTS. Hawaiian Planters' Record 32 (1) :130–142.

Imms, A. D.
    1934. A GENERAL TEXTBOOK OF ENTOMOLOGY. i–xii, 1–727, figs. 1–624. E. P. Dutton and Co.,
        New York.

Kershaw, J. C.
    1913. THE ALIMENTARY CANAL OF FLATA AND OTHER HOMOPTERA. Psyche 20 (6) :175–188, pls. 5–6.

Kirkaldy, G. W.
    1899. EINE NEUE HAWAII'SCHE FULGORIDEN–GATTUNG UND ART. Entomologische Nachrichten 25:359.

    1902. HEMIPTERA. In: Fauna Hawaiiensis, David Sharp, Ed. 3 (2) :93–174, pls. 4, 5. (Cambridge
        Univ. Press.)

    1904. A PRELIMINARY LIST OF THE INSECTS OF ECONOMIC IMPORTANCE RECORDED FROM THE HAWAIIAN
        ISLANDS. Hawaiian Forester and Agriculturist 1 (6) :152–159; 1 (7) :183–189.

1904. BIBLIOGRAPHICAL AND NOMENCLATORIAL NOTES ON THE HEMIPTERA.—NO. 3. The Entomologist 37 (498) :279–283.

1906. LEAF-HOPPERS AND THEIR NATURAL ENEMIES, PART IX. LEAF-HOPPERS—HEMIPTERA. Hawaiian Sugar Planters' Association Expt. Station, Div. Ent. Bull. 1 (9) :271–479, pls. 21–32.

1907. LEAF-HOPPERS—SUPPLEMENT. Hawaiian Sugar Planters' Association Expt. Station, Div. Ent. Bull. 3:1–186, pls. 1–20.

1907a. BIOLOGICAL NOTES ON THE HEMIPTERA OF THE HAWAIIAN ISLES NO. 1. Proc. Hawaiian Ent. Soc. 1:135–161, figs. 1–4.

1908. A LIST OF THE DESCRIBED HEMIPTERA (EXCLUDING ALEYRODIDAE AND COCCIDAE) OF THE HAWAIIAN ISLANDS. Proc. Hawaiian Ent. Soc. 1 (5) :186–208, figs. 1–3, pl. 4.

1909. A CONSPECTUS OF THE FULGORIDAE OF THE HAWAIIAN HEMIPTERA. Proc. Hawaiian Ent. Soc. 2 (2) :75–80.

1910. NOTES ON THE ANCESTRY OF THE HEMIPTERA. Proc. Hawaiian Ent. Soc. 2 (3) :116–118.

1910. FURTHER NOTES ON HEMIPTERA, CHIEFLY HAWAIIAN. Proc. Hawaiian Ent. Soc. 2 (3) :118–123.

1910. SUPPLEMENT TO HEMIPTERA. In: Fauna Hawaiiensis, David Sharp, Ed. 2 (6) :531–599. (Cambridge Univ. Press.)
———— and F. MUIR.
1913. ON SOME NEW SPECIES OF LEAF-HOPPERS. Hawaiian Sugar Planters' Association Expt. Station, Bull. Ent. Ser. 12:1–86, pls. 1–3.

KUNKEL, L. O.
1921. A POSSIBLE CAUSATIVE AGENT FOR THE MOSAIC DISEASE OF CORN. Hawaiian Sugar Planters' Association Expt. Station, Bull. Bot. Ser. 3 (1) :44–58, 2 figs.

1922. INSECT TRANSMISSION OF YELLOW STRIPE DISEASE. Hawaiian Planters' Record 26 (2) :58–64, 1 fig.

1946. LEAFHOPPER TRANSMISSION OF CORN STUNT. Proc. National Acad. Science 32:246–247.
LINNAEUS, CARL.
1758. SYSTEMA NATURAE. 10th ed. 1–823. L. Salvii, Holmiae.

1761. FAUNA SUECICA. 1–578, pls. 1–2. L. Salvii, Holmiae.
MARTIN, J. P.
1938. SUGAR CANE DISEASES IN HAWAII. i–xiv, 1–295, figs. 1–150, pls. 1–13. Hawaiian Sugar Planters' Association Expt. Station, Honolulu.
METCALF, Z. P.
1936. GENERAL CATALOGUE OF THE HEMIPTERA, FASCICLE 4, FULGOROIDEA, PART 2, CIXIIDAE. 1–269. Smith College, Massachusetts.

1938. THE FULGORINA OF BARRO COLORADO AND OTHER PARTS OF PANAMA. Mus. Comparative Zoology Harvard Mem. 82:277–423, 23 pls.

1942. BIBLIOGRAPHY OF THE HOMOPTERA AUCHENORHYNCHA. 1:1–886; 2:1–186, North Carolina State College, Raleigh.

1943. GENERAL CATALOGUE OF THE HEMIPTERA, FASCICLE 4, FULGOROIDEA, PART 3, ARAEOPIDAE (DELPHACIDAE) . 1–552. Smith College, Massachusetts.
MUIR, F. A. G.
1910. ON SOME NEW SPECIES OF LEAF-HOPPER (PERKINSIELLA) ON SUGAR CANE. Hawaiian Sugar Planters' Association Expt. Station, Bull. Ent. Ser. 9:1–11, figs. 1–5.

1913. ON SOME NEW FULGOROIDEA. Proc. Hawaiian Ent. Soc. 2 (5) :237–269, figs. 1–13.

1915. A CONTRIBUTION TOWARDS THE TAXONOMY OF THE DELPHACIDAE. Canadian Entomologist 47 (7) :208–212; (8) :261–270; (9) :296–302; (10) :317–320.

1916. REVIEW OF THE AUTOCHTHONOUS GENERA OF HAWAIIAN DELPHACIDAE. Proc. Hawaiian Ent. Soc. 3 (3) :168–221, pls. 2–4.

1917. ON THE SYNONYMY OF DELPHAX MAIDIS ASHM. Canadian Entomologist 49 (4) :147.

1917. NEW HAWAIIAN DELPHACIDAE. Proc. Hawaiian Ent. Soc. 3 (4) :298–311, pls. 5–6.

1917. HOMOPTEROUS NOTES. Proc. Hawaiian Ent. Soc. 3 (4) :311–338.

1918. TWO NEW SPECIES OF NESOSYDNE. Proc. Hawaiian Ent. Soc. 3 (5) :405–407.

1918. HOMOPTEROUS NOTES II. Proc. Hawaiian Ent. Soc. 3 (5) :414–429.

1919. NOTES ON THE DELPHACIDAE IN THE BRITISH MUSEUM COLLECTION. Canadian Entomologist
    51 (1) :6–8.

1919. ON THE GENUS ILBURNIA WHITE. Proc. Hawaiian Ent. Soc. 4 (1) :48–50.

1919. NEW HAWAIIAN DELPHACIDAE. Proc. Hawaiian Ent. Soc. 4 (1) :84–108, pls. 3–4.

1921. NEW HAWAIIAN DELPHACIDAE. Proc. Hawaiian Ent. Soc. 4 (3) :507–520, pl. 8.

1922. A NEW HAWAIIAN DELPHACID. Proc. Hawaiian Ent. Soc. 5 (1) :87–88, figs. 1–2.

1922. NEW AND LITTLE KNOWN HAWAIIAN DELPHACIDAE. Proc. Hawaiian Ent. Soc. 5 (1) :91–101, pl. 3.

1923. ON THE CLASSIFICATION OF THE FULGOROIDEA. Proc. Hawaiian Ent. Soc. 5 (2) :205–247, pls. 4–8.

1924. See MUIR, F. A. G., and W. M. GIFFARD.

1925. ON THE GENERA OF CIXIIDAE, MEENOPLIDAE AND KINNARIDAE. Pan-Pacific Entomologist 1 (3) :
    97–110; (4) :156–163.

1926. CONTRIBUTIONS TO OUR KNOWLEDGE OF SOUTH AMERICAN FULGOROIDEA. PART 1. THE FAMILY
    DELPHACIDAE. Hawaiian Sugar Planters' Association Expt. Station, Bull. Ent. Ser. 18:1–51,
    122 figs.

1926. SOME REMARKS ON DR. HEM SINGH-PRUTHI'S PAPER ON THE MORPHOLOGY OF THE MALE GENITALIA
    IN RHYNCHOTA. Proc. Hawaiian Ent. Soc. 6 (2) :323–334, pl. 11.

1927. ON SOME FULGORIDS FROM THE SOUTH PACIFIC. Ann. Mag. Nat. Hist. (IX) 20 (115) :86–91,
    7 figs.

1931. DESCRIPTIONS AND RECORDS OF FULGOROIDEA FROM AUSTRALIA AND THE SOUTH PACIFIC ISLANDS.
    NO. 1. Australian Mus. Records 18 (2) :63–83, 31 figs.

———— and W. M. GIFFARD.
1924. STUDIES IN NORTH AMERICAN DELPHACIDAE. Hawaiian Sugar Planters' Association Expt.
    Station, Bull. Ent. Ser. 15:1–53, 136 figs.

MYERS, J. G.
1922. LIFE-HISTORY OF SIPHANTA ACUTA (WALK.) , THE LARGE GREEN PLANT-HOPPER. New Zealand
    Jour. Science and Technology 5:256–263, figs. 1–4.

OSBORN, HERBERT.
1928. THE LEAFHOPPERS OF OHIO. Ohio Biological Survey Bull. 14:199–374, figs. 1–111.

1905. DESCRIPTIONS OF NEW NORTH AMERICAN FULGORIDAE. The Ohio Naturalist 5 (8) :373–376.

1934. CICADELLIDAE. In: Insects of Samoa 2 (4) :163–192, figs. 1–15. British Mus. Nat. Hist.,
    London.

1934. CICADELLIDAE FROM THE SOCIETY ISLANDS. In: Society Island Insects. Bernice P. Bishop
    Mus. Bull. 113:115–118, figs. 1–2.

1934. CICADELLIDAE OF THE MARQUESAS ISLANDS. In: Marquesan Insects—II. Bernice P. Bishop
    Mus. Bull. 114:239–269, figs. 1–23.

1935. CICADELLIDAE OF HAWAII. Bernice P. Bishop Mus. Bull. 134:1–62, figs. 1–27.

———— and E. D. BALL.

1902. A REVIEW OF THE NORTH AMERICAN SPECIES OF ATHYSANUS. The Ohio Naturalist 231–256, pls. 16–17.

———— and D. J. KNULL.

1939. MEADOW AND PASTURE INSECTS. i–viii, 1–288, 102 figs. The Educators' Press, Columbus, Ohio.

PEMBERTON, C. E.

1919. LEAFHOPPER INVESTIGATIONS ON HAWAII. Hawaiian Planters' Record 21 (4) :194–221, figs. 1–10.

———— and F. X. WILLIAMS.

1938. SOME INSECTS AND OTHER ANIMAL PESTS IN HAWAII NOT UNDER SATISFACTORY BIOLOGICAL CONTROL. Hawaiian Planters' Record 42 (3) :211–230.

PERKINS, R. C. L.

1897. THE INTRODUCTION OF BENEFICIAL INSECTS INTO THE HAWAIIAN ISLANDS. Nature 55 (1430) : 499–500.

1902. NOTES ON INSECTS INJURIOUS TO CANE IN THE HAWAIIAN ISLANDS. Hawaiian Planters' Monthly 21:593–600.

1903. THE LEAF-HOPPER OF THE SUGAR CANE. Territory of Hawaii, Board of Commissioners of Agriculture and Forestry, Div. Ent. 1:1–38.

1913. INTRODUCTION. In: Fauna Hawaiiensis. David Sharp, Ed. 1:xv–ccxxviii, pls. 1–16. (Cambridge Univ. Press.)

POOS, F. W., and N. H. WHEELER.

1943. STUDIES ON HOST PLANTS OF THE LEAFHOPPERS OF THE GENUS EMPOASCA. U. S. Dept. Agr. Tech. Bull. 850:1–51, figs. 1–21.

SAY, THOMAS.

1830–1831. DESCRIPTIONS OF NEW NORTH AMERICAN HEMIPTEROUS INSECTS BELONGING TO THE FIRST FAMILY OF THE SECTION HOMOPTERA OF LATREILLE. Jour. Philadelphia Acad. Nat. Science 6 (2) :235–244 (1830) ; 6 (2) :299–314 (1831) .

SNODGRASS, R. E.

1935. PRINCIPLES OF INSECT MORPHOLOGY. 1–667, figs. 1–319. McGraw-Hill, New York.

SPEARE, A. T.

1912. FUNGI PARASITIC UPON INSECTS INJURIOUS TO SUGAR CANE. Hawaiian Sugar Planters' Association Expt. Station, Pathological and Physiological Bull. 12:1–62, 2 figs., 6 pls.

STAL, CARL.

1859. HEMIPTERA. In: C. A. Virgin, Voyage autour du monde sur la Frégate Suédoise l'Eugénie ... 1851–1853. Zoologie, 219–298. P. A. Norstedt et Fils. Stockholm.

SWEETMAN, H. L.

1936. THE BIOLOGICAL CONTROL OF INSECTS. 1–461, figs. 1–142. Comstock Publishing Co., Ithaca, New York.

SWEZEY, O. H.

1905. LEAF-HOPPERS AND THEIR NATURAL ENEMIES (PART VII. ORTHOPTERA, COLEOPTERA, HEMIPTERA) . Hawaiian Sugar Planters' Association Expt. Station, Bull. Ent. Ser. 1 (7) :211–238, pls. 14–17.

1907. OBSERVATIONS ON THE LIFE HISTORY OF OLIARUS KOANOA KIRKALDY. Proc. Hawaiian Ent. Soc. 1 (3) :83–84.

1907. AN EXTRAORDINARY LEAF-HOPPER FROM MT. KONAHUANUI, OAHU. Proc. Hawaiian Ent. Soc. 1 (3) :104–106.

1908. NYMPH OF DICTYOPHORODELPHAX MIRABILIS SWEZEY. Proc. Hawaiian Ent. Soc. 2 (1) :2, figs. 1–5.

1936. BIOLOGICAL CONTROL OF THE SUGAR CANE LEAFHOPPER IN HAWAII. The Hawaiian Planters' Record 40 (1) :55–101, 2 pls., 23 figs.

1937. A NEW SPECIES OF DICTYOPHORODELPHAX FROM THE ISLAND OF LANAI. Proc. Hawaiian Ent. Soc. 9 (3) :431–432.

TIMBERLAKE, P. H.

1918. NOTE ON THE NON-IDENTITY OF A COMMON HAWAIIAN JASSID WITH NESOSTELES HEBE KIRKALDY OF FIJI. Proc. Hawaiian Ent. Soc. 3 (5) :381.

———
1927. BIOLOGICAL CONTROL OF INSECT PESTS IN THE HAWAIIAN ISLANDS. Proc. Hawaiian Ent. Soc. 6 (3) :529–556.

VAN DINE, D. L.
1904. A SUGAR CANE LEAF-HOPPER IN HAWAII. Hawaii Agr. Expt. Station Bull. 5:1–29, figs. 1–8.

VAN DUZEE, E. P.
1889. ON A NEW SPECIES OF PEDIOPSIS. Psyche 5:238–241.

———
1917. CATALOGUE OF THE HEMIPTERA OF AMERICA NORTH OF MEXICO. Univ. California Pubs. in Ent. 2:1–902.

———
1923. See BRITTON, W. E., et al., 1923.

WALKER, FRANCIS.
1850–1852. LIST OF THE SPECIMENS OF HOMOPTEROUS INSECTS IN THE COLLECTION OF THE BRITISH MUSEUM. PART I. 1–260 (1850) ; PART II. 261–635 (1851) ; PART III. 637–907 (1851) ; PART IV. 908–1188, 8 pls. (1852) . British Mus. Nat. Hist.

WILDERMUTH, V. L.
1915. THREE-CORNERED ALFALFA HOPPER. Jour. Agr. Research 3 (4) :343–362, pl. 43.

WILLIAMS, F. X.
1919. SOME OBSERVATIONS ON THE LEAF-HOPPER WASP, NESOMIMESA HAWAIIENSIS PERKINS, AT PAHALA, HAWAII, FEB. 11–APRIL 25, 1918. Proc. Hawaiian Ent. Soc. 4 (1) :63–68, figs. 1–3.

———
1919. SOME OBSERVATIONS ON PIPUNCULUS FLIES WHICH PARASITIZE THE CANE LEAFHOPPER AT PAHALA, HAWAII, FEB. 11–APRIL 25, 1918. Proc. Hawaiian Ent. Soc. 4 (1) :68–71, fig. 1.

———
1931. THE INSECTS AND OTHER INVERTEBRATES OF HAWAIIAN SUGAR CANE FIELDS. 1–400, figs. 1–190. Hawaiian Sugar Planters' Association Expt. Station, Honolulu.

———
1938. See PEMBERTON, C. E., and F. X. WILLIAMS.

INDEX